FREE VIDEO

FREE VIDEO

ATI TEAS Essential Test Tips Video from Trivium Test Prep!

Dear Customer,

Thank you for purchasing from Trivium Test Prep! We're honored to help you prepare for your ATI TEAS exam.

To show our appreciation, we're offering a **FREE *ATI TEAS Essential Test Tips* Video by Trivium Test Prep.*** Our video includes 35 test preparation strategies that will make you successful on the ATI TEAS. All we ask is that you email us your feedback and describe your experience with our product. Amazing, awful, or just so-so: we want to hear what you have to say!

To receive your **FREE *ATI TEAS Essential Test Tips* Video**, please email us at 5star@ triviumtestprep.com. Include "Free 5 Star" in the subject line and the following information in your email:

1. The title of the product you purchased.
2. Your rating from 1 – 5 (with 5 being the best).
3. Your feedback about the product, including how our materials helped you meet your goals and ways in which we can improve our products.
4. Your full name and shipping address so we can send your **FREE *ATI TEAS Essential Test Tips* Video**.

If you have any questions or concerns please feel free to contact us directly at 5star@trivium-testprep.com.

Thank you!

- Trivium Test Prep Team

*To get access to the free video please email us at 5star@triviumtestprep.com, and please follow the instructions above.

ATI TEAS Test Prep Study Guide 2021–2022

TEAS 6 Manual with Practice Exam Questions for the
Test of Essential Academic Skills, Sixth Edition

TABLE OF CONTENTS

ONLINE RESOURCES

To help you fully prepare for your ATI TEAS exam, Trivium includes online resources with the purchase of this study guide.

Practice Test

In addition to the practice test included in this book, we also offer an online exam. Since many exams today are computer based, getting to practice your test-taking skills on the computer is a great way to prepare.

Flash Cards

A convenient supplement to this study guide, Trivium's flash cards enable you to review important terms easily on your computer or smartphone.

Cheat Sheets

Review the core skills you need to master the exam with easy-to-read Cheat Sheets.

From Stress to Success

Watch From Stress to Success, a brief but insightful YouTube video that offers the tips, tricks, and secrets experts use to score higher on the exam.

Reviews

Leave a review, send us helpful feedback, or sign up for Trivium promotions—including free books!

Access these materials at:

www.triviumtestprep.com/ati-teas-online-resources

WANT MORE?

Try our online *ATI Teas 6 Prep Course*

Dear Reader,

Here at Trivium Test Prep, we understand how important scoring well on the ATI TEAS 6 exam is for your future. We believe you can never be "too prepared" for such a life-changing test. We are excited to offer you a comprehensive online course devoted to the ATI TEAS 6! Our *ATI Teas 6 Prep Course* includes:

- a <u>complete review</u> of all content on the ATI TEAS VI exam, with **trackable course progress** so you know exactly what you still need to review;
- <u>subject quizzes</u> at the end of each section, so you can **assess your retention** before moving on to new units;
- <u>two full practice exams</u> with **fully explained answer rationales** and **trackable scoring**, so you can measure your progress and understand what you need to improve on;
- and <u>full accessibility</u> via your computer, tablet, and mobile phone 24/7, enabling you to **learn at home or on-the-go!**

Best of all, our unique material and practice questions are available exclusively through *ATI Teas 6 Prep Course*, ensuring you get double the study time when coupled with this book!

Trivium Test Prep's *ATI Teas 6 Prep Course* is available to current customers like you at the promotional price of only **$39.99!** Many less convenient programs retail for hundreds of dollars online. To enroll today and start learning immediately, please visit:

http://course.triviumtestprep.com/

Thank you for choosing Trivium Test Prep for all your ATI TEAS 6 study needs! Best of luck with your studies,

– The Trivium Test Prep Team

INTRODUCTION

Congratulations on your decision to join the field of nursing—few other professions are so rewarding! By purchasing this book, you've already taken the first step toward succeeding in your career. The next step is to do well on the ATI Test of Essential Academic Skills (TEAS) VI, which will require you to demonstrate knowledge of high school–level reading, writing, math, and science.

This book will walk you through the important concepts in each of these subjects and also provide you with inside information on test strategies and tactics. Even if it's been years since you graduated from high school or cracked open a textbook, don't worry—this book contains everything you'll need for the ATI TEAS VI.

ABOUT THE ATI TEAS VI

The ATI TEAS VI is three hours and twenty-nine minutes long and is divided into the following sections:

SUBJECT	SUB-AREAS	TIME LIMIT
Reading 53 questions	Key ideas and details (22) Craft and structure (14) Integration of knowledge and ideas (11) Pre-test questions (6, unscored)	64 minutes
Mathematics 36 questions	Numbers and algebra (23) Measurement and data (9) Pre-test questions (4, unscored)	54 minutes
Science 53 questions	Human anatomy and physiology (32) Life and physical sciences (8) Scientific reasoning (7) Pre-test questions (6, unscored)	63 minutes
English and Language Arts 28 questions	Conventions of standard English (9) Knowledge of language (9) Vocabulary acquisition (6) Pre-test questions (4, unscored)	28 minutes
Total: 170 questions	150 scored, 20 unscored	3 hours 29 minutes

There are a total of 170 questions on the TEAS; however twenty of them are unscored, pre-test questions and used only by the test makers to gather information. That means 150 of the questions you answer will count toward your score. Keep in mind that you will not know which questions will be unscored, so you must answer all of the questions on the exam.

If you take the online version of the TEAS, you will receive your score immediately after the test. If you take the paper-and-pencil version, ATI will score your exam within forty-eight hours of receiving it from the testing site. Your scores are automatically sent to the schools you selected when you registered for the exam. You must contact the administrators of the exam, the Assessment Technologies Institute (ATI), to send your scores to any other programs.

Scoring

You cannot pass or fail the TEAS exam. Instead, you will receive a score report that details the number of questions you answered correctly in each section and also gives your percentile rank, which shows how you did in comparison with other test-takers. Each school has its own entrance requirements, so be sure to check the requirements of the institutions you want to attend so you can set appropriate goals for yourself.

Administration and Test Day

The TEAS is administered by the Assessment Technologies Institute (ATI) at testing centers nation-wide. To register for the exam, refer to the ATI website. You may take a computer-administered or pencil-and-paper test. There is no difference other than method of administration. Choose the format you are most comfortable with, but keep in mind that if you take the computer-administered version, you will receive your scores immediately.

On test day, arrive early and be sure to bring government-issued, photo identification; two No. 2 pencils; and your ATI login information. Personal belongings, cell phones, and other electronic, photographic, recording, or listening devices are not permitted in the testing center. Most testing centers offer lockers to secure your personal items, but it is a good idea to check beforehand with the facility. Calculators and scratch paper will be provided. There is a ten-minute break after the mathematics section. For the most up-to-date details on what to expect on test day, refer to the ATI website.

ABOUT TRIVIUM TEST PREP

Trivium Test Prep uses industry professionals with decades' worth of knowledge in their fields, proven with degrees and honors in law, medicine, business, education, the military, and more, to produce high quality test prep books for students.

Our study guides are specifically designed to increase any student's score. Our books are also shorter and more concise than typical study guides, so you can increase your score while significantly decreasing your study time.

How to Use This Guide

This guide is not meant to waste your time on superfluous information or concepts you've already learned. Instead, we hope you use this guide to focus on the concepts YOU need to master for the test and to develop critical test-taking skills. To support this effort, the guide provides:

- organized concepts with detailed explanations
- practice questions with worked-through solutions
- key test-taking strategies
- simulated one-on-one tutor experience
- tips, tricks, and test secrets

Because we have eliminated filler or fluff, you'll be able to work through the guide at a significantly faster pace than you would with other test prep books. By allowing you to focus only on those concepts that will increase your score, we'll make your study time shorter and more effective.

The chapters in this book are divided into a review of the topics covered on the exam. This is not intended to teach you everything you'll see on the test: there is no way to cram all of that material into one book! Instead, we are going to help you recall information that you've already learned, and even more importantly, we'll show you how to apply that knowledge. Each chapter includes an extensive review with practice questions at the end to test your knowledge. With time, practice, and determination, you'll be well prepared for test day.

PART I: READING

The ATI TEAS Reading section will require you to read both nonfiction and fiction passages and then answer questions about them. These questions will fall into three categories:

KEY IDEAS AND DETAILS questions ask about the main idea of the passage and the details that support that main idea.

CRAFT AND STRUCTURE questions ask about the craft of writing, including organization of the text, word choice, and the author's purpose.

INTEGRATION OF KNOWLEDGE AND IDEAS questions require drawing conclusions from passages and integrating information from multiple sources.

The Reading section will also include informational source comprehension questions. These questions will not refer back to a text passage; instead, they will ask you to interpret an informational source like a nutrition label, map, or thermometer.

READING PASSAGES

THE MAIN IDEA

The **MAIN IDEA** of a text is the argument that the author is trying to make about a particular **TOPIC**. Every sentence in a passage should support or address the main idea in some way.

Identifying the Main Idea

Consider a political election. A candidate is running for office and plans to deliver a speech asserting her position on tax reform, which is that taxes should be lowered. The topic of the speech is tax reform, and the main idea is that taxes should be lowered. The candidate is going to assert this in her speech, and support it with examples proving why lowering taxes would benefit the public and how it could be accomplished.

> ⚠
> **Topic**: The subject of the passage. **Main idea**: The argument the writer is making about the topic.

Other candidates may have different perspectives on the same topic; they may believe that higher taxes are necessary, or that current taxes are adequate. It is likely that their speeches, while on the same topic of tax reform, would have different main ideas supported by different examples and evidence.

Let's look at an example passage to see how to identify the topic and main idea.

Babe Didrikson Zaharias, one of the most decorated female athletes of the twentieth century, is an inspiration for everyone. Born in 1911 in Beaumont, Texas, Zaharias lived in a time when women were considered second class to men, but she never let that stop her from becoming a champion. Zaharias was one of seven children in a poor immigrant family and was competitive from an early age. As a child she excelled at most things she tried, especially sports, which continued into high school and beyond. After high school, Zaharias played amateur basketball for two years, and soon after began training in track and field. Despite the fact that women were only allowed to enter in three events, Zaharias represented the United States in the 1932 Los Angeles Olympics, and won two gold medals and one silver in track and field events.

The topic of this paragraph is obviously Babe Zaharias—the whole passage describes events from her life. Determining the main idea, however, requires a little more analysis. To figure out the main idea, consider what the writer is saying about Zaharias. The passage describes her life, but the main idea of the paragraph is what it says about her accomplishments. The writer is saying that she is someone to admire. That is the main idea and what unites all the information in the paragraph.

Example

From so far away it's easy to imagine the surface of our solar system's planets as enigmas—how could we ever know what those far-flung planets really look like? It turns out, however, that scientists have a number of tools at their disposal that allow them to paint detailed pictures of many planets' surfaces. The topography of Venus, for example, has been explored by several space probes, including the Russian Venera landers and NASA's *Magellan* orbiter. In addition to these long-range probes, NASA has also used its series of "Great Observatories" to study distant planets. These four massively powerful orbiting telescopes are the famous Hubble Space Telescope, the Compton Gamma Ray Observatory, the Chandra X-Ray Observatory, and the Spitzer Space Telescope. Such powerful telescopes aren't just found in space: NASA makes use of Earth-based telescopes as well. Scientists at the National Radio Astronomy Observatory in Charlottesville, Virginia, have spent decades using radio imaging to build an incredibly detailed portrait of Venus's surface.

Which of the following sentences best describes the main idea of the passage?

A) It's impossible to know what the surfaces of other planets are really like.

B) Telescopes are an important tool for scientists studying planets in our solar system.

C) Venus's surface has many of the same features as Earth's, including volcanoes, craters, and channels.

D) Scientists use a variety of advanced technologies to study the surfaces of the planets in our solar system.

Answer:

D) is correct. Choice A can be eliminated because it directly contradicts the rest of the passage. Choices B and C can also be eliminated because they offer only specific details from the passage. While both choices contain details from the passage, neither is general enough to encompass the passage as a whole. Only choice D provides an assertion that is both backed up by the passage's content and general enough to cover the entire passage.

Topic and Summary Sentences

The topic, and sometimes the main idea of a paragraph, is introduced in the TOPIC SENTENCE. The topic sentence usually appears early in a passage. The first sentence in the example paragraph about Babe Zaharias states the topic and main idea: *Babe Didrikson Zaharias, one of the most decorated female athletes of the twentieth century, is an inspiration for everyone.*

Even though paragraphs generally begin with topic sentences, on occasion writers build up to the topic sentence by using supporting details in order to generate interest or construct an argument. Be alert for paragraphs in which writers do not include a clear topic sentence.

There may also be a **SUMMARY SENTENCE** at the end of a passage. As its name suggests, this sentence sums up the passage, often by restating the main idea and the author's key evidence supporting it.

Example

The Constitution of the United States establishes a series of limits to rein in centralized power. "Separation of powers" distributes federal authority among three branches: the executive, the legislative, and the judicial. "Checks and balances" allow the branches to prevent any one branch from usurping power. "States' rights" are protected under the Constitution from too much encroachment by the federal government. "Enumeration of powers" names the specific and few powers the federal government has. These four restrictions have helped sustain the American republic for over two centuries.

Which of the following is the passage's topic sentence?

A)   These four restrictions have helped sustain the American republic for over two centuries.

B)   The Constitution of the United States establishes a series of limits to rein in centralized power.

C)   "Enumeration of powers" names the specific and few powers the federal government has.

D)   "Checks and balances" allow the branches to prevent any one branch from usurping power.

Answer:

B) is correct. Choice B is the first sentence of the passage and introduces the topic. Choice A is the final sentence of the passage and summarizes the passage's content. Choices C and D are supporting sentences found within the body of the passage. They include important details that support the main idea of the passage.

SUPPORTING DETAILS

SUPPORTING DETAILS reinforce the author's main idea. Let's look again at the passage about athlete Babe Zaharias.

Babe Didrikson Zaharias, one of the most decorated female athletes of the twentieth century, is an inspiration for everyone. Born in 1911 in Beaumont, Texas, Zaharias lived in a time when women were considered second class to men, but she never let that stop her from becoming a champion. Babe was one of seven children in a poor immigrant family and was competitive from an early age. As a child she excelled at most things she tried, especially sports, which continued into high school and beyond. After high school, Babe played amateur basketball for two years, and soon after began training in track and field. Despite the fact that women were only allowed to enter in three events, Zaharias represented the United States in the 1932 Los Angeles Olympics, and won two gold medals and one silver for track and field events.

Remember that the main idea of the passage is that Zaharias is someone to admire—an idea introduced in the opening sentence. The remainder of the paragraph provides details that support this assertion. These details include the circumstances of her childhood, her childhood success at sports, and the medals she won at the Olympics.

When looking for supporting details, be alert for **SIGNAL WORDS**. These signal words tell you that a supporting fact or idea will follow, and so can be helpful in identifying supporting details. Signal words can also help you rule out certain sentences as the main idea or topic sentence. If a sentence begins with one of these phrases, it will likely be too specific to be a main idea.

> ⚠️
>
> Signal words: *for example, specifically, in addition, furthermore, for instance, others, in particular, some*

Examples

From so far away it's easy to imagine the surface of our solar system's planets as enigmas—how could we ever know what those far-flung planets really look like? It turns out, however, that scientists have a number of tools at their disposal that allow them to paint detailed pictures of many planets' surfaces. The topography of Venus, for example, has been explored by several space probes, including the Russian Venera landers and NASA's *Magellan* orbiter. In addition to these long-range probes, NASA has also used its series of orbiting telescopes to study distant planets. These four massively powerful telescopes include the famous Hubble Space Telescope as well as the Compton Gamma Ray Observatory, the Chandra X-Ray Observatory, and the Spitzer Space Telescope. Such powerful telescopes aren't just found in space: NASA makes use of Earth-based telescopes as well. Scientists at the National Radio Astronomy Observatory in Charlottesville, Virginia, have spent decades using radio imaging to build an incredibly detailed portrait of Venus's surface.

1. According to the passage, which of the following is a space probe used to explore the surface of Venus?

   A) *Magellan* orbiter

   B) Hubble Space Telescope

   C) Spitzer Space Telescope

   D) National Radio Astronomy Observatory

   Answer:

   A) is correct. The passage states, "The topography of Venus, for example, has been explored by several space probes, including the Russian Venera landers and NASA's *Magellan* orbiter." The other choices are mentioned in the passage, but are not space probes.

2. If true, which detail could be added to the passage above to support the author's argument that scientists use many different technologies to study the surface of planets?

   A) Because Earth's atmosphere blocks X-rays, gamma rays, and infrared radiation, NASA needed to put telescopes in orbit above the atmosphere.

   B) In 2015, NASA released a map of Venus that was created by compiling images from orbiting telescopes and long-range space probes.

   C) NASA is currently using the *Curiosity* and *Opportunity* rovers to look for signs of ancient life on Mars.

   D) NASA has spent over $2.5 billion to build, launch, and repair the Hubble Space Telescope.

Answer:

B) is correct. Choice B is the best option because it addresses the use of multiple technologies to study the surface of planets. Choices C and D can be eliminated because they do not address the topic of studying the surface of planets. Choice A can also be eliminated because it only addresses a single technology.

FACTS VS. OPINIONS

In TEAS reading passages you might be asked to identify a statement as either a fact or an opinion. A FACT is a statement or thought that can be proven to be true. The statement *Wednesday comes after Tuesday* is a fact—you can point to a calendar to prove it. In contrast, an OPINION is an assumption, not based in fact, that cannot be proven to be true. The assertion that *television is more entertaining than feature films* is an opinion—people will disagree on this, and there is no reference you can use to prove or disprove it.

> ✔️ Which of the following phrases would be associated with opinions? *for example, studies have shown, I believe, in fact, it's possible that*

Example

Exercise is critical for healthy development in children. Today in the United States, there is an epidemic of poor childhood health; many of these children will face further illnesses in adulthood that are due to poor diet and lack of exercise now. This is a problem for all Americans, especially with the rising cost of health care.

It is vital that school systems and parents encourage children to engage in a minimum of thirty minutes of cardiovascular exercise each day, mildly increasing their heart rate for a sustained period. This is proven to decrease the likelihood of developmental diabetes, obesity, and a multitude of other health problems. Also, children need a proper diet, rich in fruits and vegetables, so they can develop physically and learn healthy eating habits early on.

Which of the following in the passage is a fact, not an opinion?

A) Fruits and vegetables are the best way to help children be healthy.

B) Children today are lazier than they were in previous generations.

C) The risk of diabetes in children is reduced by physical activity.

D) Children should engage in thirty minutes of exercise a day.

Answer:

C) is correct. Choice C is a simple fact stated by the author. It is introduced by the word *proven* to indicate that it is supported by evidence. Choice B can be discarded immediately because it is not discussed anywhere in the passage, and also because it is negative, usually a hint in multiple-choice questions that an answer choice is wrong. Choices A and D are both opinions—the author is promoting exercise, fruits, and vegetables as a way to make children healthy. (Notice that these incorrect answers contain words that hint at being an opinion such as *best* or *should*.)

MAKING INFERENCES

In addition to understanding the main idea and factual content of a passage, you will also be asked to take your analysis one step further and anticipate what other information could logically be added to the passage. In a nonfiction passage, for example, you might be asked which statement the author of the passage would agree with. In an excerpt from a fictional work, you might be asked to anticipate what the character would do next.

To answer such questions, you need to have a solid understanding of the topic and main idea of the passage. Armed with this information, you can figure out which of the answer choices best fits the criteria (or, alternatively, which do not). For example, if the author of the passage is advocating for safer working conditions in factories, any details that could be added to the passage should support that idea. You might add sentences that contain information about the number of accidents that occur in factories or that outline a new plan for fire safety.

Example

Exercise is critical for healthy development in children. Today in the United States, there is an epidemic of poor childhood health; many of these children will face further illnesses in adulthood that are due to poor diet and lack of exercise now. This is a problem for all Americans, especially with the rising cost of health care.

It is vital that school systems and parents encourage children to engage in a minimum of thirty minutes of cardiovascular exercise each day, mildly increasing their heart rate for a sustained period. This is proven to decrease the likelihood of developmental diabetes, obesity, and a multitude of other health problems. Also, children need a proper diet, rich in fruits and vegetables, so they can develop physically and learn healthy eating habits early on.

Which of the following statements might the author of this passage agree with?

A) Adults who do not have healthy eating habits should be forced to pay more for health care.

B) Schools should be required by federal law to provide vegetables with every meal.

C) Healthy eating habits can only be learned at home.

D) Schools should encourage students to bring lunches from home.

Answer:

B) is correct. Since the author argues that children need a proper diet rich in fruits and vegetables, we can infer that the author would agree with choice B. The author describes the cost of health care as a problem for all Americans, implying that he would not want to punish adults who never learned healthy eating habits (choice A). Choices C and D are contradicted by the author's focus on creating healthy habits in schools.

TYPES OF PASSAGES

Authors typically write with a purpose. Sometimes referred to as "authorial intention," an author's purpose lets us know why the author is writing and what he or she would like to accomplish. There are many reasons an author might write, but most write for one of four reasons:

- to ENTERTAIN the reader or tell a story
- to PERSUADE the reader of his or her opinion
- to DESCRIBE something, such as a person, place, thing, or event
- to EXPLAIN a process or procedure

Identifying an author's purpose can be tricky, but the writing itself often gives clues. For example, if an author's purpose is to entertain, the writing may include vivid characters, exciting plot twists, or beautiful, figurative language. On the other hand, if an author wishes to persuade the reader, the passage may present an argument or contain convincing examples that support the author's point of view. An author who wishes to describe a person, place, or event may include lots of details as well as plenty of adjectives and adverbs. Finally, the author whose purpose is to explain a process or procedure may include step-by-step instructions or might present information in a sequence.

Related to authorial intention, described above, are the different MODES of written materials. A short story, for example, is meant to entertain, while an online news article is designed to inform the public about a current event.

Each of these different types of writing has a specific name. On the ATI TEAS, you will be asked to identify which of these categories a passage fits into:

- **NARRATIVE WRITING** tells a story (novel, short story, play).
- **INFORMATIONAL** (or **EXPOSITORY**) **WRITING** informs people (newspaper and magazine articles).
- **TECHNICAL WRITING** explains something (product manual, instructions).
- **PERSUASIVE WRITING** tries to convince the reader of something (opinion column or a blog).

Examples

One of my summer reading books was *Mockingjay*. I was captivated by the adventures of the main character and the complicated plot of the book. However, I would argue that the ending didn't reflect the excitement of the story. Given what a powerful personality the main character has, I felt like the ending didn't do her justice.

1. Which of the following best captures the author's purpose?

- **A)** explain the plot of the novel *Mockingjay*
- **B)** persuade the reader that the ending of *Mockingjay* is inferior
- **C)** list the novels she read during the summer
- **D)** explain why the ending of a novel is important

Answer:

B) is correct. The purpose of the above passage is to persuade the reader of the author's opinion of the novel *Mockingjay*, specifically that the ending did not do the main character justice. The passage's use of the verb "argue" tells us that the passage is presenting a case to the reader. The passage follows this statement with evidence—that the main character had a powerful personality.

Elizabeth closed her eyes and braced herself on the armrests that divided her from her fellow passengers. Takeoff was always the worst part for her. The revving of the engines, the way her stomach dropped as the plane lurched upward: It made her feel sick. Then, she had to watch the world fade away beneath her, getting smaller and smaller until it was just her and the clouds hurtling through the sky. Sometimes (but only sometimes) it just had to be endured. She focused on the thought of her sister's smiling face and her new baby nephew as the plane slowly pulled onto the runway.

2. Which of the following best describes the mode of the passage?

A) narrative

B) expository

C) technical

D) persuasive

Answer:

A) is correct. The passage is telling a story—we meet Elizabeth and learn about her fear of flying—so it is a narrative text. There is no factual information presented or explained, nor is the author trying to persuade the reader.

TEXT STRUCTURE

Authors can structure passages in a number of different ways. These distinct organizational patterns, referred to as TEXT STRUCTURE, use the logical relationships between ideas to improve the readability and coherence of a text. The most common ways passages are organized include:

- PROBLEM-SOLUTION: The author outlines a problem and then discusses a solution.
- COMPARISON-CONTRAST: The author presents two situations and then discusses the similarities and differences.
- CAUSE-EFFECT: The author recounts an action and then discusses the resulting effects.
- DESCRIPTIVE: The author describes an idea, object, person, or other item in detail.

Example

The issue of public transportation has begun to haunt the fast-growing cities of the southern United States. Unlike their northern counterparts, cities like Atlanta, Dallas, and Houston have long promoted growth out and not up—these are cities full of sprawling suburbs and single-family homes, not densely concentrated skyscrapers and apartment buildings. What to do then, when all those suburbanites need to get into the central business districts for work? For a long time it seemed highways were the answer: twenty-lane–wide expanses of concrete that would allow commuters to move from home to work and back again. But these modern miracles have become time-sucking, pollution-spewing nightmares. The residents of these cities may not like it, but it's time for them to turn toward public transport like trains and buses if they want their cities to remain livable.

The organization of this passage can best be described as:

A) a comparison of two similar ideas

B) a description of a place

C) a discussion of several effects all related to the same cause

D) a discussion of a problem followed by a suggested solution

Answer:

D) is correct. Choice C is wrong because the author provides no root cause or a list of effects. Choices A and B are tricky, because the passage contains structures similar to those described above. For example, it compares two things (cities in the North and South) and describes a place (a sprawling city). However, if you look at the overall organization of the passage, you can see that it starts by presenting a problem (transportation) and then suggests a solution (trains and buses), making answer D the only choice that encompasses the entire passage.

RESEARCH

The ATI TEAS Reading section also includes questions about using sources for research. You will need to be able to differentiate between primary and secondary sources, and identify a useful and credible source of information.

The terms *primary source* and *secondary source* describe an author's relationship to his or her topic. A PRIMARY SOURCE is an unaltered piece of writing that was composed during the time when the events being described took place; these texts are often written by the people involved. A SECONDARY SOURCE might address the same topic but provides extra commentary or analysis. These texts can be written by people not directly involved in the events. For example, a book written by a political candidate to inform people about his or her stand on an issue is a primary source; an online article written by a journalist analyzing how that position will affect the election is a secondary source.

When researching a topic, it is necessary to determine whether or not any given source is credible. A source is credible if it is from an expert authority and is free from bias. Credible sources provide research that is trustworthy because the information has been fact-checked. Such sources include peer-reviewed journals (journals that ask other experts to review content before it is published) and websites from reputable institutions such as the World Health Organization or the American Academy of Pediatrics. Less credible sources include personal blogs, opinion pieces, and online message boards.

How can you tell if a source is credible? Ask yourself the following questions:

- Is the article from a journal that is peer-reviewed?
- Is the article recent? (Most research journals will identify themselves as peer-reviewed on their website or in the journal itself. You may also limit your library database searches to include only peer-reviewed research.)
- Is the article recent? (Articles that are over a decade old may contain information that is out-of-date or that has been proven inaccurate.)
- Is the author trustworthy? (Is the author of the article listed? Does the author have academic credentials (such as a PhD) or hold an academic post? Is the author free from bias or does he or she seem to promote a particular political view or personal agenda?)

CONTINUE

Examples

1. The students in Professor Johnson's class are searching for secondary sources for a paper on the polio vaccine. Which of the following might they consult?

   A) an interview with a person who has been diagnosed with polio

   B) pictures of patients who have received the polio vaccine

   C) a journal article on the rate of polio inoculation in the United States

   D) an interview with a doctor who specializes in the treatment of polio

   Answer:

   C) is correct. Choice C is the only secondary source listed. Choices A, B, and D, all contain firsthand information. Choice C provides extra commentary and analysis on the subject.

2. Cynthia wants to research the effectiveness of soap from different manufacturers. Where should she look for this information?

   A) a blog

   B) the manufacturer's website

   C) an independent research firm's report

   D) a magazine advertisement for dish soap

   Answer:

   C) is correct. All four sources might discuss different soaps, but choice C, an independent research firm, is the most credible because it is a professional firm and is not related to the manufacturer.

VOCABULARY

On the Reading section you may also be asked to provide definitions or intended meanings of words within passages. You may have never encountered some of these words before the test, but there are tricks you can use to figure out what they mean.

Context Clues

One of the most fundamental vocabulary skills is using the context in which a word is found to determine its meaning. Your ability to read sentences carefully is extremely helpful when it comes to understanding new vocabulary words.

Vocabulary questions on the ATI TEAS will usually include SENTENCE CONTEXT CLUES within the sentence that contains the word. There are several clues that can help you understand the context, and therefore the meaning of a word:

RESTATEMENT CLUES state the definition of the word in the sentence. The definition is often set apart from the rest of the sentence by a comma, parentheses, or a colon.

> Teachers often prefer teaching students with intrinsic motivation:
> these students have an internal desire to learn.
>
> The meaning of *intrinsic* is restated as *internal*.

CONTRAST CLUES include the opposite meaning of a word. Words like *but, on the other hand*, and *however* are tip-offs that a sentence contains a contrast clue.

> Janet was <u>destitute</u> after she lost her job, but her wealthy
> sister helped her get back on her feet.
>
> *Destitute* is contrasted with *wealthy*, so the definition of destitute is *poor*.

POSITIVE/NEGATIVE CLUES tell you whether a word has a positive or negative meaning.

> The film was <u>lauded</u> by critics as stunning, and was nominated for
> several awards.
>
> The positive descriptions *stunning* and *nominated for several awards* suggest
> that *lauded* has a positive meaning.

Examples

Select the answer that most closely matches the definition of the underlined word or phrase as it is used in the sentence.

1. The dog was <u>dauntless</u> in the face of danger, braving the fire to save the girl trapped inside the building.

    A) difficult

    B) fearless

    C) imaginative

    D) startled

    Answer:

    B) is correct. Demonstrating bravery in the face of danger would be fearless. The restatement clue (*braving*) tells you exactly what the word means.

2. Beth did not spend any time preparing for the test, but Tyrone kept a <u>rigorous</u> study schedule.

    A) strict

    B) loose

    C) boring

    D) strange

    Answer:

    A) is correct. The word *but* tells us that Tyrone studied in a different way from Beth, which means it is a contrast clue. If Beth did not study hard, then Tyrone did. The best answer, therefore, is choice A.

Analyzing Words

As you know, determining the meaning of a word can be more complicated than just looking in a dictionary. A word might have more than one **DENOTATION**, or definition, and which one the author intends can only be judged by looking at the surrounding text. For example, the word *quack* can refer to the sound a duck makes or to a person who publicly pretends to have a qualification which he or she does not actually possess.

A word may also have different **CONNOTATIONS**, which are the implied meanings and emotions a word evokes in the reader. For example, a cubicle is simply a walled desk in an office, but for many the word implies a constrictive, uninspiring workplace. Connotations can vary greatly between cultures and even between individuals.

Last, authors might make use of FIGURATIVE LANGUAGE, which is the use of a word to imply something other than the word's literal definition. This is often done by comparing two things. If you say *I felt like a butterfly when I got a new haircut*, the listener knows you do not resemble an insect but instead felt beautiful and transformed.

Examples

Select the answer that most closely matches the definition of the underlined word or phrase as it is used in the sentence.

1. The patient's uneven <u>pupils</u> suggested that brain damage was possible.

    A) part of the eye

    B) student in a classroom

    C) walking pace

    D) breathing sounds

    Answer:

    A) is correct. Only choice A matches both the definition of the word and context of the sentence. Choice B is an alternative definition for pupil, but does not make sense in the sentence. Both C and D could be correct in the context of the sentence, but neither is a definition of pupil.

2. Aiden examined the antique lamp and worried that he had been <u>taken for a ride</u>. He had paid a lot for the vintage lamp, but it looked like it was worthless.

    A) transported

    B) forgotten

    C) deceived

    D) hindered

    Answer:

    C) is correct. It is clear from the context of the sentence that Aiden was not literally taken for a ride. Instead, this phrase is an example of figurative language. From context clues you can figure out that Aiden paid too much for the lamp, so he was deceived.

Word Structure

You are not expected to know every word in the English language for your test; rather, you will need to use deductive reasoning to find the best definition of the word in question. Many words can be broken down into three main parts to help determine their meaning:

PREFIX — ROOT — SUFFIX

ROOTS are the building blocks of all words. Every word is either a root itself or has a root. The root is what is left when you strip away the prefixes and suffixes from a word. For example, in the word *unclear*, if you take away the prefix *un–*, you have the root *clear*.

Roots are not always recognizable words, because they often come from Latin or Greek words, such as *nat*, a Latin root meaning born. The word *native*, which means a person born in a referenced place, comes from this root; so does the word *prenatal*, meaning *before birth*. It is important to keep in mind, however, that roots do not always match the original definitions of words, and they can have several different spellings.

PREFIXES are elements added to the beginning of a word, and SUFFIXES are elements added to the end of the word; together they are known as affixes. They carry assigned meanings and can be attached to a word to completely change the word's meaning or to enhance the word's original meaning.

Let's use the word *prefix* itself as an example: *fix* means to place something securely and *pre–* means before. Therefore, *prefix* means to place something before or in front of. Now let's look at a suffix: in the word *feminism*, *femin* is a root which means female. The suffix *–ism* means act, practice, or process. Thus, *feminism* is the process of establishing equal rights for women.

Although you cannot determine the meaning of a word from a prefix or suffix alone, you can use this knowledge to eliminate answer choices. Understanding whether the word is positive or negative can give you the partial meaning of the word.

✔ Can you figure out the definitions of the following words using their parts? *ambidextrous, anthropology, diagram, egocentric, hemisphere, homicide, metamorphosis, nonsense, portable, rewind, submarine, triangle, unicycle*

Table 1.1. Common Roots

ROOT	DEFINITION	EXAMPLE
ast(er)	star	asteroid, astronomy
audi	hear	audience, audible
auto	self	automatic, autograph
bene	good	beneficent, benign
bio	life	biology, biorhythm
cap	take	capture
ced	yield	secede
chrono	time	chronometer, chronic
corp	body	corporeal
crac or crat	rule	autocrat
demo	people	democracy
dict	say	dictionary, dictation
duc	lead or make	ductile, produce
gen	give birth	generation, genetics
geo	earth	geography, geometry
grad	step	graduate
graph	write	graphical, autograph
ject	throw	eject
jur or jus	law	justice, jurisdiction
juven	young	juvenile
log or logue	thought	logic, logarithm
luc	light	lucidity
man	hand	manual

Table 1.1. Common Roots (continued)

ROOT	DEFINITION	EXAMPLE
mand	order	remand
mis	send	transmission
mono	one	monotone
omni	all	omnivore
path	feel	sympathy
phil	love	philanthropy
phon	sound	phonograph
port	carry	export
qui	rest	quiet
scrib or script	write	scribe, transcript
sense or sent	feel	sentiment
tele	far away	telephone
terr	earth	terrace
uni	single	unicode
vac	empty	vacant
vid or vis	see	video, vision

Table 1.2. Common Prefixes

PREFIX	DEFINITION	EXAMPLE
a– (also an–)	not, without; to, toward; of, completely	atheist, anemic, aside, aback, anew, abashed
ante–	before, preceding	antecedent, anteroom
anti–	opposing, against	antibiotic, anticlimax
belli–	warlike, combative	belligerent, antebellum
com– (also co–, col–, con–, cor–)	with, jointly, completely	combat, cooperate, collide, confide, correspond
dis– (also di–)	negation, removal	disadvantage, disbar
en– (also em–)	put into or on; bring into the condition of; intensify	engulf, embrace
hypo–	under	hypoglycemic, hypodermic
in– (also il–, im–, ir–)	not, without; in, into, toward, inside	infertile, impossible, illegal, irregular, influence, include
intra–	inside, within	intravenous, intrapersonal
out–	surpassing, exceeding; external, away from	outperform, outdoor
over–	excessively, completely; upper, outer, over, above	overconfident, overcast
pre–	before	precondition, preadolescent, prelude

PREFIX	DEFINITION	EXAMPLE
re–	again	reapply, remake
semi–	half, partly	semicircle, semiconscious
syn– (also sym–)	in union, acting together	synthesis, symbiotic
trans–	across, beyond	transdermal
trans–	into a different state	translate
under–	beneath, below; not enough	underarm, undersecretary, underdeveloped

Examples

Select the answer that most closely matches the definition of the underlined word or phrase as it is used in the sentence.

1. The <u>bellicose</u> dog will be sent to training school next week.

  A) misbehaved

  B) friendly

  C) scared

  D) aggressive

Answer:

D) is correct. Both *misbehaved* and *aggressive* look like possible answers given the context of the sentence. However, the prefix *belli–*, which means warlike, can be used to confirm that *aggressive* is the right answer.

2. The new menu <u>rejuvenated</u> the restaurant and made it one of the most popular spots in town.

  A) established

  B) invigorated

  C) improved

  D) motivated

Answer:

B) is correct. All the answer choices could make sense in the context of the sentence, so it is necessary to use word structure to find the definition. The root *juven* means young and the prefix *re–* means again, so *rejuvenate* means to be made young again. The answer choice with the most similar meaning is *invigorated*, which means to give something energy.

INFORMATIONAL SOURCES

The ATI TEAS exam also includes questions that test your comprehension of informational sources other than text passages. These questions will include visual information sources (maps, graphs, diagrams), text features (book indexes, tables of contents), printed communications (flyers, memos), or lists of instructions.

GRAPHS

Graphs are used to present numerical data in a way that is easy for the reader to understand. There are a number of different types of graphs, each of which is useful for different types of data.

BAR GRAPHS use bars of different lengths to compare amounts. The independent variable on a bar graph is grouped into categories such as months, flavors, or locations, and the dependent variable will be a quantity. Thus, comparing the lengths of the bars provides a visual guide to the relative quantities in each category.

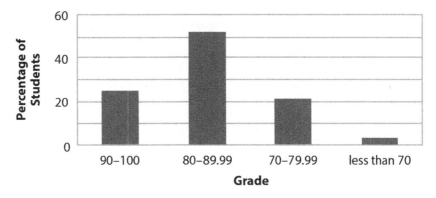

Figure 2.1. Bar Graph

SCATTERPLOTS use points to show relationships between two variables that can be plotted as coordinate points. One variable describes a position on the *x*-axis, and the other a point on the *y*-axis. Scatterplots can suggest relationships between variables. For example, both variables might increase, or one might increase when the other decreases.

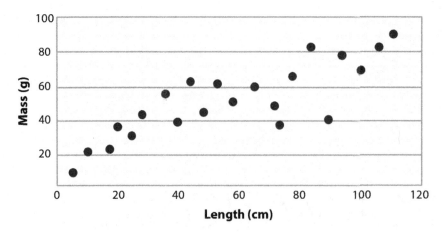

Figure 2.2. Scatterplot

LINE GRAPHS show changes in data by connecting points on a scatterplot using a line. These graphs will often measure time on the *x*-axis and are used to show trends in the data, such as temperature changes over a day or school attendance throughout the year.

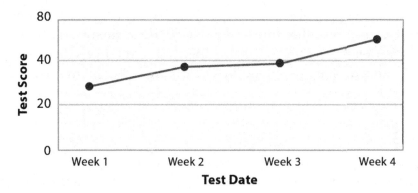

Figure 2.3. Line Graph

CIRCLE GRAPHS (also called pie charts) are used to show parts of a whole: the "pie" is the whole, and each "slice" represents a percentage or part of the whole.

Tests

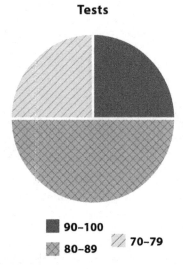

■ 90–100
▨ 80–89   ⧄ 70–79

Figure 2.4. Circle Graph

Examples

Sales at Wholesale Electronics

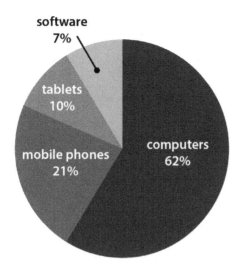

1. Which of the following products accounts for the largest share of Wholesale Electronics' total sales?

    A) mobile phones

    B) computers

    C) software and tablets

    D) software and mobile phones

    Answer:

    B) is correct. Computers account for 62 percent of sales. Mobile phones (choice A) are 21 percent, software and tablets (choice C) equal 17 percent, and software and mobile phones (choice D) equal 28 percent.

2. Mobile phones and tablets make up what percentage of Wholesale Electronics' total sales?

    A) 17 percent

    B) 28 percent

    C) 31 percent

    D) 83 percent

    Answer:

    C) is correct. Mobile phones (21 percent) and tablets (10 percent) together account for 31 percent of Wholesale Electronics' total sales.

MAPS

The LEGEND or KEY of a map explains the various symbols used on the map and their meanings and measurements. These symbols typically include a compass rose and a distance scale. A COMPASS ROSE indicates the four cardinal directions (north, south, west, and east) and the four intermediate directions (northwest, northeast, southwest, and southeast). A

DISTANCE SCALE is used to show the ratio of the distance on the page to the actual distance between objects, usually in miles or kilometers.

Examples

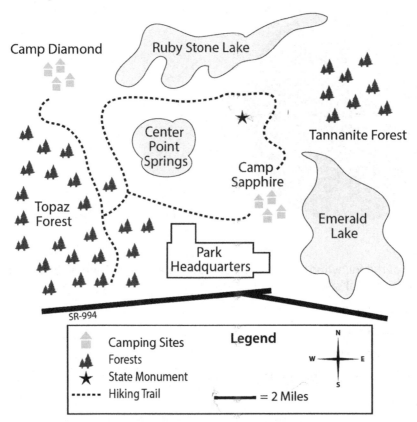

1. Which direction is Ruby Stone Lake from Park Headquarters?

    A) south

    B) northwest

    C) southwest

    D) north

    Answer:

    D) is correct. Ruby Stone Lake is north of Park Headquarters.

2. Approximately how many miles is it from the state monument to the center of Tananite Forest?

    A) 1 mile

    B) 2 miles

    C) 4 miles

    D) 5 miles

    Answer:

    C) is correct. Using the distance scale, it is possible to estimate that the center of Tananite Forest is approximately 4 miles from the state monument.

SCALE READINGS

A scale reading is a numerical value collected from a scale or measurement device. On the TEAS, you may see devices like thermometers, blood pressure cuffs, or weight scales. To prepare for the exam, familiarize yourself with the standard units and displays for these devices.

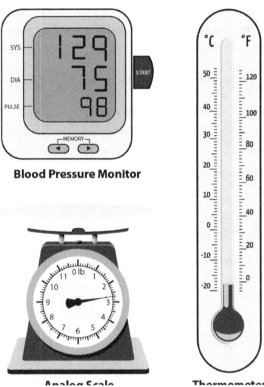

Blood Pressure Monitor

Analog Scale   **Thermometer**

Figure 2.5. Scale Readings

Examples

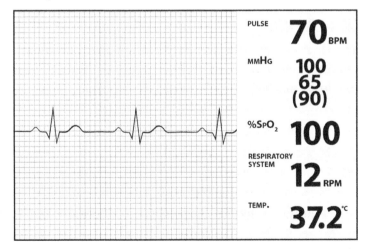

1. The figure shows the readout for a patient's EKG monitor. What is the patient's oxygen saturation?

A) 70 BPM

B) 100 mmHg

C) 100 percent

D) 37.2 °C

Answer:

C) is correct. The notation %SpO2 stands for oxygen saturation, which reads 100 percent.

The table below describes the categories for systolic blood pressure.

CATEGORIES	SYSTOLIC RANGE
Normal	< 120
Prehypertension	120 - 139
Hypertension Stage 1	140 - 159
Hypertension Stage 2	160 - 179
Hypertensive Crisis	> 180

2. The EKG monitor shows a patient who belongs in which of the following categories?

A) Normal

B) Prehypertension

C) Hypertension Stage 1

D) Hypertension Stage 2

Answer:

A) is correct. The EKG monitor shows a systolic reading of 100, which places the patient in the Normal category.

PRODUCT INFORMATION

Product information questions ask you to use given information about products, such as price, shipping, or taxes, to compare the true cost of those products. (You will be required to perform basic arithmetic for some of the problems in this section.)

Examples

Use the chart below to answer the following questions.

Shoe Prices

RETAILER	BASE PRICE	SHIPPING & HANDLING	TAXES
Wholesale Footwear	$59.99	$10.95	$7.68
Bargain Sales	$65.99	$5.95	$5.38
Famous Shoes	$79.99	$0.00	$4.89

1. Rachel wants to buy shoes and can't spend more than $80. Which retailer(s) can she shop at?

   A) Wholesale Footwear and Bargain Sales

   B) Famous Shoes

   C) Wholesale Footwear and Famous Shoes

   D) Bargain Sales and Famous Shoes

   Answer:

   A) is correct. When you add the base price, shipping and handling fees, and taxes, shoes from Famous Shoes cost $84.88, so Rachel can only shop at Wholesale Footwear ($78.62) and Bargain Sales ($77.32).

2. Allen has budgeted $6 for taxes and $6 for shipping and handling. Which retailer(s) can he shop at?

   A) Bargain Sales and Famous Shoes

   B) Wholesale Footwear and Famous Shoes

   C) Wholesale Footwear

   D) Bargain Sales and Wholesale Footwear

   Answer:

   A) is correct. Bargain Sales and Famous Shoes are both under Allen's budget for taxes and shipping and handling.

SETS OF DIRECTIONS

Some questions on the TEAS will require you to follow a set of simple directions. These directions can be given in a paragraph format or list format. Usually, each step, or direction, includes specific instructions that must be remembered in order to complete the subsequent steps. The directions will require you to manipulate quantities (such as money or numbers of items) or shapes to reach the final answer.

Write out the new answer for each step as you finish it so you can easily check your work.

Examples

1. You start with 3 red apples and 1 green apple in a basket. After following the directions below, how many apples are in the basket?

   1. Remove 1 red apple.

   2. Add 1 green apple.

   3. Add 1 red apple.

   4. Add 1 green apple.

   5. Remove 2 red apples.

   6. Remove 1 green apple.

   7. Add 3 red apples.

   8. Add 2 green apples.

A) 4 red apples and 2 green apples

B) 4 red apples and 4 green apples

C) 2 red apples and 3 green apples

D) 0 red apples and 3 green apples

Answer:

B) is correct. Starting with 3 red apples and 1 green apple, and following the directions, you have:

1. 2 red apples and 1 green apple
2. 2 red apples and 2 green apples
3. 3 red apples and 2 green apples
4. 3 red apples and 3 green apples
5. 1 red apple and 3 green apples
6. 1 red apple and 2 green apples
7. 4 red apples and 2 green apples
8. 4 red apples and 4 green apples

2. You have 12 gallons of fuel in your tank. After following the directions below, how many gallons of fuel are left in the tank?

   1. Use 1 gallon to drive to work.
   2. Use 1 gallon to drive home.
   3. Use 0.5 gallons to drive the kids to soccer practice.
   4. Use 0.5 gallons to drive to the grocery store.
   5. Use 2 gallons to drive back home.

   A) 2 gallons

   B) 5.5 gallons

   C) 7 gallons

   D) 8.5 gallons

Answer:

C) is correct. Starting with 12 gallons, and following the directions, you have:

1. 11 gallons
2. 10 gallons
3. 9.5 gallons
4. 9 gallons
5. 7 gallons

PRINTED COMMUNICATIONS

Printed communications such as invitations, advertisements, and memos can contain a lot of information. For these questions, you will need to look at sources of information other than just a plain text passage. For example, an event flyer might have important information presented graphically, or you may need to look at the subject line of a memo to find its topic.

The strategies you learned for reading passages will help you answer questions about printed communications. For example, you might need to find the purpose of a memo or identify supporting details in an advertisement.

Examples

> **MEMO**
>
> To: Human Resources Department
> From: Corporate Management
> Date: December 6, 2013
> Subject: Personal Use of Computers
>
> The corporate office has been conducting standard monitoring of computer usage, and we have been quite dismayed at the amount of personal use occurring during business hours. Employee computers are available for the sole purpose of completing company business, nothing else. Personal use should occur only in emergency situations and should be limited to thirty minutes per day. Please communicate these requirements to lower management and personnel. These rules must be respected. If not, employees will be reprimanded by Management.

1. What is the tone of the memo?

   A) derisive

   B) ambiguous

   C) enraged

   D) threatening

   Answer:

   D) is correct. The memo threatens that *employees will be reprimanded* if the given rules are not followed.

2. Which of the following are specific instructions given to the Human Resources Department?

   A) Complete company business on personal computers during business hours.

   B) Conduct standard monitoring of computer usage.

   C) Communicate that personal use of computers is to occur only in emergency situations.

   D) Communicate that personal computers should be limited to one hour per day.

   Answer:

   C) is correct. According to the memo, the Human Resources Department is to communicate to lower management and personnel that personal use of company computers is to occur only in emergency situations.

INDEXES AND TABLES OF CONTENTS

An **INDEX** is an alphabetical list of topics, and their associated page numbers, covered in a text. A **TABLE OF CONTENTS** is an outline of a text that includes topics, organized by page number. Both of these can be used to look up information, but they have slightly different purposes. An index helps the reader determine where in the text he or she can find specific details. A table of contents shows the reader the general arrangement of the text.

> When would it be appropriate to use an index but NOT a table of contents?

Examples

Use the examples to answer the following questions.

> Nursing, 189 – 296
> certification, 192 – 236
> code of ethics, 237 – 291
> procedures, 292 – 296

1. According to the index above, where might the reader find information about the nursing code of ethics?

   A) pages 237 – 291

   B) pages 189 – 296

   C) pages 292 – 296

   D) pages 189 – 236

   Answer:

   A) is correct. According to the index, this information can be found between pages 237 and 291.

TABLE OF CONTENTS

Chapter 1: Pre-Algebra	5
Chapter 2: Algebra	35
Chapter 3: Geometry	115
Chapter 4: Calculus	175

2. A student has been assigned a set of homework questions from page 125. What topic will the questions cover?

   A) Pre-Algebra

   B) Algebra

   C) Geometry

   D) Calculus

   Answer:

   C) is correct. According to the table of contents, page 125 is in Chapter 3: Geometry.

TEXT FEATURES

TEXT FEATURES are stylistic elements used to clarify, add meaning, or differentiate. Examples of text features include bold, italicized, or underlined fonts, and bulleted or numbered lists.

Bold fonts are generally used for emphasis. Italics should be used for titles of longer works, such as novels, movies, books, magazines, and plays. They are also used to denote a foreign word or phrase. Note that italicized fonts and underlined fonts serve similar purposes and are often used interchangeably. Underlining is more commonly used in handwritten documents.

Example

Which of the following sentences properly uses italics?

A) We enjoyed our vacation in *Sacramento, California*.

B) Adam ate two plates of *pasta with meatballs*.

C) Angela's favorite book is *The Art of War*.

D) The traffic on *Main Street* is terrible during rush hour.

Answer:

C) is correct. The sentence in choice C italicizes the title of a longer work and is therefore correct. Italics are not used for names of cities (choice A), foods (choice B), or streets (choice D).

PART II: MATHEMATICS

The Most Common Mistakes

People make little mistakes all the time, but during a test those tiny mistakes can make the difference between a good score and a poor one. Watch out for these common mistakes that people make on the math section of the TEAS:

- answering with the wrong sign (positive/negative)
- mixing up the order of operations
- misplacing a decimal
- providing an answer that was not asked for
- circling the wrong letter or filling in wrong circle choice

If you're thinking, *those ideas are just common sense*, that's exactly the point. Most of the mistakes made on the TEAS are simple ones. But no matter how silly the mistake, a wrong answer still means a lost point on the test.

Strategies for the Mathematics Section

Go Back to the Basics

First and foremost, practice your basic skills: sign changes, order of operations, simplifying fractions, and equation manipulation. These are the skills used most on the TEAS, though they are applied in many different contexts. Remember that when it comes down to it, all math problems rely on the four basic skills of addition, subtraction, multiplication, and division. All you need to figure out is the order in which they're used to solve a problem.

Don't Rely on Mental Math

Using mental math is great for eliminating answer choices, but ALWAYS WRITE DOWN YOUR WORK! This cannot be stressed enough. Use whatever paper is provided; by writing and/or drawing out the problem, you are more likely to catch any mistakes. The act of writing things down also forces you to organize your calculations, leading to an improvement in your TEAS score.

The Three-Times Rule

You should read each question at least three times to ensure you're using the correct information and answering the right question:

Step one: Read the question and write out the given information.

Step two: Read the question, set up your equation(s), and solve.

Step three: Read the question and check that your answer makes sense (is the amount too large or small; is the answer in the correct unit of measure, etc.).

Make an Educated Guess

Eliminate those answer choices that you are relatively sure are incorrect, and then guess from the remaining choices. Educated guessing is critical to increasing your score.

NUMBERS AND OPERATIONS

TYPES OF NUMBERS

Numbers can be categorized based on their properties. While the TEAS won't directly test you on the types of numbers, it can be helpful to understand these categories while you review mathematical terms and operations.

- A **NATURAL NUMBER** is greater than 0 and has no decimal or fraction attached. These are also sometimes called counting numbers. {1, 2, 3, 4, ...}
- **WHOLE NUMBERS** are natural numbers and the number 0. {0, 1, 2, 3, 4, ...}
- **INTEGERS** include positive and negative natural numbers and 0. {..., –4, –3, –2, –1, 0, 1, 2, 3, 4, ...}
- A **RATIONAL NUMBER** can be represented as a fraction. Any decimal part must terminate or resolve into a repeating pattern. (Examples: 0.7, $\frac{1}{2}$, –12.36)
- An **IRRATIONAL NUMBER** cannot be represented as a fraction. An irrational decimal number never ends and never resolves into a repeating pattern. (Examples: π, $\frac{3}{7}$, $-\sqrt{2}$)
- A **REAL NUMBER** is a number that can be represented by a point on a number line. Real numbers include all the rational and irrational numbers.

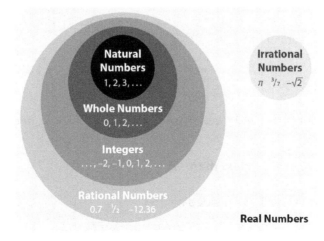

Figure 3.1. Types of Numbers

POSITIVE AND NEGATIVE NUMBERS

You can use a number line to easily find the result when adding and subtracting positive and negative numbers. When adding two numbers, whether they are positive or negative, count to the right; when subtracting, count to the left. Note that adding a negative value is the same as subtracting. Subtracting a negative value is the same as adding.

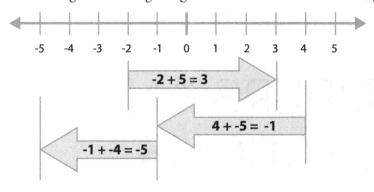

Figure 3.2. Adding and Subtracting Positive and Negative Numbers

Multiplying and dividing with negative and positive numbers is somewhat easier. Multiplying two numbers with the same sign gives a positive result, and multiplying two numbers with different signs gives a negative result. The same rules apply to division. These rules are summarized below:

(+) + (−) = the sign of the larger number

(−) + (−) = negative number

(−) × (−) or (−) ÷ (−) = positive number

(−) × (+) or (−) ÷ (+) = negative number

(+) + (+) or (+) × (+) or (+) ÷ (+) = positive number

Examples

1. Find the product of −10 and 47.

   (−) × (+) = (−)

   $−10 \times 47 = \textbf{−470}$

2. What is the sum of −65 and −32?

   (−) + (−) = (−)

   $−65 + −32 = \textbf{−97}$

3. Is the product of −7 and 4 less than −7, between −7 and 4, or greater than 4?

   (−) × (+) = (−)

   $−7 \times 4 = −28$, which is **less than −7**

4. What is the value of −16 divided by 2.5?

   (−) ÷ (+) = (−)

   $−16 \div 2.5 = \textbf{−6.4}$

ORDER OF OPERATIONS

Operations in a mathematical expression are always performed in a specific order, which is described by the acronym PEMDAS:

1. Parentheses
2. Exponents
3. Multiplication
4. Division
5. Addition
6. Subtraction

> ✔
> Can you come up with a mnemonic device to help yourself remember the order of operations?

Perform the operations within parentheses first, and then address any exponents. After those steps, perform all multiplication and division. These are carried out from left to right as they appear in the problem.

Finally, do all required addition and subtraction, also from left to right as each operation appears in the problem.

Examples

1. Solve: $-(2)^2 - (4 + 7)$

   First, complete operations within parentheses:

   $-(2)^2 - (11)$

   Second, calculate the value of exponential expressions:

   $-(4) - (11)$

   Finally, do addition and subtraction:

   $-4 - 11 = \mathbf{-15}$

2. Solve: $(5)^2 \div 5 + 4 \times 2$

   First, calculate the value of exponential expressions:

   $(25) \div 5 + 4 \times 2$

   Second, calculate division and multiplication from left to right:

   $5 + 8$

   Finally, do addition and subtraction:

   $5 + 8 = \mathbf{13}$

3. Solve the expression: $15 \times (4 + 8) - 3^3$

   First, complete operations within parentheses:

   $15 \times (12) - 3^3$

   Second, calculate the value of exponential expressions:

   $15 \times (12) - 27$

   Third, calculate division and multiplication from left to right:

   $180 - 27$

   Finally, do addition and subtraction from left to right:

   $180 - 27 = \mathbf{153}$

4. Solve the expression: $\left(\frac{5}{2} \times 4\right) + 23 - 4^2$

    First, complete operations within parentheses:

    $(10) + 23 - 4^2$

    Second, calculate the value of exponential expressions:

    $(10) + 23 - 16$

    Finally, do addition and subtraction from left to right:

    $10 + 23 - 16$

    $33 - 16 = \mathbf{17}$

DECIMALS AND FRACTIONS

Numbers are written using the base-10 system where each digit (the numeric symbols $0 - 9$) in a number is worth ten times as much as the number to the right of it. For example, in the number 37 each digit has a place value based on its location. The 3 is in the tens place, and so has a value of 30, and the 7 is in the ones place, so it has a value of 7.

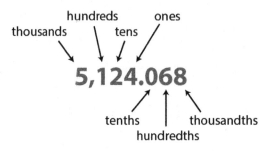

Figure 3.3. Place Value

Adding and Subtracting Decimals

When adding and subtracting decimals, write the numbers so that the decimal points are aligned. You want to subtract the ones place from the ones place, the tenths place from the tenths place, etc.

Examples

1. Find the sum of 17.07 and 2.52.

    $\begin{array}{r} 17.07 \\ +\ \ 2.52 \\ \hline = \mathbf{19.59} \end{array}$

2. Jeannette has 7.4 gallons of gas in her tank. After driving, she has 6.8 gallons. How many gallons of gas did she use?

    $\begin{array}{r} 7.4 \\ -\ 6.8 \\ \hline = \mathbf{0.6\ gal.} \end{array}$

Multiplying and Dividing Decimals

When multiplying decimals, start by multiplying the numbers normally. You can then determine the placement of the decimal point in the result by adding the number of digits after the decimal in each of the numbers you multiplied together.

When dividing decimals, you should move the decimal point in the divisor (the number you're dividing by) until it is a whole number. You can then move the decimal in the dividend (the number you're dividing into) the same number of places in the same direction. Finally, divide the new numbers normally to get the correct answer.

Examples

1. What is the product of 0.25 and 1.3?

   $25 \times 13 = 325$

   There are 2 digits after the decimal in 0.25 and one digit after the decimal in 1.3. Therefore the product should have 3 digits after the decimal: 0.325.

2. Find $0.8 \div 0.2$.

   Change 0.2 to 2 by moving the decimal one space to the right.

   Next, move the decimal one space to the right on the dividend. 0.8 becomes 8.

   Now, divide 8 by 2. $8 \div 2 = \textbf{4}$

3. Find the quotient when 40 is divided by 0.25.

   First, change the divisor to a whole number: 0.25 becomes 25.

   Next, change the dividend to match the divisor by moving the decimal two spaces to the right, so 40 becomes 4000.

   Now divide: $4000 \div 25 = \textbf{160}$

Working with Fractions

FRACTIONS are made up of two parts: the NUMERATOR, which appears above the bar, and the DENOMINATOR, which is below it. If a fraction is in its SIMPLEST FORM, the numerator and the denominator share no common factors. A fraction with a numerator larger than or equal to its denominator is an IMPROPER FRACTION; when the denominator is larger, it's a PROPER FRACTION.

Improper fractions can be converted into mixed numbers by dividing the numerator by the denominator. The resulting whole number is placed to the left of the fraction, and the remainder becomes the new numerator; the denominator does not change. The new number is called a MIXED NUMBER because it contains a whole number and a fraction. Mixed numbers can be turned into improper fractions through the reverse process: multiply the whole number by the denominator and add the numerator to get the new numerator.

Examples

1. Simplify the fraction $\frac{121}{77}$.

   121 and 77 share a common factor of 11. So, if we divide each by 11 we can simplify the fraction:

   $\frac{121}{77} = \frac{11}{11} \times \frac{11}{7} = \frac{\textbf{11}}{\textbf{7}}$

2. Convert $\frac{37}{5}$ into a mixed number.

Start by dividing the numerator by the denominator:

$37 \div 5 = 7$ with a remainder of 2

Now build a mixed number with the whole number and the new numerator:

$\frac{37}{5} = \mathbf{7\frac{2}{5}}$

Multiplying and Dividing Fractions

To multiply fractions, convert any mixed numbers into improper fractions and multiply the numerators together and the denominators together. Reduce to lowest terms if needed.

Inverting a fraction changes division to multiplication:

$\frac{a}{b} \div \frac{c}{d} = \frac{a}{b} \times \frac{d}{c} = \frac{ad}{bc}$

To divide fractions, first convert any mixed numbers into improper fractions. Then, invert the second fraction so that the denominator and numerator are switched. Finally, multiply the numerators together and the denominators together.

Examples

1. What is the product of $\frac{1}{12}$ and $\frac{6}{8}$?

Simply multiply the numerators together and the denominators together, then reduce:

$\frac{1}{12} \times \frac{6}{8} = \frac{6}{96} = \mathbf{\frac{1}{16}}$

Sometimes it's easier to reduce fractions before multiplying if you can:

$\frac{1}{12} \times \frac{6}{8} = \frac{1}{12} \times \frac{3}{4} = \frac{3}{48} = \mathbf{\frac{1}{16}}$

2. Find $\frac{7}{8} \div \frac{1}{4}$.

For a fraction division problem, invert the second fraction and then multiply and reduce:

$\frac{7}{8} \div \frac{1}{4} = \frac{7}{8} \times \frac{4}{1} = \frac{28}{8} = \mathbf{\frac{7}{2}}$

3. $\frac{2}{5} \div 1\frac{1}{5} =$

This is a fraction division problem, so the first step is to convert the mixed number to an improper fraction:

$1\frac{1}{5} = \frac{5 \times 1}{5} + \frac{1}{5} = \frac{6}{5}$

Now, divide the fractions. Remember to invert the second fraction, and then multiply normally:

$\frac{2}{5} \div \frac{6}{5} = \frac{2}{5} \times \frac{5}{6} = \frac{10}{30} = \mathbf{\frac{1}{3}}$

4. A recipe calls for $\frac{1}{4}$ cup of sugar. If $8\frac{1}{2}$ batches of the recipe are needed, how many cups of sugar will be used?

This is a fraction multiplication problem: $\frac{1}{4} \times 8\frac{1}{2}$.

First, we need to convert the mixed number into a proper fraction:

$8\frac{1}{2} = \frac{8 \times 2}{2} + \frac{1}{2} = \frac{17}{2}$

Now, multiply the fractions across the numerators and denominators, and then reduce:

$\frac{1}{4} \times 8\frac{1}{2} = \frac{1}{4} \times \frac{17}{2} = \mathbf{\frac{17}{8}}$ **cups of sugar, or** $\mathbf{2\frac{1}{8}}$

Adding and Subtracting Fractions

Adding and subtracting fractions requires a COMMON DENOMINATOR. To get a common denominator, you can multiply each fraction by the number 1. With fractions, any number over itself (e.g., $\frac{5}{5}$, $\frac{12}{12}$, etc.) is equivalent to 1, so multiplying by such a fraction can change the denominator without changing the value of the fraction. Once the denominators are the same, the numerators can be added or subtracted.

To add mixed numbers, you can first add the whole numbers and then the fractions. To subtract mixed numbers, convert each mixed number to an improper fraction, get a common denominator, and then subtract the numerators.

Examples

1. Simplify the expression $\frac{2}{3} - \frac{1}{5}$.

   First, multiply each fraction by a factor of 1 to get a common denominator. How do you know which factor of 1 to use? Look at the other fraction and use the number found in that denominator:

   $$\frac{2}{3} - \frac{1}{5} = \frac{2}{3}\left(\frac{5}{5}\right) - \frac{1}{5}\left(\frac{3}{3}\right) = \frac{10}{15} - \frac{3}{15}$$

   Once the fractions have a common denominator, simply subtract the numerators:

   $$\frac{10}{15} - \frac{3}{15} = \mathbf{\frac{7}{15}}$$

   > The phrase *simplify the expression* just means you need to perform all the operations in the expression.

2. Find $2\frac{1}{3} - \frac{3}{2}$.

   This is a fraction subtraction problem with a mixed number, so the first step is to convert the mixed number to an improper fraction:

   $$2\frac{1}{3} = \frac{2 \times 3}{3} + \frac{1}{3} = \frac{7}{3}$$

   Next, convert each fraction so they share a common denominator:

   $$\frac{7}{3} \times \frac{2}{2} = \frac{14}{6}$$
   $$\frac{3}{2} \times \frac{3}{3} = \frac{9}{6}$$

   Now, subtract the fractions by subtracting the numerators:

   $$\frac{14}{6} - \frac{9}{6} = \mathbf{\frac{5}{6}}$$

3. Find the sum of $\frac{9}{16}$, $\frac{1}{2}$, and $\frac{7}{4}$.

   For this fraction addition problem, we need to find a common denominator. Notice that 2 and 4 are both factors of 16, so 16 can be the common denominator:

   $$\frac{1}{2} \times \frac{8}{8} = \frac{8}{16}$$
   $$\frac{7}{4} \times \frac{4}{4} = \frac{28}{16}$$
   $$\frac{9}{16} + \frac{8}{16} + \frac{28}{16} = \mathbf{\frac{45}{16}}$$

4. Sabrina has $\frac{2}{3}$ of a can of red paint. Her friend Amos has $\frac{1}{6}$ of a can. How much red paint do they have combined?

   To add fractions, make sure that they have a common denominator. Since 3 is a factor of 6, 6 can be the common denominator:

$$\frac{2}{3} \times \frac{2}{2} = \frac{4}{6}$$

Now, add the numerators:

$$\frac{4}{6} + \frac{1}{6} = \frac{5}{6} \text{ of a can}$$

Converting Decimals to Fractions

To convert a fraction to a decimal, just divide the numerator by the denominator on your calculator.

To convert a decimal, simply use the numbers that come after the decimal as the numerator in the fraction. The denominator will be a power of 10 that matches the place value for the original decimal. For example, the denominator for 0.46 would be 100 because the last number is in the hundredths place; likewise, the denominator for 0.657 would be 1000 because the last number is in the thousandths place. Once this fraction has been set up, all that's left is to simplify it.

Example

Convert 0.45 into a fraction.

The last number in the decimal is in the hundredths place, so we can easily set up a fraction:

$$0.45 = \frac{45}{100}$$

The next step is to simply reduce the fraction down to the lowest common denominator. Here, both 45 and 100 are divisible by 5:

$$\frac{45}{100} = \frac{(45 \div 5)}{(100 \div 5)} = \frac{9}{20}$$

COMPARISON OF RATIONAL NUMBERS

To order numbers from least to greatest (or greatest to least), convert them to the same format and place them on a number line.

Number comparison problems present numbers in different formats and ask which is larger or smaller, or whether the numbers are equivalent. The important step in solving these problems is to convert the numbers to the same format so that it is easier to see how they compare. If numbers are given in the same format, or after they have been converted, determine which number is smaller or if the numbers are equal. Remember that for negative numbers, higher numbers are actually smaller.

Examples

1. Which of the following values is the largest? 0.49, $\frac{3}{5}$, $\frac{1}{2}$, 0.55

   Convert the fractions to decimals:

   $$\frac{3}{5} = 0.6$$
   $$\frac{1}{2} = 0.5$$

   Place the values in order from smallest to largest:

   $$0.49 < 0.5 < 0.55 < 0.6$$

   $\frac{3}{5}$ **is the largest number.**

2. Place the following numbers in order from least to greatest:

$\frac{2}{5}, -0.7, 0.35, -\frac{3}{2}, 0.46$

Convert the fractions to decimals:

$\frac{2}{5} = 0.4$

$-\frac{3}{2} = -1.5$

Place the values in order from smallest to largest:

$-1.5 < -0.7 < 0.35 < 0.4 < 0.46$

Put the numbers back in their original form:

$-\frac{3}{2} < -0.7 < 0.35 < \frac{2}{5} < 0.46$

RATIOS

A **RATIO** tells you how many of one thing exist in relation to the number of another thing. Unlike fractions, ratios do not give a part relative to a whole; instead, they compare two values. For example, if you have 3 apples and 4 oranges, the ratio of apples to oranges is 3 to 4. Ratios can be written using words (3 to 4), fractions $\left(\frac{3}{4}\right)$, or colons (3:4).

In order to work with ratios, it's helpful to rewrite them as a fraction expressing a part to a whole. For example, in the example above you have 7 total pieces of fruit, so the fraction of your fruit that are apples is $\frac{3}{7}$, and oranges make up $\frac{4}{7}$ of your fruit collection.

One last important thing to consider when working with ratios is the units of the values being compared. On the TEAS, you may be asked to rewrite a ratio using the same units on both sides. For example, you might have to rewrite the ratio 3 minutes to 7 seconds as 180 seconds to 7 seconds.

Examples

1. There are 90 voters in a room, and each is either a Democrat or a Republican. The ratio of Democrats to Republicans is 5:4. How many Republicans are there?

We know that there are 5 Democrats for every 4 Republicans in the room, which means for every 9 people, 4 are Republicans.

$5 + 4 = 9$

Fraction of Republicans: $\frac{4}{9}$

If $\frac{4}{9}$ of the 90 voters are Republicans, then:

$\frac{4}{9} \times 90 = $ **40 voters are Republicans**

2. The ratio of students to teachers in a school is 15:1. If there are 38 teachers, how many students attend the school?

To solve this ratio problem, we can simply multiply both sides of the ratio by the desired value to find the number of students that correspond to having 38 teachers:

$\frac{15 \text{ students}}{1 \text{ teacher}} \times 38 \text{ teachers} = 570 \text{ students}$

The school has **570 students**.

PROPORTIONS

A **PROPORTION** is an equation which states that 2 ratios are equal. Proportions are usually written as 2 fractions joined by an equal sign $\left(\frac{a}{b} = \frac{c}{d}\right)$, but they can also be written using colons ($a : b :: c : d$). Note that in a proportion, the units must be the same in both numerators and in both denominators.

> Proportion problems on the TEAS are usually word problems that include: distance and time, cost, or measurement.

Often you will be given 3 of the values in a proportion and asked to find the 4th. In these types of problems, you can solve for the missing variable by cross-multiplying—multiply the numerator of each fraction by the denominator of the other to get an equation with no fractions as shown below. You can then solve the equation using basic algebra. (For more on solving basic equations, see "Algebraic Expressions and Equations.")

$$\frac{a}{b} = \frac{c}{d} \rightarrow ad = bc$$

Examples

1. A train traveling 120 miles takes 3 hours to get to its destination. How long will it take for the train to travel 180 miles?

   Start by setting up the proportion:

   $$\frac{120 \text{ miles}}{3 \text{ hours}} = \frac{180 \text{ miles}}{x \text{ hours}}$$

   Note that it doesn't matter which value is placed in the numerator or denominator, as long as it is the same on both sides. Now, solve for the missing quantity through cross–multiplication:

   120 miles × x hours = 3 hours × 180 miles

   Now solve the equation:

   $$x \text{ hours} = \frac{(3 \text{ hours}) \times (180 \text{ miles})}{120 \text{ miles}}$$

   x = 4.5 hours

2. One acre of wheat requires 500 gallons of water. How many acres can be watered with 2600 gallons?

   Set up the equation:

   $$\frac{1 \text{ acre}}{500 \text{ gal.}} = \frac{x \text{ acres}}{2600 \text{ gal.}}$$

   Then solve for x:

   $$x \text{ acres} = \frac{1 \text{ acre} \times 2600 \text{ gal.}}{500 \text{ gal.}}$$

   $x = \frac{26}{5}$ or **5.2 acres**

PERCENTAGES

A **PERCENT** is the ratio of a part to the whole multiplied by 100. The equation for percentages can be rearranged to solve for either the part, the whole, or the percent:

$$percent = \frac{part}{whole}$$
$$part = whole \times percent$$

$$whole = \frac{part}{percent}$$

In the equations above, the percent should always be expressed as a decimal. In order to convert a decimal into a percentage value, simply multiply it by 100. So, if you've read 5 pages (the part) of a 10-page article (the whole), you've read $\frac{5}{10}$ = 0.5 = 50%. (The percent sign (%) is used once the decimal has been multiplied by 100.)

Note that when solving these problems, the units for the part and the whole should be the same. If you're reading a book, saying you've read 5 pages out of 15 chapters doesn't make any sense.

> ⚠️ The word *of* usually indicates what the whole is in a problem. For example, the problem might say *Ella ate two slices of the pizza*, which means the pizza is the whole.

Examples

1. 45 is 15% of what number?

   Set up the appropriate equation and solve. Don't forget to change 15% to a decimal value:

   $whole = \frac{part}{percent} = \frac{45}{0.15} = $ **300**

2. Jim spent 30% of his paycheck at the fair. He spent $15 for a hat, $30 for a shirt, and $20 playing games. How much was his check? (Round to nearest dollar.)

   Set up the appropriate equation and solve:

   $whole = \frac{part}{percent} = \frac{15 + 30 + 20}{.30} = $ **$217.00**

3. What percent of 65 is 39?

   Set up the equation and solve:

   $percent = \frac{part}{whole} = \frac{39}{65} = $ **0.6 or 60%**

4. Greta and Max sell cable subscriptions. In a given month, Greta sells 45 subscriptions and Max sells 51. If 240 total subscriptions were sold in that month, what percent were not sold by Greta or Max?

   You can use the information in the question to figure out what percentage of subscriptions were sold by Max and Greta:

   $percent = \frac{part}{whole} = \frac{(51 + 45)}{240} = \frac{96}{240} = 0.4$ or 40%

   However, the question asks how many subscriptions weren't sold by Max or Greta. If they sold 40%, then the other salespeople sold 100% − 40% = **60%**.

5. Grant needs to score 75% on an exam. If the exam has 45 questions, how many questions does he need to answer correctly?

   Set up the equation and solve. Remember to convert 75% to a decimal value:

   $part = whole \times percent = 45 \times 0.75 = 33.75$, so he needs to answer at least **34 questions correctly**.

PERCENT CHANGE

PERCENT CHANGE problems will ask you to calculate how much a given quantity changed. The problems are solved in a similar way to regular percent problems, except that instead of using the *part* you'll use the *amount of change*. Note that the sign of the *amount of change* is important: if the original amount has increased the change will be positive, and if it has decreased the change will be negative. Again, in the equations below the percent is a decimal value; you need to multiply by 100 to get the actual percentage.

Words that indicate a percent change problem: *discount, markup, sale, increase, decrease*

$$percent\ change = \frac{amount\ of\ change}{original\ amount}$$

$$amount\ of\ change = original\ amount \times percent\ change$$

$$original\ amount = \frac{amount\ of\ change}{percent\ change}$$

Examples

1. A computer software retailer marks up its games by 40% above the wholesale price when it sells them to customers. Find the price of a game for a customer if the game costs the retailer $25.

   Set up the appropriate equation and solve:

   amount of change = original amount x percent change $= 25 \times 0.4 = 10$

   If the amount of change is 10, that means the store adds a markup of $10, so the game costs:

   $25 + $10 = **$35**

2. A golf shop pays its wholesaler $40 for a certain club, and then sells it to a golfer for $75. What is the markup rate?

   First, calculate the amount of change:

   $75 - 40 = 35$

   Now you can set up the equation and solve. (Note that *markup rate* is another way of saying *percent change*):

   percent change $= \frac{amount\ of\ change}{original\ amount} = \frac{35}{40} = 0.875 = $ **87.5%**

3. A store charges a 40% markup on the shoes it sells. How much did the store pay for a pair of shoes purchased by a customer for $63?

   You're solving for the original price, but it's going to be tricky because you don't know the amount of change; you only know the new price. To solve, you need to create an expression for the amount of change:

   If *original amount* $= x$

   Then *amount of change* $= 63 - x$

   Now you can plug these values into your equation:

   original amount $= \frac{amount\ of\ change}{percent\ change}$

   $x = \frac{63 - x}{0.4}$

   The last step is to solve for x:

   $0.4x = 63 - x$

   $1.4x = 63$

   $x = 45$

   The store paid **$45 for the shoes**.

4. An item originally priced at $55 is marked 25% off. What is the sale price?

You've been asked to find the sale price, which means you need to solve for the amount of change first:

amount of change = original amount × percent change =

$55 \times 0.25 = 13.75$

Using this amount, you can find the new price. Because it's on sale, we know the item will cost less than the original price:

$55 - 13.75 = 41.25$

The sale price is $41.25.

ALGEBRA

EXPRESSIONS AND EQUATIONS

Algebraic expressions and equations include a VARIABLE, which is a letter standing in for a number. These expressions and equations are made up of TERMS, which are groups of numbers and variables (e.g., $2xy$). An EXPRESSION is simply a set of terms (e.g., $3x + 2xy$), while an EQUATION includes an equal sign (e.g., $3x + 2xy = 17$). When simplifying expressions or solving algebraic equations, you'll need to use many different mathematical properties and operations, including addition, subtraction, multiplication, division, exponents, roots, distribution, and the order of operations.

Evaluating Algebraic Expressions

To evaluate an algebraic expression, simply plug the given value(s) in for the appropriate variable(s) in the expression.

Examples

1. Evaluate $2x + 6y - 3z$ if $x = 2$, $y = 4$, and $z = -3$.

Plug in each number for the correct variable and simplify:

$2x + 6y - 3z = 2(2) + 6(4) - 3(-3) = 4 + 24 + 9 =$ **37**

2. A hat company's profits are described by the expression below, where x is the number of hats sold, and p is the average price of a hat.

$xp - 5x - 5000$

If the company sold 10,000 hats for $13 each, what was its profit?

Identify the variables:

$x = 10,000$

$p = \$13$

Plug these values into the given expression:

$xp - 5x - 5000$

$= (10,000)(13) - 5(10,000) - 5000 =$ **\$75,000**

Adding and Subtracting Terms

Only LIKE TERMS, which have the exact same variable(s), can be added or subtracted. CONSTANTS are numbers without variables attached, and those can be added and subtracted together as well. When simplifying an expression, like terms should be added or subtracted so that no individual group of variables occurs in more than one term. For example, the expression $5x + 6xy$ is in its simplest form, while $5x + 6xy - 11xy$ is not because xy appears in more than one term.

Example

1. Simplify the expression $5xy + 7y + 2yz + 11xy - 5yz$.

   Start by grouping together like terms:

   $(5xy + 11xy) + (2yz - 5yz) + 7y$

   Now you can add together each set of like terms:

   $16xy - 3yz + 7y$

2. Simplify the expression: $3ac + 4ab^2 - bc + 2ac - 7bc + 3a^3bc$

   Start by grouping like terms together, then add together each set of like terms:

   $(3ac + 2ac) + (-bc - 7bc) + 4ab^2 + 3a^3bc$

   $= 5ac - 8bc + 4ab^2 + 3a^3bc$

Multiplying and Dividing Terms

To multiply a single term by another, simply add the coefficients and then multiply the variables. Remember that when multiplying variables with exponents, those exponents are added together. For example, $(x^5y)(x^3y^4) = x^8y^5$.

When multiplying a term by a set of terms inside parentheses, you need to DISTRIBUTE to each term inside the parentheses as shown in Figure 4.1.

$$\mathbf{a(b+c) = ab + ac}$$

Figure 4.1. Distribution

When variables occur in both the numerator and denominator of a fraction, they cancel each other out. So, a fraction with variables in its simplest form will not have the same variable on the top and bottom.

Examples

1. Simplify the expression $(3x^4y^2z)(2y^4z^5)$.

   Multiply the coefficients and variables together:

   $3 \times 2 = 6$

   $y^2 \times y^4 = y^6$

   $z \times z^5 = z^6$

   Now put all the terms back together:

   $6x^4y^6z^6$

2. Simplify the expression: $(2y^2)(y^3 + 2xy^2z + 4z)$

   Multiply each term inside the parentheses by the term $2y^2$:

   $(2y^2)(y^3 + 2xy^2z + 4z)$

$(2y^2 \times y^3) + (2y^2 \times 2xy^2z) + (2y^2 \times 4z)$

$2y^5 + 4xy^4z + 8y^2z$

3. Simplify the expression: $\dfrac{2x^4y^3z}{8x^2z^2}$

Simplify by looking at each variable and crossing out those that appear in the numerator and denominator:

$\dfrac{2}{8} = \dfrac{1}{4}$

$\dfrac{x^4}{x^2} = \dfrac{x^2}{1}$

$\dfrac{z}{z^2} = \dfrac{1}{z}$

$\dfrac{2x^4y^3z}{8x^2z^2} = \dfrac{x^2y^3}{4z}$

 When multiplying terms with the same base, add the exponents. When dividing terms with the same base, subtract the exponents.

Solving Equations

To solve an equation, you need to manipulate the terms on each side to isolate the variable, meaning if you want to find x, you have to get the x alone on one side of the equal sign. To do this, you'll need to use many of the tools discussed above: you might need to distribute, divide, add, or subtract like terms, or find common denominators.

Think of each side of the equation as the two sides of a see-saw. As long as the two people on each end weigh the same amount the see-saw will be balanced: if you have a 120 lb. person on each end, the see-saw is balanced. Giving each of them a 10 lb. rock to hold changes the weight on each end, but the see-saw itself stays balanced. Equations work the same way: you can add, subtract, multiply, or divide whatever you want as long as you do the same thing to both sides.

Most equations you'll see on the TEAS can be solved using the same basic steps:

1. Distribute to get rid of parentheses.

2. Use the least common denominator to get rid of fractions.

3. Add/subtract like terms on either side.

4. Add/subtract so that constants appear on only one side of the equation.

5. Multiply/divide to isolate the variable.

Examples

1. Solve for x: $25x + 12 = 62$

This equation has no parentheses, fractions, or like terms on the same side, so you can start by subtracting 12 from both sides of the equation:

$25x + 12 = 62$

$(25x + 12) - 12 = 62 - 12$

$25x = 50$

Now, divide by 25 to isolate the variable:

$\dfrac{25x}{25} = \dfrac{50}{25}$

$x = 2$

2. Solve the following equation for x: $2x - 4(2x + 3) = 24$

Start by distributing to get rid of the parentheses (don't forget to distribute the negative):

$2x - 4(2x + 3) = 24$

$2x - 8x - 12 = 24$

There are no fractions, so now you can join like terms:

$2x - 8x - 12 = 24$

$-6x - 12 = 24$

Now add 12 to both sides and divide by -6.

$-6x - 12 = 24$

$(-6x - 12) + 12 = 24 + 12$

$-6x = 36$

$\frac{-6x}{-6} = \frac{36}{-6}$

$x = -6$

3. Solve the following equation for x: $\frac{x}{3} + \frac{1}{2} = \frac{x}{6} - \frac{5}{12}$

Start by multiplying by the least common denominator to get rid of the fractions:

$\frac{x}{3} + \frac{1}{2} = \frac{x}{6} - \frac{5}{12}$

$12\left(\frac{x}{3} + \frac{1}{2}\right) = 12\left(\frac{x}{6} - \frac{5}{12}\right)$

$4x + 6 = 2x - 5$

Now you can isolate x:

$(4x + 6) - 6 = (2x - 5) - 6$

$4x = 2x - 11$

$(4x) - 2x = (2x - 11) - 2x$

$2x = -11$

$x = -\frac{11}{2}$

4. Solve for x: $2(x + y) - 7x = 14x + 3$

This equation looks more difficult because it has 2 variables, but you can use the same steps to solve for x. First, distribute to get rid of the parentheses and combine like terms:

$2(x + y) - 7x = 14x + 3$

$2x + 2y - 7x = 14x + 3$

$-5x + 2y = 14x + 3$

Now you can move the x terms to one side and everything else to the other, and then divide to isolate x:

$-5x + 2y = 14x + 3$

$-19x = -2y + 3$

$x = \frac{2y - 3}{19}$

INEQUALITIES

INEQUALITIES look like equations, except that instead of having an equal sign, they have one of the following symbols:

> Greater than: The expression left of the symbol is larger than the expression on the right.

< Less than: The expression left of the symbol is smaller than the expression on the right.

≥ Greater than or equal to: The expression left of the symbol is larger than or equal to the expression on the right.

≤ Less than or equal to: The expression left of the symbol is less than or equal to the expression on the right.

Inequalities are solved like linear and algebraic equations. The only difference is that the symbol must be reversed when both sides of the equation are multiplied or divided by a negative number.

Example

1. Solve for x: $-7x + 2 < 6 - 5x$

   Collect like terms on each side as you would for a regular equation:

   $-7x + 2 < 6 - 5x$

   $-2x < 4$

   The direction of the sign switches when you divide by a negative number:

   $-2x < 4$

   $\boldsymbol{x > -2}$

2. A man is building a garden with an area, A, given by the equation below, where a, b, and c are the lengths of three sides of the garden:

   $A = ab + bc - ac$

   If he needs the garden to be less than 50 square feet, can he build a garden with side lengths of $a = 5$ ft, $b = 7$ ft, and $c = 3$ ft?

   The question includes the phrase less than, indicating it's an inequality problem. First, set up the inequality:

   $ab + bc - ac < A$

   Next, plug the given values in to see if the inequality is true:

   $50 > 5(7) + 7(3) - 5(3)$

   $\boldsymbol{50 > 41}$

   The inequality is true, so he can build the garden.

BUILDING EQUATIONS

Any of the math concepts discussed here can be turned into a word problem that requires you to translate words into a mathematical expression, equation, or inequality. Most of these problems can be solved using these general steps:

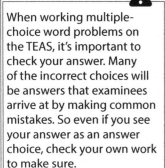

When working multiple-choice word problems on the TEAS, it's important to check your answer. Many of the incorrect choices will be answers that examinees arrive at by making common mistakes. So even if you see your answer as an answer choice, check your own work to make sure.

Step 1: Read the entire problem and determine what the question is asking for.

Step 2: List all of the given data and define the variables.

Step 3: Determine the formula needed or set up equations from the information in the problem.

Step 4: Solve.

Step 5: Check your answer. (Is the amount too large or small? Are the answers in the correct unit of measure?)

Word problems generally contain key words that can help you determine what math processes may be required in order to solve them. These will help you in Step 3, when you need to build an equation or inequality.

Table 4.1. Translating Word Problems

ENGLISH WORDS AND PHRASES	MATH TRANSLATION
is, will be, yields, amounts to, equals	$=$
y is at least (or no less than) x	$y \geq x$
y is at most (or no more than) x	$y \leq x$
in addition to, increased by, added to, perimeter, sum, total, in all	$+$
less, fewer, how much more, difference, decreased	$-$
of, times, area, product	$\times$
distribute, share, per, out of	$\div$
opposite of x	$-x$
ratio of x to y	$\frac{x}{y}$
average of $x, y, z, \ldots$	$\frac{x+y+z+\ldots}{\text{how many numbers are on top}}$

Examples

1. A store owner bought a case of 48 backpacks for $476. He sold 17 of the backpacks in his store for $18 each, and the rest were sold to a school for $15 each. What was his profit?

   Step 1: Read the entire problem and determine what the question is asking for.

   The problem is asking for the salesman's profit.

   Step 2: List all of the given data and define the variables.

   total number of backpacks = 48

   cost of backpacks = $476

   backpacks sold in store at price of $18 = 17

   income from backpacks sold in store = $18 × 17 = $306

   backpacks sold to school at a price of $15 = 48 − 17 = 31

   income from backpacks sold to school = $15 × 31 = $465

Step 3: Determine the formula needed or set up equations from the information in the problem.

profit = income − cost

Step 4: Solve.

profit = income − cost

= (306 + 465) − 476 = 295

The store owner made a profit of **$295**.

2. Twice a man's age is no more than 5 years less than his father's age. If m represents the man's age, and f his father's age, what is the inequality that would represent this situation?

Translate the words in the problem into mathematical symbols:

twice a man's age = $2m$

is no more than = $\leq$

5 years less than his father's age = $f - 5$

Use these symbols to write an inequality:

twice a man's age is no more than 5 years less than his father's age = $\mathbf{2m \leq f - 5}$

GEOMETRY

UNITS OF MEASUREMENT

The TEAS will test your knowledge of two types of units: the US customary (or American) system and the metric system. The US system includes many of the units you likely use in day-to-day activities, such as the foot, pound, and cup. The metric system is used throughout the rest of the world and is the main system used in science and medicine. Common units for the US and metric systems are shown in the table below.

Table 5.1. Units

DIMENSION	US CUSTOMARY	METRIC
length	inch/foot/yard/mile	meter
mass	ounce/pound/ton	gram
volume	cup/pint/quart/gallon	liter
temperature	Fahrenheit	kelvin

The metric system uses prefixes to simplify large and small numbers. These prefixes are added to the base units shown in the table above. For example, the measurement 1000 meters can be written using the prefix kilo– as 1 kilometer. The most commonly used metric prefixes are given in the table below.

Table 5.2. Metric Prefixes

PREFIX	SYMBOL	MULTIPLICATION FACTOR
kilo	k	1,000
hecto	h	100
deca	da	10
base unit	--	--
deci	d	0.1
centi	c	0.01
milli	m	0.001

Conversion factors can be used to convert between units both within a single system and between the US and metric systems. Some questions on the TEAS will require you to know common conversion factors, some of which are shown in the table below.

Table 5.3. Conversion Factors

1 in = 2.54 cm	1 lb = 0.454 kg
1 yd = 0.914 m	1 cal = 4.19 J
1 mi = 1.61 km	$C = \frac{5}{9}(\degree F - 32)$
1 gal = 3.785 L	1 cm³ = 1 mL
1 oz = 28.35 g	1 hr = 3600 s

To perform unit conversion, start with the initial value and multiply by a conversion factor to reach the final unit. This process is shown in Figure 5.1.

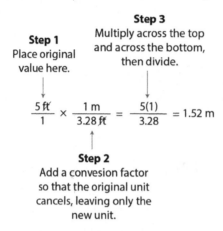

Figure 5.1. Unit Conversion

Examples

1. Convert 4.25 km to meters.

$$\frac{4.25 \text{ km}}{1} \times \frac{1000 \text{ m}}{1 \text{ km}} = \textbf{4250 m}$$

2. What is the mass in kilograms of a 150 lb man?

$$\frac{150 \text{ lb.}}{1} \times \frac{0.454 \text{ kg}}{1 \text{ lb.}} = (150)(0.454) = \textbf{68.1 kg}$$

3. A ball rolling across a table travels 6 inches per second. How many feet will it travel in 1 minute?

   This problem requires two unit conversions. Start by converting inches to feet:

$$\frac{6 \text{ in.}}{1 \text{ s.}} \times \frac{1 \text{ ft.}}{12 \text{ in.}} = \frac{0.5 \text{ ft.}}{1 \text{ s.}}$$

   Now convert seconds to minutes:

$$\frac{0.5 \text{ ft.}}{1 \text{ s.}} \times \frac{60 \text{ s.}}{1 \text{ min.}} = \frac{30 \text{ ft.}}{1 \text{ min.}}$$

   The ball will travel **30 feet** in 1 minute.

AREA AND PERIMETER

Most of the geometry problems on the TEAS will require you to find either the area inside a shape or its perimeter (the distance around it). The perimeter is found by simply adding the lengths of all the sides. (Perimeter uses units for *length*, such as feet, inches, or meters. Because area is found by multiplying two lengths, it has units of *length squared*, such as square feet, ft², or square meters, m².) You will need to memorize the formula for the area of basic shapes, including triangles, rectangles, and circles.

Table 5.4. Area and Perimeter of Basic Shapes

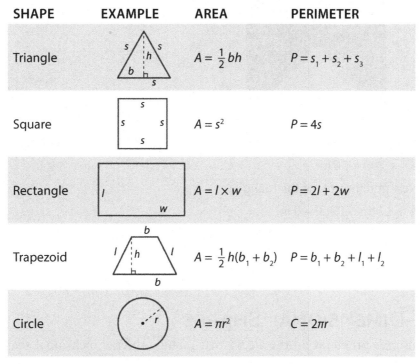

SHAPE	EXAMPLE	AREA	PERIMETER
Triangle		$A = \frac{1}{2}bh$	$P = s_1 + s_2 + s_3$
Square		$A = s^2$	$P = 4s$
Rectangle		$A = l \times w$	$P = 2l + 2w$
Trapezoid		$A = \frac{1}{2}h(b_1 + b_2)$	$P = b_1 + b_2 + l_1 + l_2$
Circle		$A = \pi r^2$	$C = 2\pi r$

The TEAS will include area and perimeter problems with compound shapes. These are complex shapes made by combining more basic shapes. While they might look complicated, they can be solved by simply breaking the compound shape apart and using the formulas given above.

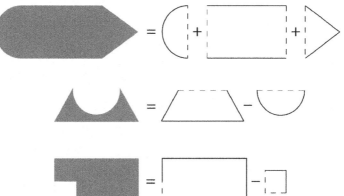

Figure 5.2. Compound Shapes

Examples

1. A farmer has purchased 100 m of fencing to put around his rectangular garden. If one side of the garden is 20 m long and the other is 28 m, how much fencing will the farmer have left over?

   The perimeter of a rectangle is equal to twice its length plus twice its width:

   $P = 2(20) + 2(28) = 96$ m

   The farmer has 100 m of fencing, so subtract to find the amount of fence left:

   $100 - 96 = $ **4** m

2. What is the area of the shaded region?

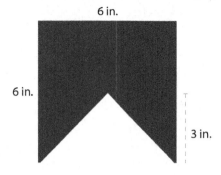

6 in.

6 in.

3 in.

The figure is a square with a triangle cut out. First, find the area of the square:

$A = s^2 = 6^2 = 36$ in^2

Now find the area of the triangle:

$A = \frac{1}{2}bh = \frac{1}{2}(6)(3) = 9$ in^2

Subtract the area of the triangle from the area of the square:

36 – 9 = 27 in^2

THREE-DIMENSIONAL SHAPES

You may also see problems on the TEAS that include three-dimensional shapes. These problems will ask you to find the volume of the shape or its surface area (the area of all its sides). Surface area is found by adding the area of each face on the shape. The formulas for the volume of common three-dimensional shapes are given in the table below.

Table 5.5. Volume of Basic Solids

SOLID	VOLUME
sphere (r is radius)	$V = \frac{4}{3}\pi r^3$
cube (s is side)	$V = s^3$
cylinder (r is radius of base; h is height)	$V = \pi r^2 h$
right rectangular prism (h is height; B is area of base)	$V = Bh$

Examples

1. What is the surface area of a cube with a side length of 5 mm?

A cube has six faces, each of which is a square:

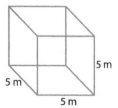

5 m

5 m

5 m

Find the area of each side using the formula for the area of a square:

$A = s^2 = 5^2 = 25 \text{ m}^2$

Multiply the area by 6 (because the cube has six faces):

SA = 25(6) = 150 m²

2. What is the volume of a sphere with a radius of 3 cm?

Use the formula for the volume of a sphere:

$V = \frac{4}{3}\pi r^3 = \frac{4}{3}\pi(3)^3 = \mathbf{36\pi}$ **cm³**

PYTHAGOREAN THEOREM

Shapes with 3 sides are known as TRIANGLES. In addition to knowing the formulas for their area and perimeter, you should also know the Pythagorean theorem, which describes the relationship between the three sides (*a*, *b*, and *c*) of a right triangle:

$$a^2 + b^2 = c^2$$

Example

Erica is going to run a race in which she'll run 3 miles due north and 4 miles due east. She'll then run back to the starting line. How far will she run during this race?

One leg of her route (the triangle) is missing, but you can find its length using the Pythagorean theorem:

$a^2 + b^2 = c^2$

$3^2 + 4^2 = c^2$

$25 = c^2$

$c = 5$

Adding all 3 sides gives the length of the whole race:

$3 + 4 + 5 =$ **12 miles**

STATISTICS

GRAPHS AND CHARTS

These questions require you to interpret information from graphs and charts; they will be pretty straightforward as long as you pay careful attention to detail. There are several different graph and chart types that may appear on the TEAS.

Bar Graphs and Histograms

BAR GRAPHS present the numbers of an item that exist in different categories. The categories are shown on one axis, and the number of items is shown on the other axis. Bar graphs are usually used to easily compare amounts.

> 🔒 On the test you'll need to both read graphs and determine what kinds of graphs are appropriate for different situations.

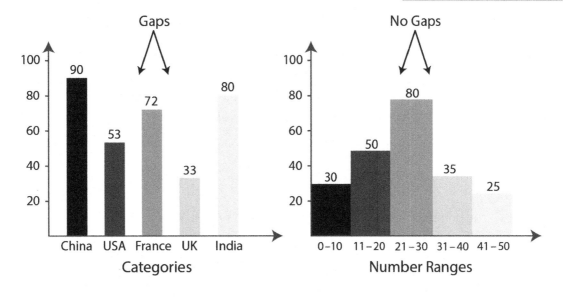

Bar Graph

Histogram

Figure 6.1. Bar Graph versus Histogram

Histograms similarly use bars to compare data, but the independent variable is a continuous variable that has been "binned" or divided into categories. For example, the time of day can be broken down into 8:00 a.m. to 12:00 p.m., 12:00 p.m. to 4:00 p.m., and so on. Usually (but not always), a gap is included between the bars of a bar graph but not a histogram.

Histograms can be symmetrical, skewed left or right, or multimodal (data spread around). Note that SKEWED LEFT means the peak of the data is on the *right*, with a tail to the left, while SKEWED RIGHT means the peak is on the *left*, with a tail to the right. This seems counterintuitive to many; the "left" or "right" always refers to the tail of the data. This is because a long tail to the right, for example, means there are high outlier values that are skewing the data to the right.

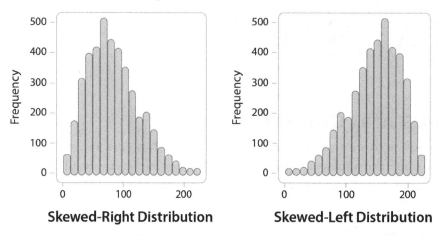

Figure 6.2. Histogram Skew

Examples

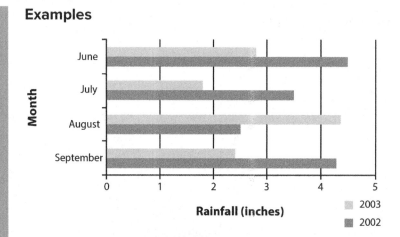

1. The graph above shows rainfall in inches per month. Which month had the least amount of rainfall? Which had the most?

   The shortest bar represents the month with the least rain, and the longest bar represents the month with the most rain: **July 2003 had the least**, and **June 2002 had the most**.

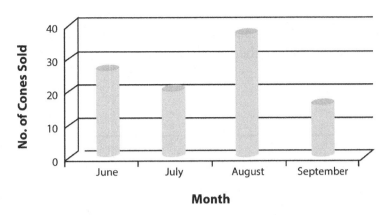

2. According to the graph above, how many more ice cream cones were sold in July than in September?

Tracing from the top of each bar to the scale on the left shows that sales in July were 20 and September sales were 15. So, **5 more cones were sold in July**.

Pie Charts

PIE CHARTS present parts of a whole and are often used with percentages. Together, all the slices of the pie add up to the total number of items, or 100%.

Examples

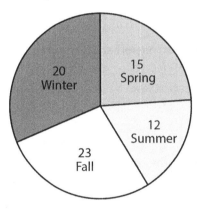

1. The pie chart above shows the distribution of birthdays in a class of students. How many students have birthdays in the spring or summer?

Fifteen students have birthdays in spring and 12 in summer, so there are **27 students** with birthdays in spring or summer.

2. Using the same Birthday Pie Chart in the example before, what percentage of students have birthdays in winter? Round to the nearest tenth of a percent.

Use the equation for percent:

$$percent = \frac{part}{whole} = \frac{winter\ birthdays}{total\ birthdays} =$$

$$\frac{20}{20 + 15 + 23 + 12} = \frac{20}{70} = \frac{2}{7} = .286 \text{ or } \textbf{28.6\%}$$

Line Graphs

LINE GRAPHS show trends over time. The number of each item represented by the graph will be on the *y*-axis, and time will be on the *x*-axis.

Examples

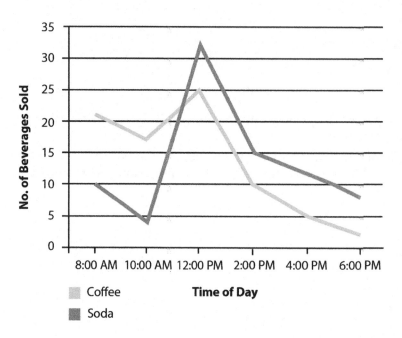

1. The line graph above shows beverage sales at an airport snack shop throughout the day. Which beverage sold more at 4:00 p.m.?

   At 4:00 p.m., approximately 12 sodas and 5 coffees were sold, so more **soda** was sold.

2. At what time of day were the most beverages sold?

   This question is asking for the time of day with the most sales of coffee and soda combined. It is not necessary to add up sales at each time of day to find the answer. Just from looking at the graph, you can see that sales for both beverages were highest at noon, so the answer must be **12:00 p.m.**

MEASURES OF CENTRAL TENDENCY

MEAN is a math term for average. To find the mean, total all the terms and divide by the number of terms. The MEDIAN is the middle number of a given set. To find the median, put the terms in numerical order; the middle number will be the median. In the case of a set of even numbers, the middle two numbers are averaged. MODE is the number which occurs most frequently within a given set.

> It is possible to have more than one mode.

Examples

1. Find the mean of 24, 27, and 18.

Add the terms, then divide by the number of terms:

$$mean = \frac{24 + 27 + 18}{3} = \textbf{23}$$

2. The mean of three numbers is 45. If two of the numbers are 38 and 43, what is the third number?

Set up the equation for mean with x representing the third number, then solve:

$$mean = \frac{38 + 43 + x}{3} = 45$$

$$38 + 43 + x = 135$$

$$x = \textbf{54}$$

3. What is the median of 24, 27, and 18?

Place the terms in order, then pick the middle term:

18, 24, 27

The median is **24**.

4. What is the median of 24, 27, 18, and 19?

Place the terms in order. Because there are an even number of terms, the median will be the average of the middle 2 terms:

18, 19, 24, 27

$$median = \frac{19 + 24}{2} = \textbf{21.5}$$

5. What is the mode of 2, 5, 4, 4, 3, 2, 8, 9, 2, 7, 2, and 2?

The mode is 2 because it appears the most within the set.

PART III: SCIENCE

The ATI TEAS Science test includes fifty-three questions on a range of topics from the life and physical sciences. The majority of the questions (around thirty-five) will ask about human anatomy and physiology, so it's important to focus your study time on reviewing the basic structure and function of the body's organ systems.

Around ten of the questions will cover life science (biology) and the physical sciences (chemistry and physics). Fortunately, the ATI TEAS focuses on only a few important concepts from these fields, making it easier to prepare. These topics include:

- macromolecules (e.g., carbohydrates and proteins)
- genetics
- atomic structure
- physical properties and states of matter
- chemical reactions and bonding

Finally, the Science test will include questions about scientific reasoning. These questions will cover topics like measurement and experimental design.

ANATOMY AND PHYSIOLOGY

TERMINOLOGY

Directional Terms

Anatomical science uses common terms to describe spatial relationships, often in pairs of opposites. These terms generally refer to the position of a structure in an organism that is upright with respect to its environment (e.g., in its typical orientation while moving forward).

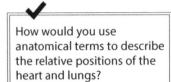

How would you use anatomical terms to describe the relative positions of the heart and lungs?

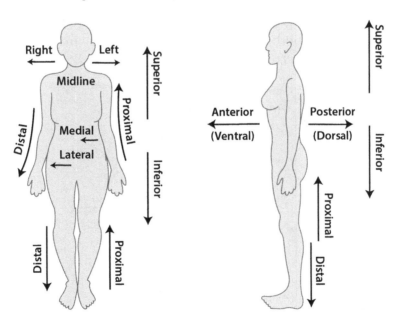

Figure 7.1. Directional Terms

Table 7.1. Directional Terms

TERM	DEFINITION
superior	toward the head, or toward the upper body region
inferior	toward the lower body region
anterior (ventral)	on the belly or front side of the body
posterior (dorsal)	on the buttocks or back side of the body
proximal	near the trunk or middle part of the body
distal	farthest away from the point of reference
medial	close to the midline of the body
lateral	away from the midline of the body

Body Cavities

The internal structure of the human body is organized into compartments called CAVITIES, which are separated by membranes. There are two main cavities in the human body: the dorsal cavity and the ventral cavity (both named for their relative positions).

The DORSAL CAVITY is further divided into the CRANIAL CAVITY, which holds the brain, and the SPINAL CAVITY, which surrounds the spine. The two sections of the dorsal cavity are continuous. Both sections are lined by the MENINGES, a three-layered membrane that protects the brain and spinal cord.

The VENTRAL CAVITY houses most of the body's organs. It also can be further divided into smaller cavities. The THORACIC CAVITY holds the heart and lungs, the ABDOMINAL CAVITY holds the digestive organs and kidneys, and the PELVIC CAVITY holds the bladder and reproductive organs. Both the abdominal and pelvic cavities are enclosed by a membrane called the PERITONEUM.

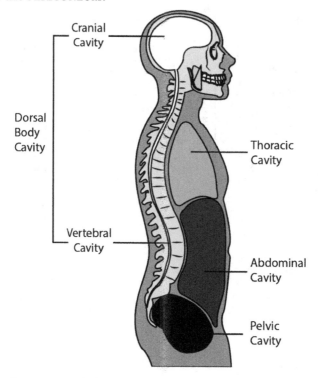

Figure 7.2. Body Cavities

Examples

1. Which of the following terms describes the location of the wrist relative to the elbow?

   A) distal

   B) proximal

   C) anterior

   D) posterior

   Answer:

   A) is correct. The wrist is distal, or farther from the trunk, than the elbow.

2. Which of the following cavities holds the ovaries?

   A) ventral

   B) thoracic

   C) abdominal

   D) pelvic

   Answer:

   D) is correct. The pelvic cavity holds the reproductive organs, which, in females, include the ovaries.

THE CIRCULATORY SYSTEM

The **CIRCULATORY SYSTEM** circulates nutrients, gases, wastes, and other substances throughout the body. This system includes the blood, which carries these substances; the heart, which powers the movement of blood; and the blood vessels, which carry the blood.

The Pulmonary and Systemic Loops

The circulatory system includes two loops. In the **PULMONARY LOOP**, deoxygenated blood is carried from the heart to the lungs, where gas exchange takes place. The newly oxygenated blood then travels back to the heart. In the **SYSTEMIC LOOP**, oxygenated blood is pushed out of the heart and travels through larger blood vessels until it reaches the capillaries, where gas exchange takes place. The deoxygenated blood is then carried back to the heart by veins, and the process starts again. A healthy resting heart can pump around five liters per minute through this cycle.

 The veins of the stomach and intestines do not carry blood directly to the heart. Instead, they divert it to the liver (through the hepatic portal vein) so that the liver can store sugar, remove toxins, and process the products of digestion.

CONTINUE

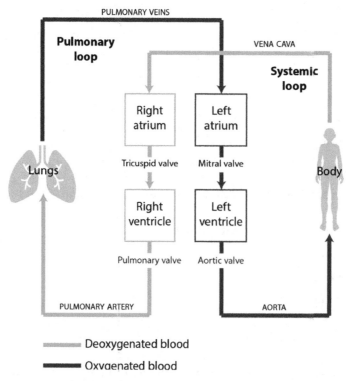

Figure 7.3. The Path of Blood in the Circulatory System

The Heart

The circulatory system relies on the **HEART**, a cone-shaped muscular organ that is no bigger than a closed fist. The heart must pump the blood low in oxygen to the lungs; once the blood is in the lungs, it is oxygenated and returned to the heart. The heart then pumps the oxygenated blood through the whole body.

The cavity that holds the heart is called the **PERICARDIAL CAVITY**. It is filled with serous fluid produced by the pericardium, which is the lining of the pericardial cavity. The serous fluid acts as a lubricant for the heart. It also keeps the heart in place and empties the space around the heart.

The heart wall has three layers:

- **EPICARDIUM**: the protective outermost layer of the heart composed of connective tissue.
- **MYOCARDIUM**: the middle layer of the heart that contains the cardiac muscular tissue. It performs the pumping function to circulate blood.
- **ENDOCARDIUM**: the smooth innermost layer that keeps the blood from sticking to the inside of the heart.

The heart wall is uneven because some parts of the heart—like the atria—do not need a lot of muscle power to perform their duties. Other parts, like the ventricles, require a thicker muscle to pump the blood.

There are four **CHAMBERS** in the heart: the right and left atria, and the right and left ventricles. The **ATRIA** (plural for *atrium*) are smaller than the ventricles, and they have thin walls, as their function is to receive blood from the lungs and the body and pump it to the ventricles. The **VENTRICLES** have to pump the blood to the lungs and the rest of the body, so they are larger and have thicker walls. The left half of the heart, which is responsible for pumping the blood through the body, has a thicker wall than the right half, which pumps the deoxygenated blood to the lungs.

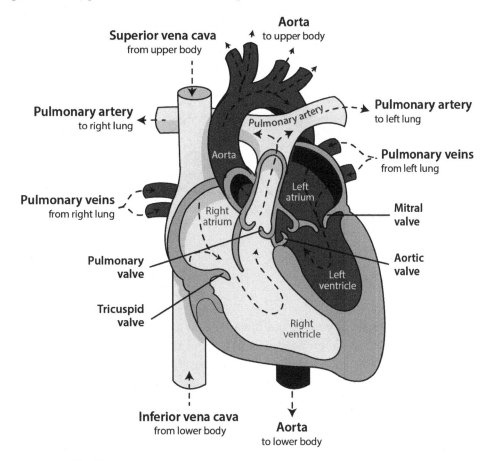

Figure 7.4. The Heart

The heart has one-way valves allowing the blood to flow in only one direction. The valves that keep the blood from going back into the atria from the ventricles are called the ATRIOVENTRICULAR VALVES, and the valves that keep the blood from going back into the ventricles from the arteries are called the SEMILUNAR VALVES.

The pumping function of the heart is made possible by two groups of cells that set the heart's pace and keep it well-coordinated: the sinoatrial and the atrioventricular node. The SINOATRIAL NODE sets the pace and signals the atria to contract. The ATRIOVENTRICULAR NODE picks up the signal from the sinoatrial node, and this signal tells the ventricles to contract.

The Heart Valves
Try Pulling My Aorta
- Tricuspid
- Pulmonary
- Mitral
- Aorta

The Blood Vessels

The BLOOD VESSELS carry the blood from the heart throughout the body and then back. They vary in size depending on the amount of the blood that needs to flow through them. The hollow part in the middle, called the LUMEN, is where the blood actually flows. The vessels are lined with endothelium, which is made out of the same type of cells as the endocardium and serves the same purpose—to keep the blood from sticking to the walls and clotting.

ARTERIES are blood vessels that transport the blood away from the heart. They work under a lot more pressure than the other types of blood vessels; hence, they have a thicker, more muscular wall, which is also highly elastic. The smaller arteries are usually more muscular, while the larger are more elastic.

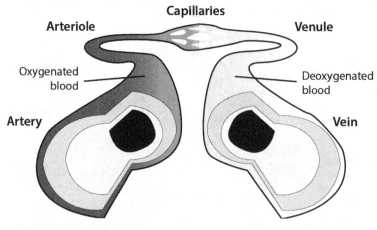

Figure 7.5. Blood Vessels

The largest artery in the body is called the **AORTA**. It ascends from the left ventricle of the heart, arches to the back left, and descends behind the heart. Narrower arteries that branch off of main arteries and carry blood to the capillaries are called **ARTERIOLES**. The descending aorta carries blood to the chest and abdomen, but not to the lungs. The lungs get blood through the **PULMONARY ARTERY** that comes out of the right ventricle.

The arching part of the aorta (called the **AORTIC ARCH**) branches into three arteries: the brachiocephalic artery, the left common artery, and the left subclavian artery. The **BRACHIOCEPHALIC ARTERY** carries blood to the brain and head; it further divides into the right subclavian artery, which brings the blood to the right arm. The **LEFT COMMON CAROTID ARTERY** carries blood to the brain; the **LEFT SUBCLAVIAN ARTERY** carries blood to the left arm.

The **DESCENDING AORTA** bends away from the aortic arch and carries blood to the abdomen and lower body. At the fourth lumbar vertebra, the descending aorta splits into the two **ILIAC ARTERIES**, which further divide into the **INTERNAL** and **EXTERNAL ILIAC ARTERIES**. These vessels bring blood to the pelvis and legs.

VEINS are blood vessels that bring the blood from the body back to the heart. As they do not work under the same pressure as the arteries, they are much thinner and not as muscular or elastic. The veins also have a number of one-way valves that stop the blood from going back through them.

> ⚠
> The pulmonary veins are the only veins in the human body that carry oxygenated blood.

Veins use inertia, muscle work, and gravity to get the blood to the heart. Thin veins that connect to the capillaries are called **VENULES**. The lungs have their own set of veins: the **LEFT** and **RIGHT SUPERIOR** and **INFERIOR PULMONARY VEINS**. These vessels enter the heart through the left atrium.

The two main veins are called the superior vena cava and the inferior vena cava. The **SUPERIOR VENA CAVA** ascends from the right atrium and connects to the head and neck, delivering the blood supply to these structures. The superior vena cava also connects to the arms via both the subclavian and brachiocephalic veins. The **INFERIOR VENA CAVA** descends from the right atrium, carrying the blood from the lumbar veins, gonadal veins, hepatic veins, phrenic veins, and renal veins.

CAPILLARIES are the smallest blood vessels, and the most populous in the body. They can be found in almost every tissue. They connect to arterioles on one end and the venules on the other end. Also, capillaries carry the blood very close to the cells and thus enable cells to exchange gases, nutrients, and cellular waste. The walls of capillaries have to be very thin for this exchange to happen.

The Blood

BLOOD is the medium for the transport of substances throughout the body. There are four to five liters of this liquid connective tissue in the human body. Blood is comprised of red blood cells, hemoglobin, white blood cells, platelets, and plasma.

Also called ERYTHROCYTES, RED BLOOD CELLS (RBCs) are produced inside the red bone marrow and transport oxygen. HEMOGLOBIN (HGB) is a red pigment found in the red blood cells, and it is rich in iron and proteins, which both allow these cells to transport the oxygen. RBCs also have a biconcave shape, which means they are round and thinner in the middle. This shape gives them a larger surface area, making them more effective.

The blood also contains many immune system components, including white blood cells (or LEUKOCYTES). PLATELETS, also called THROMBOCYTES, circulate in the blood and are vital for blood clotting. They are formed in the red bone marrow and serve many functions in the body.

Finally, PLASMA is the liquid part of blood, and it forms 55 percent of the total blood volume. Plasma consists of up to 90 percent water, as well as proteins, including antibodies and albumins. Other substances circulating in the blood plasma include glucose, nutrients, cell waste, and various gases.

Examples

1. Which of the following layers of the wall of the heart contains cardiac muscles?

    A) myocardium only

    B) epicardium only

    C) endocardium only

    D) myocardium and epicardium only

    Answer:

    A) is correct. The myocardium is the muscular layer of the heart that contains cardiac muscle.

2. The blood from the right ventricle goes to

    A) the left atria.

    B) the vena cava.

    C) the aorta.

    D) the lungs.

    Answer:

    D) is correct. The right ventricle pumps deoxygenated blood from the heart to the lungs.

3. The blood vessels that carry the blood from the heart are called

A) veins.

B) venules.

C) capillaries.

D) arteries.

Answer:

D) is correct. Blood leaves the heart in arteries.

THE RESPIRATORY SYSTEM

The human body needs oxygen in order to function. The **RESPIRATORY SYSTEM** is responsible for intake of this gas. This system is also in charge of removing carbon dioxide from the body, an equally important function. The respiratory system can be divided into two sections: the upper respiratory tract and the lower respiratory tract.

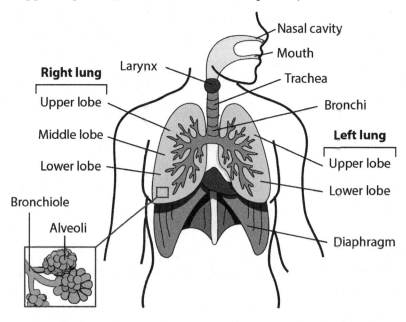

Figure 7.6. The Respiratory System

The Upper Respiratory Tract

The **UPPER RESPIRATORY TRACT** consists of the nose, nasal cavity, olfactory membranes, mouth, pharynx, epiglottis, and the larynx.

The **NOSE** is the primary body part for air intake and removing carbon dioxide. The nose itself is made out of bone, cartilage, muscle, and skin, and it serves as a protector of the hollow space behind it called the **NASAL CAVITY**. The nasal cavity is covered with hair and mucus, which together serve an important function—they stop contaminants from the outside. Common contaminants include dust, mold, and other particles. The nasal cavity prevents the contaminants from entering further into the respiratory system; it also warms and moisturizes air.

The nose and the nasal cavity also contain **OLFACTORY MEMBRANES**, which are small organs responsible for our sense of smell. They are located on the top of the nasal cavity, just under the bridge of the nose.

We can also breathe through the **MOUTH**, although it is not the primary breathing opening. The mouth does not perform as well when it comes to the three functions of the primary opening (filtering, moisturizing, and warming of air). However, the mouth does have advantages over the nose when it comes to breathing, including its larger size and proximity to the lungs.

The next part of the respiratory system is the **THROAT**, which is also called the **PHARYNX**. The pharynx is a smooth, muscular structure lined with mucus and divided into three regions: the nasopharynx, the oropharynx, and the laryngopharynx.

Air comes in through the nose and then passes through the **NASOPHARYNX**, which is also where the Eustachian tubes from the middle ears connect with the pharynx. The air then enters the **OROPHARYNX**, which is where air from the mouth enters the pharynx; this is the same passageway used for transporting food when eating. Both air and food also pass through the **LARYNGOPHARYNX**, where these substances are diverted into different systems.

The **EPIGLOTTIS** is responsible for ensuring that air enters the trachea and food enters the esophagus. The epiglottis is a flap made of elastic cartilage. It remains open while the body breaths to allow air to enter the trachea. When food or liquid is swallowed, the epiglottis closes over the trachea, preventing any material from entering the respiratory tract.

The **LARYNX** is the part of the airway that sits between the pharynx and the trachea. It is also called the *voice box*, because it contains mucus membrane folds (vocal folds) that vibrate when air passes through them to produce sounds. The larynx is made out of three cartilage structures: the epiglottis, the thyroid cartilage (also called the Adam's apple), and the cricoid cartilage, a ring-shaped structure that keeps the larynx open.

The Lower Respiratory Tract

The **LOWER RESPIRATORY TRACT** consists of the trachea, bronchi, lungs, and the muscles that help with breathing.

The lower respiratory tract begins with the **TRACHEA**, also known as the *windpipe*. The trachea stretches between the larynx and the bronchi. As its name suggests, the windpipe resembles a pipe, and its flexibility allows it to follow various head and neck movements. The trachea is made out of fibrous and elastic tissues, smooth muscle, and about twenty cartilage rings.

The inner lining of the windpipe is composed of epithelial tissue, which contains mucus-producing cells called **GOBLET CELLS**, as well as cells that have small, hair-like fringes. These structures, called **CILIA**, allow air to pass through the windpipe, where it is further filtered by the mucus. The fringes also help to move mucus up the airways and out, keeping the air passage clear.

Connecting to the trachea are the **BRONCHI**. The **PRIMARY BRONCHI**, consisting of many *C*-shaped cartilage rings, branch into the secondary bronchi. Two branches extend from the left primary bronchi, and three branches extend from the right, corresponding to the number of lobes in the lungs.

The **SECONDARY BRONCHI** contain less cartilage and have more space between the rings. The same goes for the **TERTIARY BRONCHI**, which are extensions of the secondary bronchi as they divide throughout the lobes of the lungs. Like the trachea, the bronchi are lined with epithelium that contains goblet cells and cilia.

BRONCHIOLES branch from the tertiary bronchi. They contain no cartilage at all; rather, they are made of smooth muscle and elastic fiber tissue, which allows them to be quite small yet still able to change their diameter. For example, when the body needs more oxygen, they expand, and when there is a danger of pollutants entering the lungs, they constrict.

Bronchioles end with **TERMINAL BRONCHIOLES**, which connect them with **ALVEOLI**, which is where the gas exchange happens. Alveoli are small cavities located in alveolar sacs and surrounded by capillaries. The inner surface of alveoli is coated with **ALVEOLAR FLUID**, which plays a vital role in keeping the alveoli moist, the lungs elastic, and the thin wall of the alveoli stable. The wall of the alveoli is made out of alveolar cells and the connective tissue that forms the respiratory membrane where it comes into contact with the wall of the capillaries.

The **LUNGS** themselves are two spongy organs that contain the bronchi, bronchioles, alveoli, and blood vessels. The lungs are contained in the rib cage, and are surrounded by the pleura, a double-layered membrane consisting of the outer **PARIETAL PLEURA** and the inner **VISCERAL PLEURA**. Between the layers of the pleura is a hollow space called the **PLEURAL CAVITY**, which allows the lungs to expand.

In anatomy, the terms *right* and *left* are used with respect to the subject, not the observer.

The lungs are wider at the bottom, which is referred to as the **BASE**, and they are narrower at the top part, which is called the **APEX**. The lungs are divided into **LOBES**, with the larger lung (the right one) consisting of three lobes, and the smaller lung (the left lung) consisting of two lobes.

Respiration

The muscles that play a major role in respiration are the diaphragm and the intercostal muscles. The **DIAPHRAGM** is a structure made of skeletal muscle, and it is located under the lungs, forming the floor of the thorax. The **INTERCOSTAL MUSCLES** are located between the ribs. The **INTERNAL INTERCOSTAL MUSCLES** help with breathing out (expiration) by depressing the ribs and compressing the thoracic cavity; the **EXTERNAL INTERCOSTAL MUSCLES** help with breathing in (inspiration).

Breathing in and out is also called **PULMONARY VENTILATION**. The two types of pulmonary ventilation are inhalation and exhalation.

During **INHALATION** (also called inspiration), the diaphragm contracts and moves a few inches toward the stomach, making more space for the lungs to expand. This movement pulls the air into the lungs. The external intercostal muscles also contract to expand the rib cage and pull more air into the lungs. The lungs are now at a lower pressure than the atmosphere, (called negative pressure), which causes air to come into the lungs until the pressure inside the lungs and the atmospheric pressure are the same.

During **EXHALATION** (expiration), the diaphragm and the external intercostal muscles relax, and the internal intercostal muscles contract. This causes the thoracic cavity to become smaller and the pressure in the lungs to climb higher than the atmospheric pressure, which moves air out of the lungs.

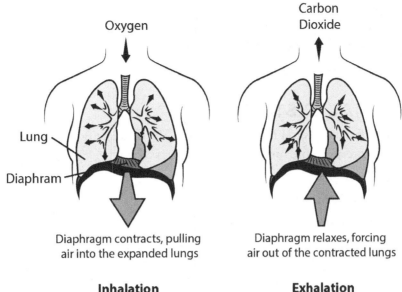

Oxygen

Carbon Dioxide

Lung

Diaphram

Diaphragm contracts, pulling air into the expanded lungs

Diaphragm relaxes, forcing air out of the contracted lungs

Inhalation

Exhalation

Figure 7.7. Pulmonary Ventilation

Types of Breathing

In shallow breathing, around 0.5 liters of air is circulated, a capacity called TIDAL VOLUME. During deep breathing, a larger amount of air is moved, usually three to five liters, a volume known as VITAL CAPACITY. The abdominal, as well as other muscles, are also involved in breathing in and out during deep breathing.

EUPNEA is a term for the breathing our body does when resting, which consists of mostly shallow breaths with an occasional deep breath. The lungs are never completely without air—around a liter of air is always present in the lungs.

Examples

1. Which of the following is the opening in the throat through which air passes after it enters the mouth?

   A) nasopharynx

   B) oropharynx

   C) laryngopharynx

   D) larynx

   Answer:

   B) is correct. Air that enters through the mouth passes through the oropharynx to reach the larynx.

2. During respiration, the epiglottis prevents air from entering which of the following organs?

   A) bronchi

   B) pharynx

   C) larynx

   D) esophagus

THE SKELETAL SYSTEM

The skeletal system plays several roles in the body. The bones and joints that make up the skeletal system are responsible for:

- providing support and protection
- allowing movement
- generating blood cells
- storing fat, iron, and calcium
- guiding the growth of the entire body

Generally, the skeleton can be divided into two parts: the axial skeleton and the appendicular skeleton. The AXIAL SKELETON consists of eighty bones placed along the body's midline axis and grouped into the skull, ribs, sternum, and vertebral column. The APPENDICULAR SKELETON consists of 126 bones grouped into the upper and lower limbs and the pelvic and pectoral girdles. These bones anchor muscles and allow for movement.

Bone Components

On the cellular level, the bone consists of two distinctively different parts: the matrix and living bone cells. The BONE MATRIX is the nonliving part of the bone, which is made out of water, collagen, protein, calcium phosphate, and calcium carbonate crystals. The LIVING BONE CELLS (OSTEOCYTES) are found at the edges of the bones and throughout the bone matrix in small cavities. Bone cells play a vital part in the growth, development, and repair of bones, and can be used for the minerals they store.

Looking at a cross section of a bone, you can see that it is made out of layers. These include the PERIOSTEUM, which is the topmost layer of the bone, acting as a layer of connective tissue. The periosteum contains collagen fibers that anchor the tendons and the muscles; it also holds the stem and the osteoblast cells that are necessary for growth and repair of the bones. Nervous tissue, nerve endings, and blood vessels are also present in the periosteum.

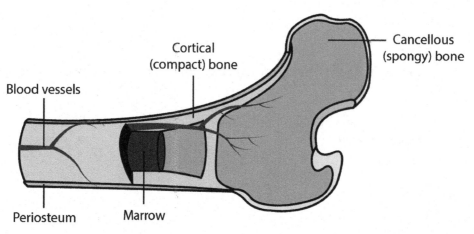

Figure 7.8. The Structure of Bone

Under the periosteum is a layer of **COMPACT BONE**, which gives the bone its strength. Made out of mineral salts and collagen fibers, it also contains many cavities where osteocytes can be found. **CANCELLOUS (SPONGY) BONE** is found under the compact bone at the ends of long bones and in vertebrae. This layer of bone is less dense than compact bone but includes a much larger surface area, making it ideal for exchange. The functional unit of cancellous bone is the **TRABECULA**, which holds red bone marrow and provides structural support.

Bone Cell Processes

New bone is formed by osteoblasts during **OSSIFICATION**. This process occurs in fetal development and is ongoing as bones grow and repair themselves. **OSTEOCLASTS**, another type of bone cell, are responsible for breaking down bone tissue. They are located on the surface of bones and help balance the body's calcium levels by degrading bone to release stored calcium.

> ✔
> How might diet affect the body's ability to rebuild bone after a fracture?

Inside the red bone marrow, which is located in the medullar cavity of the bones, a process called **HEMATOPOIESIS** occurs. In the process, white and red blood cells are made from stem cells. The amount of the red bone marrow declines at the end of puberty, as a significant part of it is replaced by the yellow bone marrow.

The Five Types of Bones

The **LONG BONES** make up the major bones of the limbs. They are longer than they are wide, and they are responsible for most of our height. The long bones can be divided in two regions: the **EPIPHYSES**, located at the ends of the bone, and **DIAPHYSIS**, located in the middle. The middle of the diaphysis contains a hollow medullary cavity, which serves as storage for bone marrow.

The **SHORT BONES** are roughly as long as they are wide, and are generally cube shaped or round. Short bones in the body include the carpal bones of the wrist and tarsal bones of the foot. The **FLAT BONES** do not have the medullary cavity because they are thin and usually thinner on one end region. Flat bones in the body include the ribs, the hip bones, and the frontal, the parietal, and the occipital bones of the skull. The **IRREGULAR BONES** are those bones that do not fit the criteria to be classified as long, short, or flat bones. The vertebrae and the sacrum, among others, are irregular bones.

There are only two **SESAMOID BONES** that are actually counted as proper bones: the patella and the pisiform bone. Sesamoid bones are formed inside the tendons located across the joints, and apart from the two mentioned, they are not present in all people.

The Skull

Composed of twenty-two bones, the **SKULL** protects the brain and the sense organs for vision, hearing, smell, taste, and balance. The skull has only one movable joint; this joint connects it with the **MANDIBLE**, or the *jaw bone*, which is the only movable bone of the skull. The other twenty-one bones are fused together.

The upper part of the skull is known as the **CRANIUM**, which protects the brain, while the lower and frontal parts of the skull form the facial bones. Located just under the mandible, and not a part of the skull, is the **HYOID BONE**. The hyoid is the only bone in the body that is not attached to any other bone. It helps keep the trachea open and anchors the tongue muscles.

Other bones closely connected to, but not part of the skull, are the AUDITORY OSSICLES: the malleus, incus, and stapes. These bones play an important role in hearing.

The Vertebral Column

The VERTEBRAL COLUMN, or the spine, begins at the base of the skull and stretches through the trunk down the middle of the back to the coccyx. It supports the weight of the upper body and protects the spinal cord. It is made up of twenty-four vertebrae, plus the SACRUM and the COCCYX (the *tailbone*). These twenty-four vertebrae are divided into three groups:

- the CERVICAL, or the neck vertebrae (seven bones)
- the THORACIC, or the chest vertebrae (twelve bones)
- the LUMBAR, or the lower back vertebrae (five bones)

Furthermore, each vertebra has its own name, which is derived from the first letter of the group to which it belongs (for example, *L* for lumbar vertebrae). The letter is placed first, followed by a number (the first of the lumbar vertebrae is thus called *L1*).

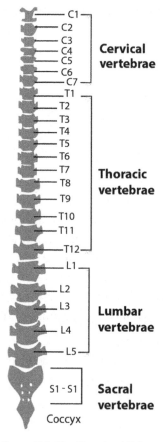

Figure 7.9. The Vertebral Column

The Ribs and the Sternum

The ribs and the sternum are the bones that form the rib cage of the thoracic region. The STERNUM, also known as the *breastbone*, is a thin bone along the midline of the thoracic region. Most of the ribs are connected to this bone via the COSTAL CARTILAGE, a thin band of cartilage.

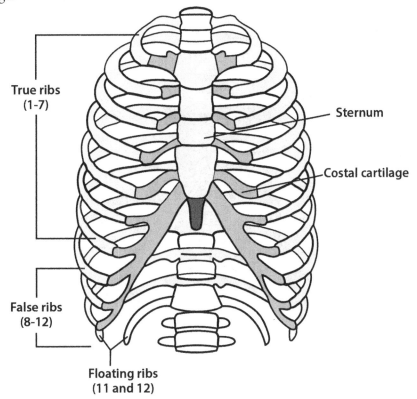

Figure 7.10. The Ribs

The human skeleton has twelve pairs of RIBS. On the back side, they are attached to the thoracic vertebrae. On the front, the first seven of them attach directly to the sternum, the next three attach to the cartilage between the seventh rib and the sternum, and the remaining two do not attach to the sternum at all. These ribs protect the kidneys, not the lungs and heart. The first seven ribs are known as the *true ribs*, and the rest are known as *false ribs*. Together, these bones form the THORACIC CAGE, which supports and protects the heart and lungs.

The Appendicular Skeleton

The upper limbs, which belong to the APPENDICULAR SKELETON, are connected with the axial skeleton by the PECTORAL GIRDLE. The pectoral girdle is formed from the left and right CLAVICLE and SCAPULA. The scapula and the HUMERUS, the bones of the upper arm, form the ball and socket of the shoulder joint. The upper limbs also include the ULNA, which forms the elbow joint with the humerus, and the RADIUS, which allows the turning movement at the wrist.

The WRIST JOINT is formed out of the forearm bones and the eight CARPAL bones, which themselves are connected with the five METACARPALS. Together, these structures form the bones of the hand. The metacarpals connect with the fingers. Each finger is composed of three bones called PHALANGES, except the thumb, which only has two phalanges.

The lower limbs are connected to the axial skeleton by the PELVIC GIRDLE, which includes the left and right hip bones. The hip joint is formed by the hip bone and the

FEMUR, which is the largest bone in the body. On its other end, the femur forms the knee joint with the PATELLA (the kneecap) and the TIBIA, which is one of the bones of the lower leg.

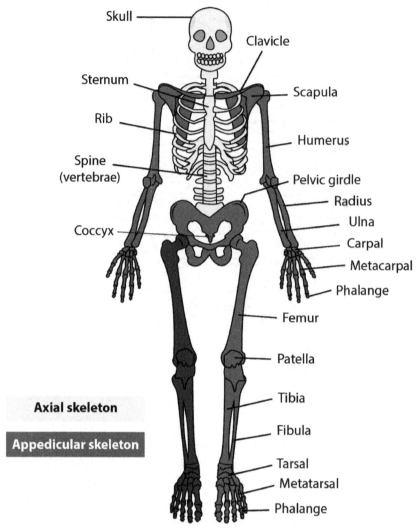

Figure 7.11. The Axial and Appendicular Skeletons

Of the two lower leg bones, the TIBIA is the larger, and it carries the weight of the body. The FIBULA, the other leg bone, serves mostly to anchor the muscle. Together, these two bones form the ankle joint with a foot bone called the TALUS. The talus is one of seven tarsal bones that form the back part of the foot and the heel. They connect to the five long METATARSALS, which form the foot itself and connect to the toes. Each toe is made out of three phalanges, except the big toe, which has only two phalanges.

The Joints

The JOINTS, also known as *articulations*, are where the bones come into contact with each other, with cartilage, or with teeth. There are three types of joints: synovial, fibrous, and cartilaginous joints.

The SYNOVIAL JOINTS feature a small gap between the bones that is filled with synovial fluid, which lubricates the joint. They are the most common joints in the body, and they allow the most movement. **FIBROUS JOINTS**, found where bones fit tightly together, permit little to no movement. These joints also hold teeth in their sockets. In a **CARTILAGINOUS JOINT**, two bones are held together by cartilage; these joints allow more movement than fibrous joints but less than synovial ones.

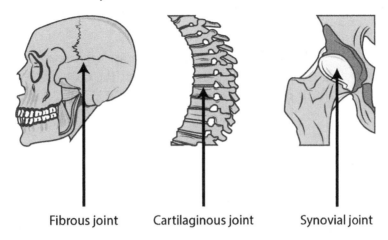

Fibrous joint   Cartilaginous joint   Synovial joint

Figure 7.12. Types of Joints

Examples

1. Stem cells are found in which of the following tissues?

   A) red bone marrow

   B) cartilage

   C) compact bones

   D) bone matrix

   Answer:

   A) is correct. Stem cells are found in red bone marrow.

2. Which of the following parts of the skeletal system is formed from long bones?

   A) limbs

   B) thoracic cage

   C) skull

   D) vertebral column

   Answer:

   A) is correct. Long bones are the main bones composing the arms and legs.

THE MUSCULAR SYSTEM

Movement is the main function of the **MUSCULAR SYSTEM**; muscles are attached to the bones in our bodies and allow us to move our limbs. They also work in the heart, blood vessels, and digestive organs, where they facilitate movement of substances through the body. In addition to movement, muscles also help support the body's posture and create heat. There are three types of muscle: visceral, cardiac, and skeletal.

Visceral Muscle

VISCERAL MUSCLE is the weakest type of muscle. It can be found in the stomach, intestines, and blood vessels, where it helps contract and move substances through them. We cannot consciously control visceral muscle—it is controlled by the unconscious part of the brain. That's why it is sometimes referred to as *involuntary muscle.*

Some skeletal muscles, such as the diaphragm and those that control blinking, can be voluntarily controlled but usually operate involuntarily.

Visceral muscle is also called **SMOOTH MUSCLE** because of its appearance under the microscope. The cells of the visceral muscle form a smooth surface, unlike the other two types of muscle.

Cardiac Muscle

CARDIAC MUSCLE is only found in the heart; it makes the heart contract and pump blood through the body. Like visceral muscle, cardiac muscle cannot be voluntarily controlled. Unlike visceral muscle, however, the cardiac muscle is quite strong.

Cardiac muscle is composed of individual muscle cells called **CARDIOMYOCYTES** that are joined together by **INTERCALATED DISCS**. These discs allow the cells in cardiac muscle to contract in sync. When observed under a microscope, light and dark stripes are visible in the muscle: this pattern is caused by the arrangement of proteins.

Skeletal Muscle

The last type of muscle is **SKELETAL MUSCLE**, which is the only type of muscle that contracts and relaxes by voluntary action. Skeletal muscle is attached to the bone by tendons. Tendons are formed out of connective tissue rich in collagen fibers.

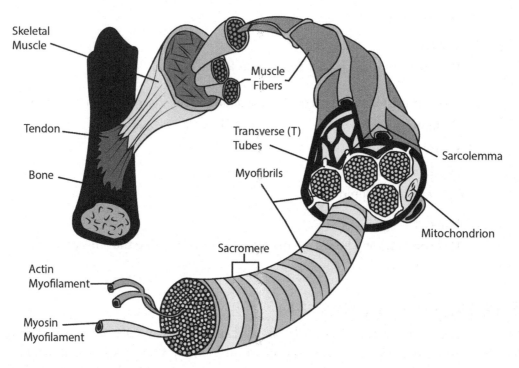

Figure 7.13. The Structure of Skeletal Muscle

Skeletal muscle is made out of cells that are lumped together to form fiber structures. These fibers are covered by a cell membrane called the **SARCOLEMMA**, which serves as a conductor for electrochemical signals that tell the muscle to contract or expand. The **TRANSVERSE TUBES**, which are connected to the sarcolemma, transfer the signals deeper into the middle of the muscle fiber.

Calcium ions, which are necessary for muscle contraction, are stored in the **SARCOPLAS-MIC RETICULUM**. The fibers are also rich in **MITOCHONDRIA**, which act as power stations fueled by sugars and provide the energy necessary for the muscle to work. Muscle fibers are mostly made out of **MYOFIBRILS**, which do the actual contracting. Myofibrils are in turn made out of protein fibers arranged into small subunits called **SARCOMERES**.

Muscle contraction is explained by the **SLIDING FILAMENT THEORY**. When the sarcomere is at rest, the thin filaments containing **ACTIN** are found at both ends of the muscle, while the thick filaments containing **MYOSIN** are found at the center. Myosin filaments contain "heads," which can attach and detach from actin filaments. The myosin attaches to actin and pulls the thin filaments to the center of the sarcomere, forcing the thin filaments to slide inward and causing the entire sarcomere to shorten, or contract, creating movement. The sarcomere can be broken down into zones that contain certain filaments.

- The **Z-LINE** separates the sarcomeres: a single sarcomere is the distance between two Z-lines.
- The **A-BAND** is the area of the sarcomere in which thick myosin filaments are found and does not shorten during muscular contraction.
- The **I-BAND** is the area in the sarcomere between the thick myosin filaments in which only thin actin filament is found.
- The **H-ZONE** is found between the actin filaments and contains only thick myosin filament.

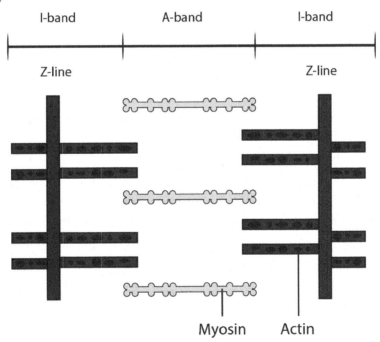

Figure 7.14. Sliding Filament Theory

Skeletal muscle can be divided into two types, according to the way it produces and uses energy. **TYPE I** fibers contract slowly and are used for stamina and posture. They produce energy from sugar using aerobic respiration, making them resistant to fatigue.

TYPE II muscle fibers contract more quickly. Type IIA fibers are found in the legs, and are weaker and show more endurance than Type IIB fibers, which are found mostly in the arms.

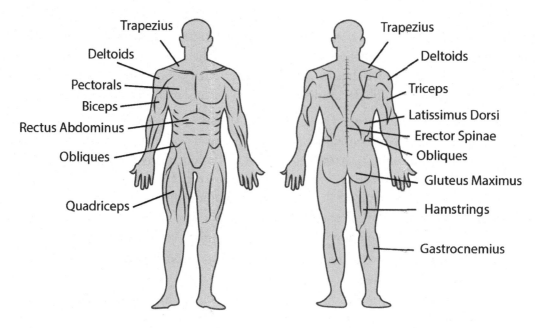

Figure 7.15. Important Skeletal Muscles

Skeletal muscles work by contracting. This shortens the length in their middle part, called the *muscle belly*, which in turn pulls one bone closer to another. The bone that remains stationary is called the **ORIGIN**. The other bone, the one that is actually moving toward the other, is called the **INSERTION**.

Skeletal muscles usually work in groups. The muscle mainly responsible for the action is called the **AGONIST**, and it is always paired with another muscle that does the opposite action, called the **ANTAGONIST**. For example, the biceps are the agonist when the elbow is flexed—they contract to pull the lower arm up. The triceps are the antagonist and remain relaxed. When the elbow is extended, the opposite is true—the triceps are the agonist and the biceps are the antagonist.

Other muscles that support the agonist include **SYNERGISTS**, which are found near the agonist, attach to the same bones, stabilize the movement, and reduce unnecessary movement. **FIXATORS** are other support muscles that keep the origin stable.

There are several different ways to name the more than 600 skeletal muscles found in the human body. Muscles can be named according to:

- the region of the body in which they are located (e.g., transverse abdominis)
- number of origins (e.g., biceps)
- bones to which they are attached (e.g., occipitofrontalis)
- function (e.g., flexor)
- relative size (e.g., gluteus maximus)

Motor Neurons and Contractions

The neurons that control muscles are called MOTOR NEURONS. Motor neurons control a number of muscle cells that together are called the MOTOR UNIT. The number of cells in the motor unit is larger in big muscles that need more strength, like those in the arms and legs. In small muscles where precision is more important than strength, like the muscles in fingers and around the eyes, the number of cells in motor units is smaller.

When signaled by motor neurons, muscles can contract in several different ways:

- Isotonic muscle contractions produce movement.
- Isometric muscle contractions maintain posture and stillness.
- Muscle tone is naturally occurring constant semi-contraction of the muscle.
- Twitch contraction is a short contraction caused by a single, short nerve impulse.
- Temporal summation is a phenomenon in which a few short impulses delivered over time build up the muscle contraction in strength and duration.
- Tetanus is a state of constant contraction caused by many rapid short impulses.

Muscle Metabolism

There are two ways muscles get energy: through aerobic respiration, which is most effective, and through LACTIC ACID FERMENTATION, which is a type of anaerobic respiration. The latter is less effective and it only happens when blood cannot get into the muscle due to very strong or prolonged contraction.

In both these methods, the goal is to produce ADENOSINE TRI-PHOSPHATE (ATP) from glucose. ATP is the most important energy molecule for our bodies. During its conversion to ADENOSINE DI-PHOSPHATE (ADP), energy is released.

Muscles also use other molecules to help in the production of energy. MYOGLOBIN stores oxygen, allowing muscles to use aerobic respiration even when there is no blood coming into the muscles. CREATINE PHOSPHATE creates ATP by giving its phosphate group to the energy-depleted adenosine di-phosphate. Lastly, muscles use GLYCOGEN, a large molecule made out of several glucose molecules, which helps muscles make ATP.

When it runs out of energy, a muscle goes into a state called MUSCLE FATIGUE. This means it contains little to no oxygen, ATP, or glucose, and that it has high levels of lactic acid and ADP. When a muscle is fatigued, it needs more oxygen to replace the oxygen used up from myoglobin sources, and to rebuild its other energy supplies.

Examples

1. Which of the following types of muscle is found in blood vessels?

   A) cardiac muscle

   B) visceral muscle

   C) Type I muscle fibers

   D) Type II muscle fibers

   Answer:

   B) is correct. Blood is moved through blood vessels by visceral, or smooth, muscle that cannot be voluntarily controlled.

2. Which of the following processes are performed by myofibrils?

   A) sugar storage

   B) electrochemical communication

   C) lactic acid fermentation

   D) muscle contractions

Answer:

D) is correct. Myofibrils are the muscle fibers that contract.

THE NERVOUS SYSTEM

The NERVOUS SYSTEM consists of the brain, the spinal cord, the nerves, and the sensory organs. This system is responsible for gathering, processing, and reacting to information from both inside and outside of the body. It is divided into two parts: the central nervous system and the peripheral nervous system. The CENTRAL NERVOUS SYSTEM (CNS) is made of the brain and spinal cord and is responsible for processing and storing information, as well as deciding on the appropriate action and issuing commands.

The PERIPHERAL NERVOUS SYSTEM (PNS) is responsible for gathering information, transporting it to the CNS, and then transporting commands from the CNS to the appropriate organs. Sensory organs and nerves do the gathering and transporting of information, while the efferent nerves transport the commands.

Nervous System Cells

The nervous system is mostly made out of nervous tissue, which in turn consists of two classes of cells: neurons and neuralgia. NEURONS are the nerve cells. They can be divided into several distinct parts. The SOMA is the body of the neuron; it contains most of the cellular organelles. DENDRITES are small, treelike structures that extend from the soma. Their main responsibility is to carry information to the soma, and sometimes away from it. Also extending from the soma is the long, thin AXON. There is usually one axon per soma, but the axon can branch out farther. It is responsible for sending information from the soma, rarely to it. Lastly, the places where two neurons meet, or where they meet other types of cells, are called SYNAPSES.

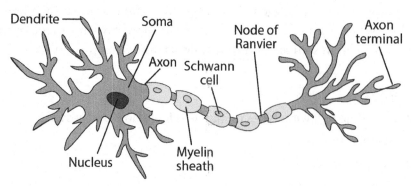

Figure 7.16. Neuron

NEUROGLIA are the maintenance cells for neurons. Neurons are so specialized that they almost never reproduce. Therefore, they need the neuroglial cells, a number of which surround every neuron, to protect and feed them. Neuroglia are also called the GLIAL CELLS.

In the peripheral nervous system, the primary glial cell is a SCHWANN CELL. Schwann cells secrete a fatty substance called MYELIN that wraps around the neuron and allows much faster transmission of the electrical signal the neuron is sending. Gaps in the myelin sheath are called NODES OF RANVIER.

Protecting the Central Nervous System (CNS)

The CNS consists of the brain and spinal cord. Both are placed within cavities in protective skeletal structures: the brain is housed in the cranial cavity of the skull, and the spinal cord is enclosed in the vertebral cavity in the spine. The BRAIN serves as the control system for the nervous system, while the SPINAL CORD carries signals and processes some reflexes to stimuli.

Since the organs that form the CNS are vital to our survival, they are also protected by two other important structures: the meninges and the cerebrospinal fluid. The MENINGES are a protective covering of the CNS made up of three distinct layers. The first is the DURA MATER, which, as its name suggests, is the most durable, outer part of the meninges. It is made out of collagen fibers—rich and thick connective tissue—and it forms a space for the cerebrospinal fluid around the CNS.

Next is the ARACHNOID MATER, which is the thin lining on the inner side of the dura mater. It forms many tiny fibers that connect the dura mater with the next layer, the PIA MATER, which is separated from the arachnoid mater by the SUBARACHNOID SPACE. The pia mater directly covers the surface of the brain and spinal cord, and it provides sustenance to the nervous tissue through its many blood vessels.

The subarachnoid space is filled with CEREBROSPINAL FLUID (CSF), a clear fluid formed from blood plasma. CSF can also be found in the ventricles (the hollow spaces in the brain) and in the central canal (a cavity found in the middle of the spinal cord).

As the CNS floats in the cerebrospinal fluid, it appears lighter than it really is. This is especially important for the brain, because the fluid keeps it from being crushed by its own weight. The floating also protects the brain and the spinal cord from shock—like sudden movements and trauma. Additionally, the CSF contains the necessary chemical substance for the normal functioning of the nervous tissue, and it removes the cellular waste from the neurons.

The Brain

The nervous tissue that makes up the brain is divided into two classes. The GRAY MATTER, which consists mostly of interneurons that are unmyelinated, is the tissue where the actual processing of signals happens. It is also where the connections between neurons are made. The WHITE MATTER, which consists mostly of myelinated neurons, is the tissue that conducts signals to, from, and between the gray matter regions.

The brain can be divided into three distinct parts: the forebrain (prosencephalon), the midbrain (mesencephalon), and the hindbrain (rhombencephalon).

The **FOREBRAIN** is broken down into two more regions: the cerebrum and the diencephalon. The **CEREBRUM** is the outermost and largest part of the brain. It is divided through the middle by the longitudinal fissure into the left and the right hemisphere, each of which is further divided into four lobes: the frontal, parietal, temporal, and occipital. The two hemispheres are connected by a bundle of white matter called the **CORPUS CALLOSUM**.

The surface of the cerebrum, called the **CEREBRAL CORTEX**, is made out of gray matter with characteristic **SULCI** (grooves) and **GYRI** (bulges). The cerebral cortex is where the actual processing happens in the cerebrum: it is responsible for the higher brain functions like thinking and using language.

The **DIENCEPHALON** is a structure formed by the thalamus, hypothalamus, and the pineal gland. The **THALAMUS**, composed of two gray matter masses, routes the sensory signals to the correct parts of the cerebral cortex. The hypothalamus and the pineal gland are both endocrine glands.

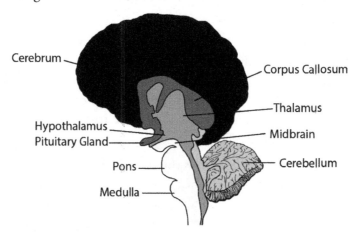

Figure 7.17. The Brain

The **MIDBRAIN** is the topmost part of the brain stem. It is involved in reflex reactions to visual and auditory information, muscle movement, reward-seeking, and learning.

The **HINDBRAIN** consists of the brain stem and the cerebellum. The brain stem is further broken down into the medulla oblongata and the pons. The **MEDULLA OBLONGATA** is mostly made out of white matter, but it also contains gray matter that processes involuntary body functions like blood pressure, level of oxygen in the blood, and reflexes like sneezing. The **PONS** is in charge of transporting signals to and from the cerebellum, and between the upper regions of the brain, the medulla, and the spinal cord.

The **CEREBELLUM** looks like a smaller version of the cerebrum—it has two spheres and is wrinkled. The cerebellum's role is to control and coordinate complex muscle activities; it also helps maintain posture and balance.

Peripheral Nervous System (PNS)

The nerves that form the **PERIPHERAL NERVOUS SYSTEM** (**PNS**) are made of bundled axons whose role is to carry signals to and from the spinal cord and the brain. A single axon, covered with a layer of connective tissue called the **ENDONEURIUM**, bundles with other axons to form **FASCICLES**. These are covered with another sheath of connective tissue called the **PERINEURIUM**. Groups of fascicles wrapped together in another layer of connective tissue, the **EPINEURIUM**, form a whole nerve.

There are five types of peripheral nerves.

1. **Efferent neurons** (also called motor neurons) signal effector cells in muscles and glands to react to stimuli.

2. **Afferent neurons** (also called sensory neurons) take in information from inside and outside the body through the sensory organs and receptors.

3. **Interneurons** transmit information to the CNS where it is evaluated, compared to previously stored information, stored or discarded, and used to make a decision (a process called integration).

4. **Spinal nerves**—thirty-one pairs in total—extend from the side of the spinal cord. They exit the spinal cord between the vertebrae, and they carry information to and from the spinal cord and the neck, the arms, the legs, and the trunk. Spinal nerves are grouped and named according to the region they originate from: eight pairs of cervical, twelve pairs of thoracic, five pairs of lumbar, five pairs of sacral, and one pair of coccygeal nerves.

5. **Cranial nerves**—twelve pairs in total—extend from the lower side of the brain. They are identified by their number, and they connect the brain with the sensory organs, head muscles, neck and shoulder muscles, the heart, and the gastrointestinal track.

The Divisions of the Peripheral Nervous System

The PNS is divided into two parts based on our ability to exert conscious control. The part of the PNS we can consciously control is the **somatic nervous system (SNS)**, which stimulates the skeletal muscles. The **autonomic nervous system (ANS)** cannot be consciously controlled; it stimulates the visceral and cardiac muscle, as well as the glandular tissue.

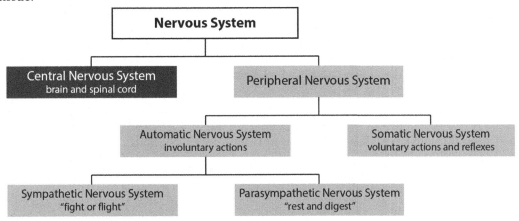

Figure 7.18. Divisions of the Nervous System

The ANS itself is further divided into the sympathetic, parasympathetic, and enteric nervous systems. The **sympathetic nervous system** forms the *fight-or-flight* reaction to stimuli like emotion, danger, and exercise. It increases respiration and heart rate, decreases digestion, and releases stress hormones. The **parasympathetic nervous system** is responsible for stimulating activities that occur when the body is at rest, including digestion and sexual arousal.

The *fight-or-flight* reaction includes accelerated breathing and heart rate, dilation of blood vessels in muscles, release of energy molecules for use by muscles, relaxation of the bladder, and slowing or stopping movement in the upper digestive tract.

Lastly, the ENTERIC NERVOUS SYSTEM is responsible for the digestive system and its processes. This system works mostly independently from the CNS, although it can be regulated through the sympathetic and parasympathetic systems.

Examples

1. Which of the following parts of a neuron is responsible for carrying information away from the cell?

    A) soma

    B) axon

    C) dendrite

    D) myelin

    Answer:

    B) is correct. The axon carries information away from the soma, or body of the cell.

2. Which of the following neurons signals muscles to contract?

    A) efferent neuron

    B) afferent neurons

    C) interneurons

    D) efferent and afferent neurons

    Answer:

    A) is correct. Efferent neurons signal muscles to contract.

THE DIGESTIVE SYSTEM

The DIGESTIVE SYSTEM is a system of organs in the body that is responsible for the intake and processing of food and the removal of food waste products. The digestive system ensures that the body has the nutrients and the energy it needs to function.

The digestive system includes the GASTROINTESTINAL (GI) TRACT, which consists of the organs through which food passes on its way through the body:

1. oral cavity
2. pharynx
3. esophagus
4. stomach
5. small intestines
6. large intestines

Throughout the digestive system there are also organs that have a role in processing food, even though food does not pass through them directly. These include the teeth, tongue, salivary glands, liver, gallbladder, and pancreas.

The Mouth

The digestive system begins with the ORAL CAVITY, also known as the MOUTH. The mouth contains other organs that play a role in digestion. The TEETH are small organs that cut and grind food. They are located on the edges of the mouth, are made out of dentin, which is a substance that resembles bone, and are covered by enamel. The teeth are very hard organs, and each of them has its own blood vessels and nerves, which are located in the matter that fills the tooth, called the pulp.

Also in the mouth is the TONGUE, which is a muscle located behind the teeth. The tongue contains the taste buds and moves food around the mouth as it is processed by the teeth. It then moves food toward the pharynx in order to swallow. The SALIVARY GLANDS, located around the mouth, produce saliva. There are three pairs of salivary glands, and the saliva they produce lubricates and digests carbohydrates.

The Pharynx

The PHARYNX is a tube that enables the passage of food and air further into the body. This structure performs two functions. The pharynx needs the help of the epiglottis, which allows food to pass to the esophagus by covering the opening of the larynx, a structure that carries air into the lungs. When you need to breathe in, the esophagus is closed, so the air passes only into the larynx.

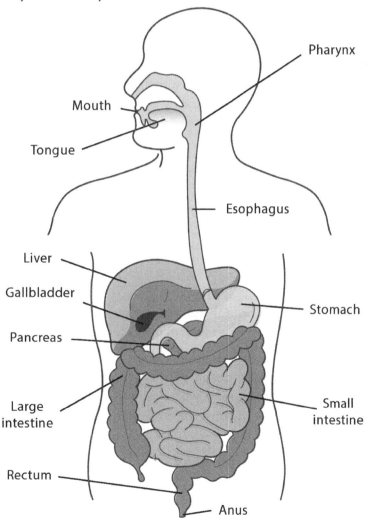

Figure 7.19. The Digestive System

The Esophagus

A sphincter is any circular muscle that controls movement of substances through passageways. Sphincters are found throughout the human body, including in the bladder, esophagus, and capillaries.

The ESOPHAGUS begins at the pharynx and continues to carry food all the way to the stomach. The esophagus is a muscular tube, and the muscles in its wall help to push food down. During vomiting, it pushes food up.

The esophagus has two rings of muscle, called SPHINCTERS. These sphincters close at the top and the bottom ends of the esophagus when food is not passing through it. Heartburn occurs when the bottom sphincter cannot close entirely and allows the contents of the stomach to enter the esophagus.

The Stomach

The stomach is a round organ located on the left side of the body just beneath the diaphragm. It is divided into four different regions. The CARDIA connects the stomach to the esophagus, transitioning from the tube-like shape of the esophagus into the sack shape of the rest of the stomach. The cardia is also where the lower sphincter of the esophagus is located.

The BODY of the stomach is its largest part, and the FUNDUS is located above the body. The last part of the stomach is the PYLORUS, a funnel-shaped region located beneath the body of the stomach. It controls the passage of partially digested food further down the GI tract through the PYLORIC SPHINCTER.

The stomach is made out of four layers of tissue. The innermost layer, the MUCOSA, contains a smooth muscle and the mucus membrane that secretes digestive enzymes and hydrochloric acid. The cells that secrete these products are located within the small pores called the GASTRIC PITS. The mucus membrane also secretes mucus to protect the stomach from its own digestive enzymes.

The SUBMUCOSA is located around the mucosa and is made of connective tissue; it contains nerves and blood vessels. The MUSCULARIS layer enables the movement of the stomach; it is made up of three layers of smooth muscle. The outermost layer of the stomach is the SEROSA. It secretes SEROUS FLUID that keeps the stomach wet and reduces friction between the stomach and the surrounding organs.

The Small Intestine

The SMALL INTESTINE continues from the stomach and takes up most of the space in the abdomen. Attached to the wall of the abdomen, it measures around twenty-two feet long.

The small intestine can be divided into three parts. The DUODENUM is the part of the small intestine that receives the food and chemicals from the stomach. The JEJUNUM, which continues from the duodenum, is where most of the nutrients are absorbed into the blood. Lastly, the ILEUM, which continues from the jejunum, is where the rest of the nutrients are absorbed.

Absorption in the small intestine is helped by the VILLI, which are small protrusions that increase the surface area available for absorption. The villi are made out of smaller microvilli.

The Liver and Gallbladder

The LIVER is not a part of the GI tract. However, it performs roles that are vital for digestion and life itself. It is involved in detoxification of the blood, storage of nutrients, and production of components of blood plasma. Its role in digestion is to produce BILE, a fluid that aids in the digestion of fats. After its production, bile is carried through the bile ducts to the GALLBLADDER, a small, muscular, pear-shaped organ that stores and releases bile.

The liver is located just beneath the diaphragm and is the largest organ in the body after the skin. Triangular in shape, it extends across the whole width of the abdomen. It is divided into four lobes: the left lobe, the right lobe, the caudate lobe (which wraps around the inferior vena cava), and the quadrate lobe (which wraps around the gallbladder).

The Pancreas

The PANCREAS is another organ that is not part of the GI tract but which plays a role in digestion. It is located below and to the left of the stomach. The pancreas secretes both the enzymes that digest food and the hormones *insulin* and *glucagon*, which control blood sugar levels.

The pancreas is known as a HETEROCRINE GLAND, which means it contains both endocrine tissue, which produces insulin and glucagon that move directly into the bloodstream, and exocrine tissue, which produces digestive enzymes that pass into the small intestine. These enzymes include:

- pancreatic amylase that breaks large polysaccharides into smaller sugars
- trypsin, chymotrypsin, and carboxypeptidase that break down proteins into amino acid subunits
- pancreatic lipase that breaks down large fat molecules into fatty acids and monoglycerides
- ribonuclease and deoxyribonuclease that digest nucleic acids

The Large Intestine

The LARGE INTESTINE continues from the small intestine and loops around it. No digestion actually takes place in the large intestine. Rather, it absorbs water and some leftover vitamins. The large intestine carries waste (*feces*) to the RECTUM, where it is stored until it is expelled through the ANUS.

Examples

1. Which of the following organs does food NOT pass through as part of digestion?

    A) stomach

    B) large intestine

    C) esophagus

    D) liver

    Answer:

    D) is correct. The liver is an accessory organ of the digestive system: it produces fluids that aid in digestion, but food does not pass through it.

2. Which layer of the stomach contains blood vessels and nerves?

A) the mucosa

B) the submucosa

C) the serosa

D) the cardia

Answer:

B) is correct. The submucosa, which surrounds the inner mucosa layer, contains the blood vessels and nerves that serve the stomach.

THE IMMUNE SYSTEM

The immune system is primarily responsible for acting as a line of defense against pathogens that enter the body. **PATHOGENS** are any foreign substances that cause disease or infection, including microbes such as viruses, bacteria, and fungi. Most microorganisms are harmless; however, there are still many that can cause disease by dissolving, blocking, or destroying human cells. The immune system works both by keeping pathogens out and by destroying pathogens that do enter the body.

The immune system is divided into the innate and adaptive systems. The innate system uses nonspecific defenses to prevent diseases while the adaptive system targets specific pathogens.

The Innate Immune System

The **INNATE IMMUNE SYSTEM** uses nonspecific defenses that target any microorganism or injured cell that could pose a pathogenic threat to the body. The body's first line of defense are physical barriers: the skin acts as a barrier to pathogens, and cilia, tears, mucus, and saliva trap pathogens that enter the body via the mouth, eyes, or nose.

INFLAMMATION is initiated by the innate immune system as a response to pathogens that enter the body. When body tissue is injured or damaged, the localized tissue surrounding the damage releases **HISTAMINES** that raise the temperature and increase blood flow into the area in order to stimulate more neutrophils, a type of white blood cell, to enter the tissue for repair. Other innate responses include **ANTIMICROBIAL PEPTIDES**, which destroy bacteria by interfering with the functions of their membranes or DNA, and **INTERFERON**, which causes nearby cells to increase their defenses.

Fever is another innate response to potential infection. This occurs when pathogens enter and affect the body in multiple locations, triggering the release of enough histamines to raise the overall body temperature in response. Low to moderate fevers are beneficial to the immune system, killing any pathogens that are negatively impacting the body.

The Adaptive Immune System

The body's **ADAPTIVE IMMUNE SYSTEM** specifically targets pathogens and attacks them based on their specific properties. These properties are expressed by **ANTIGENS**—substances that exist on the surface of pathogenic cells that the immune system does not recognize. When antigens are detected on a foreign substance, the immune system is triggered to attack the cell. The series of events that occurs next is collectively referred to as the IMMUNE RESPONSE.

Immune responses are performed by two distinct kinds of white blood cells called LYMPHOCYTES. T-CELLS are the first type of lymphocyte that detects antigens. After a phagocyte ingests a pathogen cell, T-cells are alerted to the presence of antigens that now exist in the phagocyte membrane. T-cells rapidly divide and form different kinds of T-cells that perform different functions. HELPER T-CELLS are activated to seek out and bind to the antigen. These helper T-cells are known as the coordinators of immune response due to their ability to stimulate one of two different kinds of immune responses.

Helper T-cells can stimulate CYTOTOXIC T-CELLS to actively destroy the infected cells in a CELL-MEDIATED RESPONSE. This response differs from a nonspecific response because the cytotoxic cells bind to the targeted cell's surface in order to kill it.

Helper T-cells can also stimulate the production of **B-cells** in order to trigger an ANTIBODY-MEDIATED RESPONSE. Two kinds of B-cells arise in this response: plasma cells and memory cells. Rather than respond by killing the cell, the PLASMA CELLS produce ANTIBODIES, proteins that bind to the antigen to neutralize it and stimulate phagocytes to ingest the entire structure. The MEMORY CELLS then store the information for producing the antibody and are quickly sprung into action if and when the same antigen appears in the body. This resistance to a now-known pathogen is called IMMUNITY.

> ⚠ Memory B-cells are the underlying mechanisms behind vaccines, which introduce a harmless version of a pathogen into the body to active the body's adaptive immune response.

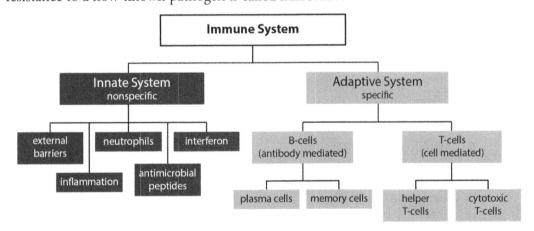

Figure 7.20. Divisions of the Immune System

White Blood Cells

WHITE BLOOD CELLS (WBCs), also called LEUKOCYTES, are an integral part of the both the innate and adaptive immune systems. There are two classes of white blood cells: granular and agranular leukocytes. GRANULAR LEUKOCYTES are divided into three types: the neutrophils that digest bacteria, the eosinophils that digest viruses, and the basophils that release histamine. AGRANULAR LEUKOCYTES are divided into two classes: the lymphocytes, which fight off viral infections and produce antibodies for fighting pathogen-induced infection, and the monocytes, which play a role in removing pathogens and dead cells from wounds.

> ✔ In humans, white blood cells are produced by the endocrine system and are transported through the cardiovascular and lymphatic systems. In what other ways do organ systems work together to prevent disease?

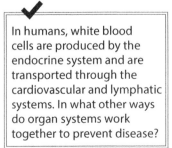

Table 7.2. Types of White Blood Cells

TYPE OF CELL	NAME OF CELL	ROLE	INNATE OR ADAPTIVE?	PREVALENCE
Granulocytes	Neutrophil	first responders that quickly migrate to the site of infections to destroy bacterial invaders	innate	very common
	Eosinophil	attack multicellular parasites	innate	rare
	Basophil	large cell responsible for inflammatory reactions, including allergies	innate	very rare
Lymphocyte	B-cells	respond to antigens by releasing antibodies	adaptive	
	T-cells	respond to antigens by destroying invaders and infected cells	adaptive	common
	Natural killer cells	destroy virus-infected cells and tumor cells	innate and adaptive	
Monocyte	Macrophage	engulf and destroy microbes, foreign substances, and cancer cells	innate and adaptive	rare

Examples

1. Which of the following immune system processes is NOT considered a nonspecific defense of the innate immune system?

    A) fever

    B) inflammation

    C) phagocyte production

    D) antibody production

    Answer:

    D) is correct. Antibodies are produced by B-cells as part of an adaptive immunity response.

2. Which of the following types of cells coordinates both cell-mediated and antibody-mediated responses?

    A) helper T-cells

    B) memory cells

    C) B-cells

    D) phagocytes

    Answer:

    A) is correct. Helper T-cells are lymphocytes that attach to antigens and can trigger either cell-mediated or antibody-mediated responses.

THE ENDOCRINE SYSTEM

The ENDOCRINE SYSTEM consists of many GLANDS that produce and secrete hormones, which send signals to molecules that are traveling through the bloodstream. HORMONES allow cells, tissues, and organs to communicate with each other. Hormones play a role in almost all bodily functions, including growth, sleeping, digestion, response to stress, and sexual functioning. The glands of the endocrine system are scattered throughout the body, and each has a specific role to play.

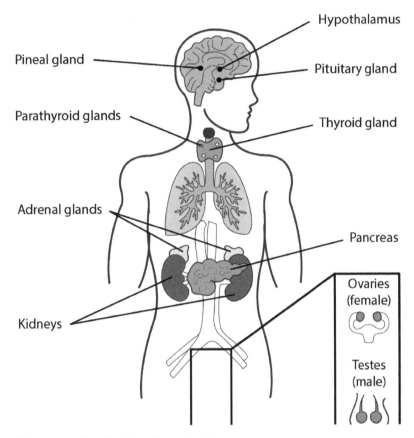

Figure 7.21. Glands of the Endocrine System

- The **PITUITARY GLAND** hangs from the base of your brain and produces the hormone which controls growth and some aspects of sexual functioning. (Hormones produced: growth hormone, thyroid-stimulating hormone, oxytocin, follicle-stimulating hormone)

- The **HYPOTHALAMUS** is also located in the brain. Its main function is to control the pituitary gland, and many of the hormones it releases stimulate the pituitary gland to in turn release hormones itself. (Hormones produced: dopamine, thyrotropin-releasing hormone, growth-hormone–releasing hormone)

- The **PINEAL GLAND**, located in the brain, releases melatonin, a hormone that induces drowsiness and lowers body temperature. (Hormone produced: melatonin)

- The **THYROID GLAND** is found in the neck just below the Adam's apple. It controls protein production and the body's use of energy. The thyroid is regulated by the thyroid-stimulating hormone, which is released by the pituitary gland. (Hormones produced: T3 and thyroxine)

- The four **PARATHYROID GLANDS** are located on the back of the thyroid. They produce parathyroid hormone, which regulates calcium and phosphate levels in the body. (Hormone produced: parathyroid hormone)

- The **PANCREAS**, discussed above, is located behind the stomach and releases hormones that regulate digestion and blood-sugar levels. (Hormones produced: insulin, glucagon, somatostatin)

- The **ADRENAL GLANDS** sit atop the kidneys. The adrenal glands have two regions that produce two sets of hormones: the adrenal cortex releases corticosteroids and androgens, while the adrenal medulla regulates the fight-or-flight response. (Hormones produced: cortisol, testosterone, adrenaline, noradrenaline, dopamine)

- The **TESTES** are glands found in males; they regulate maturation of sex organs and the development of secondary sex characteristics like muscle mass and growth of axillary hair. (Hormones produced: testosterone, estradiol)

- The **OVARIES** are glands found in females; they regulate the menstrual cycle, pregnancy, and secondary sex characteristics like enlargement of the breasts and the widening of the hips. (Hormones produced: progesterone, estrogen)

Examples

1. Which of the following glands indirectly controls growth by acting on the pituitary gland?
   A) hypothalamus
   B) thyroid gland
   C) adrenal glands
   D) parathyroid glands

   Answer:

   A) is correct. The hypothalamus releases hormones that in turn cause the pituitary gland to release growth-related hormones.

2. Which hormone is primarily responsible for the development of male secondary sexual characteristics?
   A) melatonin
   B) follicle-stimulating hormone
   C) estrogen
   D) testosterone

   Answer:

   D) is correct. Testosterone is produced by the testes, which are only found in males. It is responsible for the development of male secondary sexual characteristics.

3. A patient experiencing symptoms such as kidney stones and arthritis due to a calcium imbalance probably has a disorder of which of the following glands?

A) hypothalamus

B) thyroid gland

C) parathyroid glands

D) adrenal glands

Answer:

C) is correct. The parathyroid glands regulate levels of calcium and phosphate in the body.

THE REPRODUCTIVE SYSTEM

Reproductive systems are the groups of organs that enable the successful reproduction of a species. In humans, fertilization is internal, with sperm being transferred from the male to the female during copulation.

The Male Reproductive System

The male reproductive system consists of the organs that produce and ejaculate SPERM, the male gamete. Sperm are produced in the TESTES, specifically in bodies called SEMINIFEROUS TUBULES; mature sperm are stored in the EPIDIDYMIS. The testes are housed in the SCROTUM, located under the PENIS.

During sexual arousal, the VAS DEFERENS carry sperm to the URETHRA, the tube which runs through the penis and carries semen (and urine) out of the body. Along the way, the sperm is joined by fluids from three glands to form SEMEN. The SEMINAL VESICLES secrete the bulk of the fluid which makes up semen, which is

> The Path of Sperm: **SEVEn UP**
> - **S**eminiferous tubes
> - **E**pididymis
> - **V**as deferens
> - **E**jaculatory duct
> - **U**rethra
> - **P**enis

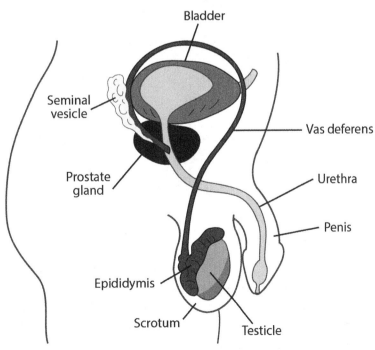

Figure 7.22. The Male Reproductive System

composed of various proteins, sugars, and enzymes. The **PROSTATE** contributes an alkaline fluid that counteracts the acidity of the vaginal tract. Finally, the **COWPER'S GLAND** secretes a protein-rich fluid that acts as a lubricant.

The main hormone associated with the male reproductive system is **TESTOSTERONE**, which is released by the testes (and in the adrenal glands in much smaller amounts). Testosterone is responsible for the development of the male reproductive system and male secondary sexual characteristics, including muscle development and facial hair growth.

The Female Reproductive System

Sexual reproduction in animals occurs in cycles that depend on the production of an **OVULE**, or egg, by the female of the species. In humans, the reproductive cycle occurs approximately once a month, when an egg is released from the female's ovaries.

The female reproductive organs, or gonads, are called **OVARIES**. Each ovary has a follicle that contains **OOCYTES**, or undeveloped eggs. The surrounding cells in the ovary help to protect and nourish the oocyte until it is needed. During the menstrual cycle, one or more oocytes will mature into an egg with help from the **CORPUS LUTEUM**, a mass of follicular tissue that provides nutrients to the egg and secretes estradiol and progesterone.

✔
> What type of muscle is most likely found in the uterus?

Once it has matured, the egg will be released into the **FALLOPIAN TUBE**, where fertilization will take place if sperm are present. The egg will then travel into the **UTERUS**. Unfertilized eggs are shed along with the uterine lining during **MENSTRUATION**. Fertilized eggs, known as **ZYGOTES**, implant in the lining of the uterus where they continue to develop.

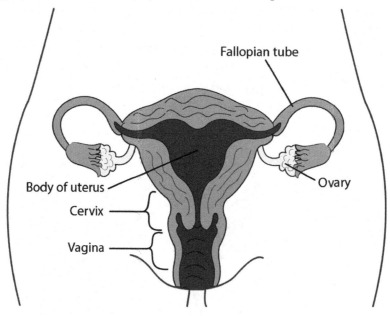

Figure 7.23. The Female Reproductive System

Embryo Fertilization and Development

After fertilization, the cell will start to divide and, after four to five days, become a ball of cells known as a **BLASTOCYST**. The blastocyst is then implanted into the **ENDOMETRIUM** of the uterus. After the blastocyst has been implanted into the endometrium, the placenta develops. The PLACENTA is a temporary organ that attaches the embryo to the mother; it provides nutrients to the fetus, carries waste away from the fetus, protects the fetus from infection, and produces hormones that support pregnancy. The placenta develops from cells called the TROPHOBLAST, which come from the outer layer of the blastocyst.

In humans, the gestation period of the EMBRYO (also called the FETUS), is 266 days or roughly 8.8 months. The human development cycle in the womb is divided into three trimesters. In the first trimester, the organs responsible for the embryo's growth develop. These include the placenta and umbilical cord. During this time, ORGANOGENESIS occurs, and the various stem cells from the blastocyst differentiate into the organs of the body. The organs are not fully developed at this point, but they do exist.

In the second trimester, the fetus experiences rapid growth, up to about twenty-five to thirty centimeters in length. At this point, it is usually apparent that the woman is pregnant, as the uterus grows and extends, and the woman's belly becomes slightly distended. In the third trimester, the fetus finishes developing. The baby exits the uterus through the CERVIX and leaves the body through the VAGINA.

Examples

1. Which of the following organs does NOT contribute material to semen?

   A) the prostate

   B) the Cowper's glands

   C) the penis

   D) the testes

   Answer:

   C) is correct. Semen travels through the penis to exit the body, but the penis does not itself produce any material to contribute to semen.

2. Fertilization typically takes place in the:

   A) fallopian tube

   B) ovaries

   C) uterus

   D) cervix

   Answer:

   A) is correct. Fertilization take place when a sperm enters an egg in the fallopian tube.

THE GENITOURINARY SYSTEM

The URINARY SYSTEM excretes water and waste from the body and is crucial for maintaining the body's electrolyte balance (the balance of water and salt in the blood). Because many organs function as part of both the reproductive and urinary systems, the two are sometimes referred to collectively as the GENITOURINARY SYSTEM.

The main organs of the urinary system are the KIDNEYS, which filter waste from the blood; maintain the electrolyte balance in the blood; and regulate blood volume, pressure, and pH. The kidneys also function as an endocrine organ and release several important hormones. These include RENIN, which regulates blood pressure, and CALCITRIOL, the active form of vitamin D. The kidney is divided into two regions: the RENAL CORTEX, which is the outermost layer, and the RENAL MEDULLA, which is the inner layer.

The functional unit of the kidney is the NEPHRON, which is a series of looping tubes that filter electrolytes, metabolic waste, and other water-soluble waste molecules from the blood. These wastes include UREA, which is a nitrogenous byproduct of protein catabolism, and URIC ACID, a byproduct of nucleic acid metabolism. Together, these waste products are excreted from the body in URINE.

Filtration begins in a network of capillaries called a GLOMERULUS which is located in the renal cortex of each kidney. This waste is then funneled into COLLECTING DUCTS in the renal medulla. From the collecting ducts, urine passes through the RENAL PELVIS and then through two long tubes called URETERS.

The two ureters drain into the urinary bladder, which holds up to 1,000 milliliters of liquid. The bladder exit is controlled by two sphincters, both of which must open for urine to pass. The internal sphincter is made of smooth involuntary muscle, while the external sphincter can be voluntarily controlled. In males, the external sphincter also closes to prevent movement of seminal fluid into the bladder during sexual activity.

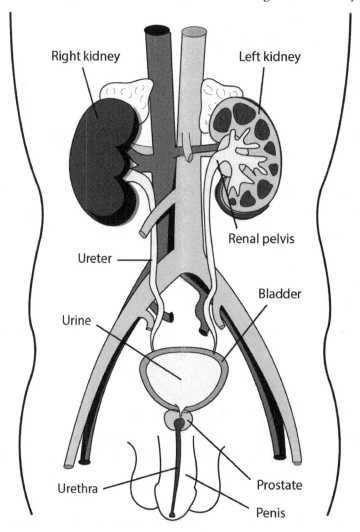

Figure 7.24. The Male Genitourinary System

Urine exits the bladder through the URETHRA. In males, the urethra goes through the penis and also carries semen. In females, the much shorter urethra ends just above the vaginal opening.

Examples

1. Which of the following is the outermost layer of the kidney?

A) renal cortex

B) renal medulla

C) renal pelvis

D) nephron

Answer:

A) is correct. The outermost layer of the kidney is the renal cortex.

2. Which of the following organs holds urine before it passes into the urethra?

A) prostate

B) kidney

C) ureter

D) urinary bladder

Answer:

D) is correct. The urinary bladder holds urine before it passes to the urethra to be excreted.

THE INTEGUMENTARY SYSTEM

The INTEGUMENTARY SYSTEM refers to the skin (the largest organ in the body) and related structures, including the hair and nails. Skin is composed of three layers. The EPIDERMIS is the outermost layer of the skin. This waterproof layer contains no blood vessels and acts mainly to protect the body. Under the epidermis lies the DERMIS, which consists of dense connective tissue that allows skin to stretch and flex. The dermis is home to blood vessels, glands, and HAIR FOLLICLES. The HYPODERMIS is a layer of fat below the dermis that stores energy (in the form of fat) and acts as a cushion for the body. The hypodermis is sometimes called the SUBCUTANEOUS LAYER.

The skin has several important roles. It acts as a barrier to protect the body from injury, the intrusion of foreign particles, and the loss of water and nutrients. It is also important for THERMOREGULATION. Blood vessels near the surface of the skin can dilate, allowing for higher blood flow and the release of heat. They can also constrict to reduce the amount of blood that travels near the surface of the skin, which helps conserve heat. Finally, the skin produces vitamin D when exposed to sunlight.

Because the skin covers the whole body, it plays a vital role in allowing organisms to interact with the environment. It is home to nerve endings that sense temperature, pressure, and pain; it also houses glands that help maintain homeostasis. ECCRINE glands, which are located primarily in the palms of the hands and soles of the feet (and to a lesser degree in other areas of the body), release

> Why would flushing—the reddening of the skin caused by dilating blood vessels—be associated with fevers?

the water and salt (NaCl) mixture called SWEAT. These glands help the body maintain the appropriate salt/water balance. Sweat can also contain small amounts of other substances the body needs to expel, including alcohol, lactic acid, and urea.

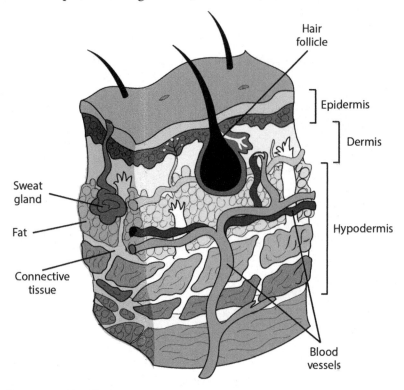

Figure 7.25. The Skin

APOCRINE glands, which are located primarily in the armpit and groin, release an oily substance that contains pheromones. They are also sensitive to adrenaline, and are responsible for most of the sweating that occurs due to stress, fear, anxiety, or pain. Apocrine glands are largely inactive until puberty.

Examples

1. Which of the following is NOT a function of the skin?
   A) regulating body temperature
   B) protecting against injury
   C) producing adrenaline
   D) maintaining water/salt balance

   Answer:

   C) is correct. The skin does not produce adrenaline. (Adrenaline is produced and released by the adrenal glands.)

2. Which of the following is the outermost layer of the skin?
   A) hypodermis
   B) dermis
   C) epidermis
   D) apocrine

Answer:

C) is correct. The epidermis is the outermost layer of the skin. It is waterproof and does not contain any blood vessels.

LIFE SCIENCE

BIOLOGICAL MACROMOLECULES

ORGANIC compounds are those that contain carbon. These compounds, such as glucose, triacylglycerol, and guanine, are used in day-to-day metabolic processes. Many of these molecules are POLYMERS formed from repeated smaller units called MONOMERS. INORGANIC compounds are those that do not contain carbon. These make up a very small fraction of mass in living organisms and are usually minerals such as potassium, sodium, and iron.

There are several classes of organic compounds commonly found in living organisms. These biological molecules include carbohydrates, proteins, lipids, and nucleic acids, which, when combined, make up more than 95 percent of non-water material in living organisms.

Carbohydrates

CARBOHYDRATES, also called sugars, are molecules made of carbon, hydrogen, and oxygen. Sugars are primarily used in organisms as a source of energy: they can be catabolized (broken down) to create energy molecules such as adenosine triphosphate (ATP) or nicotinamide adenine dinucleotide (NAD$^+$), providing a source of electrons to drive cellular processes.

The monomer of carbohydrates is the MONOSACCHARIDE, a sugar with the formula $C_nH_{2n}O_n$. Glucose, for example, is the monosaccharide $C_6H_{12}O_6$. Simple sugars like glucose can bond together to form polymers called POLYSACCHARIDES. Some polymers of glucose include starch, which is used to store excess sugar, and cellulose, which is a support fiber responsible in part for the strength of plants.

Glucose: $C_6H_{12}O_6$

Figure 8.1. A Carbohydrate

Lipids

LIPIDS are compounds primarily composed of carbon and hydrogen with only a small percentage of oxygen. Lipids contain a HEAD, usually formed of glycerol or phosphate, and a TAIL, which is a hydrocarbon chain. The composition of the head, whether it is a carboxylic acid functional group, a phosphate group, or some other functional group, is usually polar, meaning it is hydrophilic. The tail is composed of carbon and hydrogen and is usually nonpolar, meaning it is hydrophobic.

The combined polarity of the lipid head and the non-polarity of the lipid tail are unique features of lipids critical to the formation of the phospholipid bilayer in the cell membrane. The fatty acid tails are all pointed inward, and the heads are pointed outward. This provides a semipermeable membrane that allows a cell to separate its contents from the environment.

Lauric Acid: $C_{12}H_{24}O_2$

polar head
(hydrophilic)

nonpolar tail
(hydrophobic)

Figure 8.2. A Lipid (Lauric Acid)

The **SATURATION** of a lipid describes the number of double bonds in the tail of the lipid. The more double bonds a lipid tail has, the more unsaturated the molecule is, and the more bends there are in its structure. As a result, unsaturated fats (like oils) tend to be liquid at room temperature, whereas saturated fats (like lard or butter) are solid at room temperature.

Proteins

PROTEINS are large molecules that play an important role in almost every cellular process in the human body. They act as catalysts, transport molecules across membranes, facilitate DNA replication, and regulate the cell cycle, including mitosis and meiosis.

Proteins are composed of a chain of **AMINO ACIDS**. The sequence of amino acids in the chain determines the protein's structure and function. Each amino acid is composed of three parts:

- Amino group ($-NH_2$): The amino group is found on all amino acids.
- Carboxyl group ($-COOH$): The carboxyl group is found on all amino acids.
- R group: The R group is a unique functional group that is different for each amino acid.

There are twenty-two amino acids used to produce proteins. It is not necessary to know each amino acid, but it is important to know that sequences of these amino acids form proteins, and that each amino acid has a unique R-functional group.

Histidine

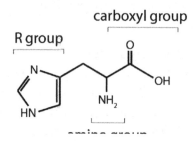

Figure 8.3. An Amino Acid (Histidine)

Nucleic Acids

The major differences between DNA and RNA include:
- Uracil replaces thymine in RNA.
- RNA can exist as a single strand, while DNA is double stranded.
- RNA contains ribose, while DNA contains deoxyribose.

NUCLEIC ACIDS, which include DNA and RNA, store all information necessary to produce proteins. These molecules are built using smaller molecules called **NUCLEOTIDES**, which are composed of a 5-carbon sugar, a phosphate group, and a nitrogenous base.

DNA is made from four nucleotides: adenine, guanine, cytosine, and thymine. Together, adenine and guanine are classified as **PURINES**, while thymine and cytosine are classified as **PYRIMIDINES**. These nucleotides bond together in pairs; the pairs are then bonded together in a chain to create a double helix shape with the sugar as the outside and the nitrogenous base on the inside. In DNA, adenine and thymine always bond together, as do guanine and cytosine. In RNA, thymine is replaced by a nucleotide called uracil, which bonds with adenine. RNA also differs from DNA in that it often exists as a single strand.

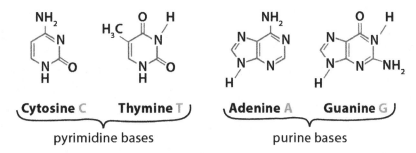

Figure 8.4. DNA Nucleotides

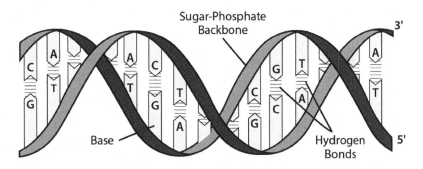

Figure 8.5. DNA Double Helix

The individual strands of DNA are directional, meaning it matters in which direction the DNA is read. The two ends of a DNA strand are called the 3' end and the 5' end, and these names are included when describing a section of DNA, as shown below:

5'-ATGAATTGCCT-3'

For two complementary strands of DNA, one end starts at 5', and the other starts at 3':

5'-ATGAATTGCCT-3'

3'-TACTTAACGGA-5'

This naming convention is needed to understand the direction of DNA replication and where the enzymes bind during the process.

Examples

1. Which of the following polymers is created by joining amino acids?

   A) DNA

   B) lipid

   C) protein

   D) carbohydrate

   Answer:

   C) is correct. Proteins are built by joining amino acids.

2. Which of the following nucleotides is NOT found in DNA?

A) adenine

B) uracil

C) thymine

D) cytosine

Answer:

B) is correct. Uracil is a nucleotide found in RNA, not DNA.

3. Which of the following compounds is NOT created by joining monosaccharides?

A) glycogen

B) starch

C) cellulose

D) guanine

Answer:

D) is correct. Guanine is a nucleic acid, not a polysaccharide.

THE BASICS OF THE CELL

The CELL is the smallest unit of life that can reproduce on its own. All higher organisms are composed of cells, which are specialized to perform the many processes that keep organisms alive and allow them to reproduce.

Parts of the Cell

Although the cell is the smallest unit of life, there are many small bodies, called ORGAN-ELLES, which exist in the cell. These organelles are required for the many processes that take place inside a cell.

- The MITOCHONDRIA are the organelles responsible for making ATP within the cell. Mitochondria have several layers of membranes used to assist the electron transport chain. This pathway uses energy provided by molecules such as glucose or fat (lipid) to generate ATP through the transfer of electrons.

- A VACUOLE is a small body used to transfer materials within and out of the cell. It has a membrane of its own and can carry things such as cell wastes, sugars, or proteins.

- The NUCLEUS of a eukaryotic cell contains all of its genetic information in the form of DNA. In the nucleus, DNA replication and transcription occur. In the eukaryotic cell, after transcription, the mRNA is exported out of the nucleus into the cytosol for use.

- The ENDOPLASMIC RETICULUM (ER) is used for translation of mRNA into proteins and for the transport of proteins out of the cell. The rough endoplasmic reticulum has many ribosomes attached to it, which function as the cell's machinery in transforming RNA into protein. The smooth endoplasmic reticulum is associated with the production of fats and steroid hormones.

- A RIBOSOME is a small two-protein unit that reads mRNA and, with the assistance of transport proteins, creates an amino acid.
- The GOLGI APPARATUS collects, packages, and distributes the proteins produced by ribosomes.
- CHLOROPLASTS are plant organelles where the reactions of photosynthesis take place.

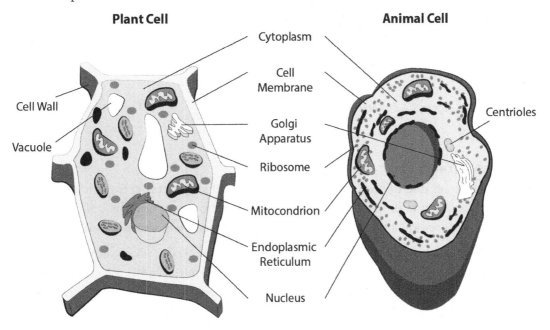

Figure 8.6. Plant and Animal Cell Organelles

Cell Membrane

The CELL MEMBRANE surrounds the cell and controls what enters and leaves. It is composed of compounds called PHOSPHOLIPIDS that consist of an alkane tail and a phospho-group head. The alkane lipid tail is hydrophobic, meaning it will not allow water to pass through, and the phosphate group head is hydrophilic, which allows water to pass through. The arrangement of these molecules forms a bilayer, which has a hydrophobic middle layer. In this manner, the cell is able to control the import and export of various substances into the cell.

In addition to the phospholipid bilayer, the cell membrane often includes proteins, which perform a variety of functions. Some proteins are used as receptors, which allow the cell to interact with its surroundings. Others are TRANSMEMBRANE PROTEINS, meaning they cross the entire membrane. These types of proteins are usually channels that allow the transportation of molecules into and out of the cell.

Membrane proteins are also used in cell-to-cell interaction. This includes functions such as cell-cell joining or recognition, in which a cell membrane protein contacts a protein from another cell. A good example of this is the immune response in the human body. Due to the proteins found on the cell membrane of antigens, immune system cells can contact, recognize, and attempt to remove them.

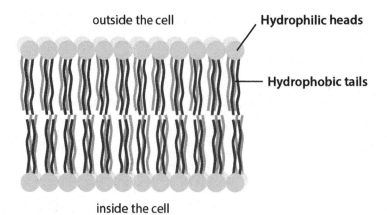

outside the cell — Hydrophilic heads

Hydrophobic tails

inside the cell

Figure 8.7. Cell Membrane Bilayer

Membrane Transport

A cell needs to be able to both import and export vital substances across the membrane while at the same time preventing harmful substances from entering the cell. Two major classes of transportation allow this process to occur: active transport and passive transport.

ACTIVE TRANSPORT uses ATP to accomplish one of two tasks: it can move a molecule against the concentration gradient (from low concentration to high), or it can be used to import or export a bulky molecule, such as a sugar or a protein, across the cell membrane. Active transport requires the use of proteins and energy in the form of ATP. The ATP produced by the cell binds to the proteins in the cell membrane and is hydrolyzed, producing the energy required to change the conformational structure of the protein. This change in the structure of the protein allows the protein to funnel molecules across the cell membrane.

PASSIVE TRANSPORT does not require energy and allows molecules such as water to passively diffuse across the cell membrane. Facilitated diffusion is a form of passive transport that does not require energy but does require the use of proteins located on the cell membrane. These transport proteins typically have a "channel" running through the core of a protein specific to a certain type of molecule. For example, a transport protein for sodium only allows sodium to flow through the channel.

Tonicity

The balance of water in the cell is one of the most important regulatory mechanisms for the cell. Water enters or exits the cell through a process called **OSMOSIS**. This movement of water does not usually require energy, and the movement is regulated by a factor called tonicity.

TONICITY is the concentration of solutes in the cell. Solutes can be salt ions, such as sodium or chlorine, or other molecules, such as sugar, amino acids, or proteins. The difference in tonicity between the cell and its outside environment governs the transportation of water into and out of the cell. For example, if there is a higher tonicity inside the cell, then water will enter the cell. If there is a higher tonicity outside the cell, the water will leave the cell. This is due to a driving force called the **CHEMIOSMOTIC POTENTIAL**, which attempts to make tonicity equal across a membrane.

There are three terms used to describe a cell's tonicity:

- When a cell is in an **ISOTONIC** environment, the same concentration of solutes exists inside and outside the cell. There will be no transport of water in this case.

- When a cell is in a **HYPERTONIC** environment, the concentration of solutes outside the cell is higher than that inside the cell. The cell will lose water to the environment and shrivel. This is what happens if a cell is placed into a salty solution.

- When a cell is in a **HYPOTONIC** environment, the concentration of solutes outside the cell is lower than that inside the cell. The cell will absorb water from the environment and swell, becoming turgid.

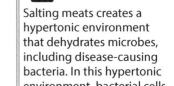

Salting meats creates a hypertonic environment that dehydrates microbes, including disease-causing bacteria. In this hypertonic environment, bacterial cells lose so much water they can no longer function, which protects the meat from infection.

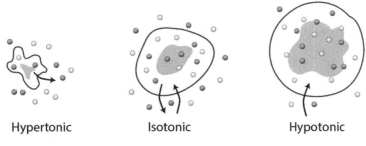

Hypertonic   Isotonic   Hypotonic

Figure 8.8. Tonicity

Cell Interactions

With the vast number of cells in living organisms (an estimated 100 trillion in the human body), how do they all interact and talk with one another? Cells are able to communicate with one another through cell signaling, which occurs via chemical signals excreted by the cell. It is also possible to have direct cell-to-cell communication through protein receptors located in the cell membrane. Important signaling molecules include **CYCLIC AMP**, which is best known for its function in the signaling cascade when epinephrine binds to a cell, and **NEUROTRANSMITTERS** such as dopamine and serotonin, among many others.

LOCAL, or **DIRECT**, **SIGNALING** is a signal that occurs between cells that are either right next to each other or within a few cells' distance. This communication can occur by two methods. First, **GAP JUNCTIONS** exist between the membranes of two cells that can allow signaling molecules to directly enter the cells. Second, the receptors on the membrane can bind with other cells that have membrane receptors to communicate.

The primary chemical used in long-range, or endocrine, signaling is called a **HORMONE**. In humans and animals, hormones are produced by organs and cells in the endocrine system such as the testes, hypothalamus, and pituitary glands. These hormones, once released, can travel throughout the organism through the circulatory system (blood). The hormones can then bind to other cells that have the appropriate receptor and cause a signal to start inside the cell.

One example of long-range signaling in the human body is the production of insulin by the pancreas. Insulin spreads through the body via the blood, and when it binds to an insulin receptor on a cell, the cell begins to take in more glucose. This process is called long-range signaling because insulin is produced by cells in only one location (the pancreas) but is able to affect nearly all other cells in the body.

An example of long-distance signaling in plants is the production of ethylene, a ripening chemical. It can be present in the air or can diffuse through cell walls, and the production of ethylene by one plant can produce a chain reaction that causes nearby plants to also start ripening.

Examples

1. The Golgi apparatus is responsible for which of the following tasks?

    A) protein synthesis

    B) intracellular and extracellular transport

    C) storage and replication of DNA

    D) production of ATP

    Answer:

    B) is correct. The Golgi apparatus packages and transports proteins produced on the endoplasmic reticulum.

2. Which of the following structures is embedded in the cell membrane to facilitate the movement of molecules across the membrane?

    A) proteins

    B) ATP

    C) glucose

    D) lipids

    Answer:

    A) is correct. Proteins embedded in the cell membrane are integral to many cell functions, including active transport and some types of passive transport.

3. A student places a cell with a 50 mM intracellular ion content into a solution containing a 20 mM ion content. Which of the following will happen in this system?

    A) Water will move out of the cell, decreasing the size of the cell.

    B) Water will move into the cell, increasing the size of the cell.

    C) Ions will move into the cell.

    D) There will be no movement of water or ions across the cell membrane.

    Answer:

    B) is correct. The concentration of ions is higher inside the cell than outside, so water will move into the cell from the environment, increasing the size of the cell.

4. Which of the following substances cannot travel across a cell membrane without the use of energy?

    A) water

    B) potassium

    C) sodium

    D) glucose

Answer:

D) is correct. A glucose molecule is too large to pass through the cell membrane without the help of specialized proteins.

THE CELL CYCLE

The cell cycle is the process cells go through as they live, grow, and divide to produce new cells. The cell cycle can be divided into four primary phases:

1. G1 phase: growth phase one
2. S phase: DNA replication
3. G2 phase: growth phase two
4. Mitotic phase: The cell undergoes mitosis and splits into two cells.

The Cell Cycle
Go Sally Go, Make Children!
- Growth phase 1
- DNA Synthesis
- Growth phase 2
- Mitosis
- Cytokinesis

Together, the G1, S, and G2 phases are known as **INTERPHASE**. During these phases, which usually take up 80 to 90 percent of the total time in a cell cycle, the cell is growing and conducting normal cell functions.

Mitosis

The process of cell division is called **MITOSIS**. When a cell divides, it needs to make sure that each copy of the cell has a roughly equal amount of the necessary elements, including DNA, proteins, and organelles. In multicellular organisms, mitosis occurs in somatic (body) cells that contain a pair of homologous chromosomes. The two resulting daughter cells will have identical genetic material.

The mitotic phase is separated into five substages:

Mitosis
I Passed My Anatomy Test
- Interphase
- Prophase
- Metaphase
- Anaphase
- Telophase

- Prophase: In prophase, the DNA in the cell winds into chromatin, and each pair of duplicated chromosomes becomes joined. The mitotic spindle, which pulls apart the chromosomes later, forms and drifts to each end of the cell.

- Prometaphase: In this phase, the nuclear membrane, which holds the DNA, dissolves, allowing the chromosomes to come free. The chromosomes now start to attach to microtubules linked to the centrioles.

- Metaphase: The centrioles, with microtubules attached to the chromosomes, are now on opposite sides of the cell. The chromosomes align in the middle of the cell, and the microtubules begin contracting.

- Anaphase: In anaphase, the chromosomes move to separate sides of the cell, and the cell structure begins to lengthen, pulling apart as it goes.

- Telophase and Cytokinesis: In this last part of the cell cycle, the cell membrane splits, and two new daughter cells are formed. The nucleolus, containing the DNA, re-forms.

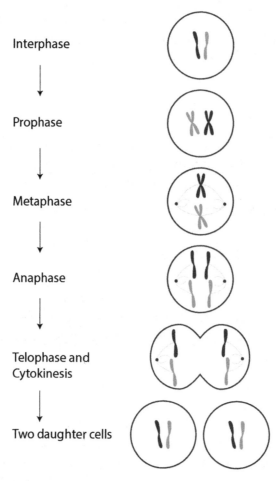

Interphase

Prophase

Metaphase

Anaphase

Telophase and
Cytokinesis

Two daughter cells

Figure 8.9. Mitosis

Meiosis

Meiosis is cellular division that creates gametes (sex cells). The dividing cell starts with a set of homologous chromosomes (2n), but the four resulting daughter cells will each have only one set of chromosomes (1n). There are two consecutive stages of meiosis known as Meiosis I and Meiosis II. These two stages are further broken down into four stages each.

MEIOSIS I

1. Prophase I: The chromosomes condense, using histone proteins, and become paired. Microtubules attach to the chromosomes and centrioles and begin to align them in the middle of the cell.
2. Metaphase I: The chromosomes align in the middle of the cell and begin to pull apart from one another.
3. Anaphase I: The homologous chromosomes separate and move toward opposite sides of the cell.
4. Telophase I: The cells separate, and each cell now has one copy each of a homologous chromosome.

MEIOSIS II

1. Prophase II: A spindle forms and aligns the chromosomes. No crossing-over occurs.

2. Metaphase II: The chromosomes again align at the metaphase plate.

3. Anaphase II: The sister chromatids pull apart to opposite ends of the cell.

4. Telophase II: The cell splits apart, resulting in four unique daughter cells.

Examples

1. A scientist takes DNA samples from a cell culture at two different times, each sample having the same cell count. In the first sample, he finds that there is 6.5 pg of DNA, whereas in the second sample, he finds that there is 13 pg of DNA. Which stage of the cell cycle is the first sample in?

   A) interphase G1

   B) interphase S

   C) interphase G2

   D) mitotic phase

   Answer:

   A) is correct. During the G1 phase of interphase, the cell has not replicated its DNA. During the other three phases listed, the cell would have replicated its DNA, doubling the amount of DNA in the cell.

2. At the end of which phase of mitosis are chromosomes first clearly visible under a light microscope?

   A) interphase

   B) prophase

   C) metaphase

   D) anaphase

   Answer:

   B) is correct. During prophase, the DNA replicated during interphase condenses into chromosomes, which are clearly visible under a light microscope.

NUCLEIC ACIDS

The Structure of DNA

A cell has a lot of DNA: even the smallest human cell contains a copy of the entire human genome. In human cells, this copy of the genome is nearly two meters in length—quite long, considering the average cell is only 100 μm in diameter.

In the nucleus, DNA is organized around proteins called HISTONES; together, this protein and DNA complex is known as CHROMATIN. During interphase, chromatin is usually arranged loosely to allow access to DNA. During mitosis, however, DNA is tightly packaged into units called CHROMOSOMES. When DNA has replicated, the chromosome is composed of two CHROMATIDS joined together at the CENTROMERE.

Each somatic cell is DIPLOID ($2n$), meaning it has two sets of homologous chromosomes, one from each parent. For example, humans have twenty-three pairs of chromosomes, for a total of forty-six chromosomes. Gametes (sex cells) have only one set of chromosomes, so a human sex cell has twenty-three chromosomes. Cells with one set of chromosomes are referred to as HAPLOID ($1n$).

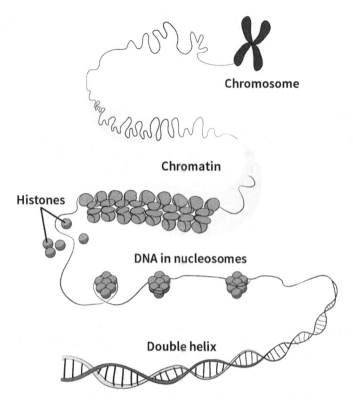

Figure 8.10. Structure of DNA

DNA Replication

DNA REPLICATION is the process by which a copy of DNA is created in a cell. During DNA replication, three steps will occur. The first step is INITIATION, in which an initiator protein binds to regions of DNA known as origin sites. Once the initiation protein has been bound, the DNA polymerase complex will be able to attach. At this point, the enzyme helicase unwinds DNA into two separate single strands.

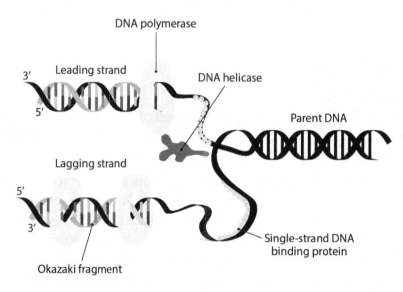

Figure 8.11. DNA replication

During the next step, ELONGATION, new strands of DNA are created. Single-strand binding proteins (SSBs) will bind to each strand of the DNA. Then, DNA polymerase will attach and start replicating the strands by synthesizing a new, complementary strand. DNA polymerase reads the DNA in the 3' to 5' direction, meaning the new strand is synthesized in the 5' to 3' direction. This creates a problem, because the DNA can only be read in the 3' to 5' direction on one strand, known as the LEADING STRAND. The LAGGING STRAND, which runs from 5' to 3', has to be synthesized piece by piece in chunks called OKAZAKI FRAGMENTS. The breaks between these fragments are later filled in by DNA ligase.

The last step in the process of DNA replication is TERMINATION. After DNA polymerase completes the copying process, the replication forks meet, and the process is terminated. There is one catch to this: because the DNA polymerase enzyme can never read or replicate the very end of a strand of DNA, every time a full chromosome is replicated, a small part of DNA is lost at the end. This piece of DNA is usually noncoding and is called a TELOMERE. The shortening of the telomeres is the reason why replication can occur only a limited number of times in somatic cells before DNA replication is no longer possible.

Table 8.1. Important Enzymes in DNA Replication

DNA Helicase	This unwinds a section of DNA to create a segment with two single strands.
DNA Polymerase	DNA polymerase I is responsible for synthesizing Okasaki fragments. DNA polymerase III is responsible for the primary replication of the 5' to 3' strand.
DNA Ligase	Ligase fixes small breaks in the DNA strand and is used to seal the finished DNA strands.
DNA Telomerase	In some cells, DNA telomerase lengthens the telomeres at the end of each strand of DNA, allowing it to be copied additional times.

Transcription and Translation

The "message" contained in DNA and RNA is encoded in the nucleotides. Each amino acid is represented by a set of three base pairs in the nucleotide sequence called a CODON. There are sixty-four possible codons (4 × 4 × 4), which means many of the twenty-two amino acids are coded for with more than one codon. There are also three stop codons, which instruct the ribosome to stop processing the mRNA.

The processing of information stored in DNA to produce a protein takes place in two stages: transcription and translation. In transcription, an mRNA copy of the DNA is created. In translation, the mRNA strand is read by a ribosome to create an amino acid chain, which is folded into a protein.

DNA TRANSCRIPTION is the process of making messenger RNA (mRNA) from a DNA strand. The steps for DNA transcription are similar to those of DNA replication, although different enzymes are used. The DNA strand provides a template for RNA polymerase: the DNA is first unwound, and

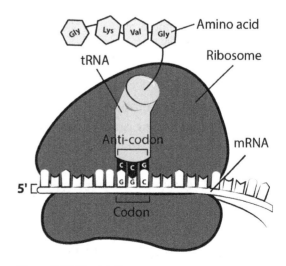

Figure 8.12. Translation

then RNA polymerase makes a complementary transcript of the DNA sequence, called mRNA.

The TRANSLATION process converts the mRNA transcript into a useable protein. This process occurs in a ribosome, which lines up the mRNA so it can bind to the appropriate tRNA (transfer RNA). Each tRNA includes an amino acid and an ANTICODON, which matches to the complementary codon on the mRNA. When the tRNA is in place, a bond is formed between the growing amino acid strand and the new amino acid brought by the tRNA.

The translation process stops when a stop codon is reached in the sequence. These codons activate a protein called a release factor, which binds to the ribosome. The ribosome, which is made of two proteins, will split apart after the release factor binds. This releases the newly formed amino acid chain.

Mutations

The DNA sequence can sometimes undergo a MUTATION, which is a change in the base-pair sequence of the DNA strand. A mutation can be benign, or silent, meaning it has no effect, or it can cause a change in the protein structure.

> ✔
> How would the consequences of a mutation in a gamete cell be different from those resulting from a mutation in a somatic cell?

> ⚠
> Sickle cell anemia is caused by a point mutation. A single change in the base-pair sequence from a T to an A changes a codon from GAA to GUA, which changes the amino acid from glutamate to valine. The resulting hemoglobin protein is elongated and cannot carry oxygen as effectively.

One way a gene can be changed permanently is through a POINT MUTATION, where a single base in the sequence of a gene changes. This can happen through a single base substitution, insertion, or deletion. If one base (or a few bases) in the sequence changes, this is called a BASE SUBSTITUTION. An INSERTION occurs when one base (or a few bases) is added to the sequence, and a deletion occurs when one nucleotide (or a few nucleotides) is lost from the sequence.

Adding or removing nucleotides from a stretch of DNA changes the total amount of DNA, which can influence how the gene is read by RNA polymerase and, ultimately, by ribosomes. This type of mutation is called a FRAME-SHIFT MUTATION. Occasionally, two breaks may occur in a chromosome, and the fragment that breaks away flips around and reattaches. This type of mutation is called a CHROMOSOME INVERSION.

Many mutations will not result in any change in the protein sequence at all. For example, if the sequence CCG mutated to CCA, there would be no change, because the codon produced by both sequences corresponds to the amino acid glycine.

Gene Regulation

An important part of understanding metabolism is learning how genes are activated and deactivated. Studying gene expression and regulation is easier in bacteria due to their simple genomes and the simplicity of extracting their plasmids. Although human gene regulation is becoming more thoroughly understood, the vast complexity of the human metabolism and number of genes makes it difficult to get a full picture of all the interactions.

To understand gene regulation, it is necessary to understand the structure of the genetic code. Proteins are not produced from a single gene; instead, a set of genes, called an OPERON, is required. The operon includes a PROMOTER, which initiates transcription; an

OPERATOR, to which an enzyme can bind to regulate transcription; and the protein coding sequence.

Either negative or positive regulation is used to control the operon. In negative regulation, a gene will be expressed unless a repressor becomes attached. In positive regulation, genes are expressed only when an activator attaches to initiate expression.

In addition to interactions with the operon, the expression of DNA can be controlled by modifications to the chromatin. Because the location of the promoters in the chromatin sequence greatly affects access to the gene, expression can be regulated by managing how tightly bound the chromatin is in the nucleus. Modifications to histone proteins, small amino acid structures found only in eukaryotic cell nuclei, can also inhibit or allow access to DNA.

Examples

1. Which of the following sequences is the complementary segment of this section of DNA: 5' AAGCCCTATAC 3'?

   A) 3' UUCGGGAUAUG 5'

   B) 3' TTCGGGATATG 5'

   C) 3' GTATAGGGCTT 5'

   D) 3' GUAUAGGGCUU 5'

   Answer:

   B) is correct. This sequence correctly matches each nucleotide, has the correct orientation, and does not contain the nucleotide uracil (which is found in RNA).

2. Which of the following describes why small sections of DNA are lost during replication?

   A) The sections of DNA between Okazaki fragments cannot be recovered.

   B) DNA polymerase cannot replicate the end of the DNA strand.

   C) DNA cannot be read in the 5' to 3' direction.

   D) The initiator proteins bind to only one strand of DNA.

   Answer:

   B) is correct. DNA polymerase cannot replicate the end of a DNA strand, so that section of the DNA is lost during replication.

3. At an ACU codon, the amino acid threonine will be inserted in the polypeptide. Which of the following anticodons would be found on the tRNA molecule that carries threonine?

   A) ACU

   B) UCA

   C) TGA

   D) UGA

   Answer:

   D) is correct. Anticodons and codons are complementary: the complement of the codon ACU is the anticodon UGA.

GENETICS

GENETICS is the study of genes and how they are passed down to offspring. Before the discovery of genes, there were many theories about how traits are passed to offspring. One of the dominant theories in the nineteenth century was blending inheritance, which stated that the genetic material from the parents would mix to form that of the children in the same way that two colors might mix.

The idea was eventually displaced by the current theory, which is based on the concept of a GENE, which is a region of DNA that codes for a specific protein. Multiple versions of the same gene, called ALLELES, account for variation in a population.

During sexual reproduction, offspring receive a single copy of every gene from each parent. These two genes may be identical, making the individual HOMOZYGOUS, or they may be different, making the individual HETEROZYGOUS for that gene. In a heterozygous individual, the genes do not blend; instead they act separately, with one often being completely or partially suppressed.

Natural selection acts on an organism's phenotype, not its genotype. Only alleles that affect an organism's fitness will be selected for or against.

An organism's GENOTYPE is its complete genetic code. PHENOTYPE is an organism's observable characteristics, such as height, eye color, skin color, and hair color. Although the genotype of two different people might be different, each person could have the same phenotype, depending on which alleles are dominant or recessive. For example, the two types of roses Rr and RR are both red, meaning they have the same phenotype. However, they have a different genotype, with one rose type being heterozygous and the other being homozygous.

Mendel's Laws

The idea that individual genes are passed down from parents to their children was conceived by GREGOR MENDEL. Mendel used various plants to test his ideas, but his best-known work is with pea plants.

Mendel became an Augustinian monk at the age of twenty-one. He studied briefly at the University of Vienna and, after returning to the monastery, started work on breeding plants. During the course of his work, he discovered that the plants had heritable features, meaning features that were passed from parent to offspring. Because of the short generation time of peas, Mendel started working on identifying the traits that could be passed on in the pea plant. He tracked two characteristics: pea flower color and pea shape. From this, he found that the traits were independent of one another, meaning that the pea's flower color in no way affected the pea shape.

If an organism is described as true-breeding for a specific trait, it is homozygous for that trait and will pass it on to its offspring.

During the course of his work, Mendel came up with three laws to describe genetic inheritance: the law of segregation, the law of independent assortment, and the law of dominance. The LAW OF SEGREGATION states that genes come in allele pairs (if the organism is diploid, which most are) and that each parent can pass only a single allele down to its child. Thus, for a pair of alleles in a gene, one comes from the father, and one comes from the mother in sexual reproduction. The law of segregation also states that the alleles must separate during the course of meiosis so that only one is given to each gamete.

The **LAW OF INDEPENDENT ASSORTMENT** states that genes responsible for different traits are passed on independently. Thus, there is not necessarily a correlation between two genes. For example, if a mother is tall and has brown hair, she might pass on her genes for tallness to her child, but perhaps not the ones for brown hair. This law can be seen in the use of the Punnett square, in which gene alleles are separated to determine inheritance.

Lastly, the **LAW OF DOMINANCE** states that some alleles are dominant and some are recessive. Dominant alleles will mask the behavior of recessive ones. For example, red might be dominant in a rose, and white might be recessive. Thus, if a homozygous red rose mates with a homozygous white rose, all of their offspring will be red. Although the white gene allele will be present, it will not be expressed.

> ⚠️
> When writing the genetic information for a genotype, the dominant allele is written as a capital letter (A), while the recessive is written as a lowercase (a). A homozygous genotype can be AA or aa, and a heterozygous genotype will be Aa.

Monohybrid and Dihybrid Crosses

A **GENETIC CROSS** is a method in genetic experimentation in which a scientist intentionally breeds two individual parent organisms in order to produce an offspring that carries genetic material from both parents. The pair of parents is called the parental generation, or **P GENERATION**. The offspring of this initial breeding is known as the first filial generation, or **F1 GENERATION**. If the F1 generation is intentionally bred as well, the offspring of this generation is known as the second filial generation, or **F2 GENERATION**. This pattern of naming continues on as more generations are bred during experimentation.

The purpose of these genetic crosses is to isolate and study traits as they are passed through the generations. In **MONOHYBRID** crosses, the P generation is selected based on one particular trait—one parent possesses the dominant trait, while the other possesses the recessive trait. For example, in one of his pea experiments, Mendel selectively bred one plant with the dominant yellow seed trait with another plant that had the recessive green seed trait. The parent with the dominant trait can have a genotype that is either homozygous (YY) or heterozygous (Yy), while the parent with the recessive trait has a homozygous genotype (yy).

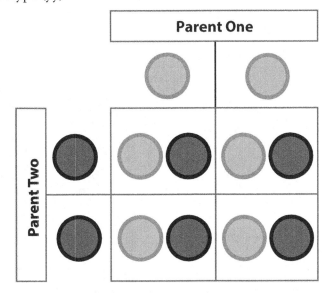

Figure 8.13. Punnett Square: Monohybrid Cross of Seed Color

The phenotype of the resulting F1 generation can be predicted using a **PUNNETT SQUARE**. This diagram determines the probability that an offspring will inherit a particular genotype. For monohybrid crosses, the Punnett square has only four possible combinations for a genotype, each with a 25 percent chance of occurring.

The probability that a certain genotype combination will occur is the Punnett ratio. For example, if two heterozygous yellow pea plants (Yy) are crossed, the Punnett square shows that there is a 3/4 probability that the offspring will be yellow and a 1/4 probability the offspring will be green. This gives this monohybrid cross a Punnett ratio of 3:1.

	Y	y
Y	YY	Yy
y	Yy	yy

Figure 8.14. Punnet Square: Monohybrid Cross of Seed Color

In a **DIHYBRID CROSS**, the P generation is selected for two traits that differ between the two parents. One of Mendel's pea experiments included the dihybrid cross of a P generation that bred one parent with the two dominant traits (yellow and smooth) with a parent that had two recessive traits (green and wrinkled). The resulting Punnett square displays sixteen possible combinations of genotypes for these two traits. The Punnett ratio for this is 9:3:3:1 because there is a:

- 9/16 probability that the offspring will be yellow and smooth
- 3/16 probability that the offspring will be yellow and wrinkled
- 3/16 probability that the offspring will be green and smooth
- 1/16 probability that the offspring will be green and wrinkled

> ✔
> If the parent with the dominant yellow seed trait has a homozygous trait of YY, then there is a 100 percent chance that the F1 generation will express the yellow seed trait. How does this change if the YY parent instead has a Yy genotype?

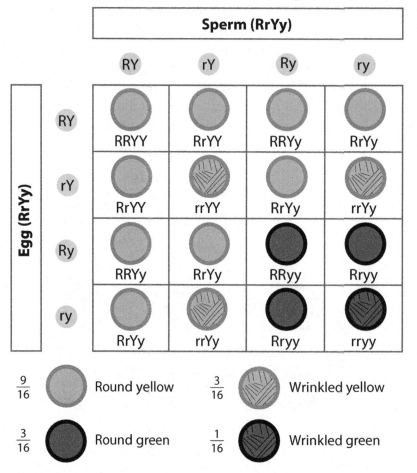

Figure 8.15. Punnett Square: Dihybrid Cross of Seed Color and Shape

Non-Mendelian Genetics

Mendel's laws apply to traits that are controlled by only one gene that has two possible alleles with a dominant/recessive relationship. Many traits do not fit these qualifications and will show inheritance patterns that are different from what Mendelian genetics would predict.

GENE LINKAGE occurs with genes that are situated close together on a chromosome and thus are more likely to be inherited together. Tracking the frequency of linked genes being transmitted together can help researchers determine the physical relationship between genes. All genes have a 50 percent chance of being inherited with any other gene. Genes that are paired with another gene more than 50 percent of the time are more likely to be linked; the higher the percentage, the closer the genes are in distance to one another.

SEX-LINKED genes are located on the SEX CHROMOSOME of each individual. All females have two X CHROMOSOMES, while all males have both an X and a Y CHROMOSOME. Genes that are located on the Y chromosome result in traits that are expressed only in the males of a species. Because females have two X chromosomes (and thus carry two alleles), the dominant allele will express itself for X-linked traits. Males, however, have only one allele for every X gene. As a result, the trait will be expressed regardless of whether it is dominant or recessive.

Non-Mendelian inheritance patterns can also be seen when alleles do not have a binary dominant/recessive relationship. The appearance of two dominant alleles creates an effect called CODOMINANCE, in which both dominant genes are expressed in the individual. This effect is responsible for the human blood type AB, as the gene for blood types A and B are both dominant.

Color blindness and hemophilia are both X-linked disorders: they are carried by females but appear more frequently in males.

INCOMPLETE DOMINANCE occurs when one allele is not completely dominant over the other. For example, if the flower color red is incompletely dominant over the color white, offspring with both alleles will have pink flowers (a blend of red and white).

Introduction of Genetic Variation

Sexual reproduction introduces genetic variation into each generation. During meiosis, the INDEPENDENT ASSORTMENT of chromosomes gives each gamete a unique subset of genes from the parent. When a gamete combines with another to form a zygote, the result is a genetically unique organism that has a different gene composition from either of the parents.

The process of meiosis also introduces genetic variation during CROSSING-OVER, which occurs in prophase I when homologous chromosomes pair along their lengths. Each gene on each chromosome becomes aligned with its sister gene. When crossing-over occurs, a DNA sequence is broken and crisscrossed, creating a new chromatid with pieces of each of the original homologous chromosomes.

RANDOM FERTILIZATION, the random pairing of sperm and egg, also produces genetic variation. Organisms produce millions of gametes, so no matter how many times a pair breeds, it is next to impossible to get two children that have the same genotype (except identical twins).

Examples

1. In a certain plant, having the dominant allele R results in bright-red seeds, and the recessive allele r results in pale-pink seeds. In the first generation, a scientist crosses a true-breeding RR plant with a recessive rr plant. The F1 plant is then crossed with itself, resulting in the F2 generation. In the F2 generation, what percentage of the plants will have bright-red seeds?

    A) 25 percent

    B) 50 percent

    C) 75 percent

    D) 100 percent

    Answer:

    C) is correct. Use Punnett squares to find the result of each cross. The F1 generation will all have the genotype Rr:

F1	R	R
r	Rr	Rr
r	Rr	Rr

    In the F2 generation, 75 percent of the plants will carry the dominant R allele:

F2	R	r
R	RR	Rr
r	Rr	rr

2. Which of the following statements describes the expression of X-linked traits?

    A) X-linked traits are expressed more often in men.

    B) X-linked traits are expressed more often in women.

    C) X-linked traits are expressed equally in men and women.

    D) X-linked traits are expressed only in men who carry the dominant allele.

    Answer:

    A) is correct. X-linked traits are expressed more often in men because they carry only one copy of the gene and so will express the gene whether the allele is dominant or recessive.

3. Which of the following is NOT a way that meiosis increases genetic variation?

    A) creating haploid sex cells that will be randomly fertilized

    B) allowing for the exchange of genetic material between chromosomes

    C) increasing the probability of mutations in the nucleotide sequence of DNA

    D) sorting each set of homologous chromosomes independently

    Answer:

    C) is correct. Meiosis does not increase the probability of mutations. Mutations are caused by environmental factors (such as radiation) or mistakes in DNA replication.

PHYSICAL SCIENCE

THE STRUCTURE OF THE ATOM

The **ATOM** is the basic building block of all physical matter. It is composed of three subatomic particles: protons, electrons, and neutrons. A **PROTON** is a positively charged subatomic particle with a mass of approximately 1.007 atomic mass units. The number of protons in an atom determines which **ELEMENT** it is. For example, an atom with one proton is hydrogen, and an atom with twelve protons is carbon.

A **NEUTRON** is a non-charged subatomic particle with a mass of approximately 1.008 atomic mass units. The number of neutrons in an atom does not affect its chemical properties but will influence its rate of radioactivity. Both protons and neutrons are found in the center, or **NUCLEUS**, of the atom.

Lastly, an **ELECTRON** is a negatively charged subatomic particle with a mass of approximately 0.00055 atomic mass units. The number of electrons in an atom, in conjunction with the protons, determines the atom's charge. An atom with more protons than electrons

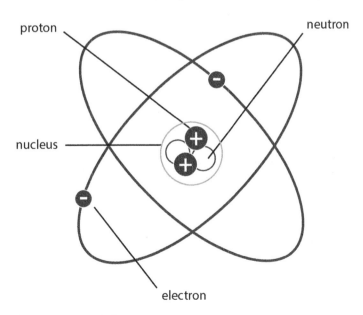

Figure 9.1. Atomic Structure

is a positive CATION, and an atom with more electrons than protons is a negative ANION. Cations and anions are collectively referred to as IONS.

The modern concept of the atom, which provided the basis for all of chemistry, was first laid out in John Dalton's ATOMIC THEORY, which was developed in 1808. Atomic theory states the following:

1. An element is composed of atoms, which are extremely small, indivisible particles. Although we now know that atoms are composed of smaller units such as protons, electrons, and neutrons, it is still recognized that atoms are the basic building blocks of matter.

2. Each individual element has a set of properties that are distinct and different from that of other elements.

3. Atoms cannot be created, destroyed, or transformed through physical changes. We now know that atoms can be created or destroyed, although this requires a massive amount of energy. Furthermore, radioactive elements can be transformed into other elements.

4. Compounds are defined by a specific ratio of atoms that are combined with one another, and the relative numbers and types of atoms are constant in any given compound.

Examples

1. Which of the following subatomic particles are found in the nucleus of an atom?

    A) protons only

    B) electrons only

    C) protons and neutrons only

    D) protons, electrons, and neutrons

    Answer:

    C) is correct. The nucleus of an atom includes protons and neutrons. Electrons orbit around the nucleus.

2. What is the charge of an atom with five protons and seven electrons?

    A) 12

    B) −12

    C) 2

    D) −2

    Answer:

    D) is correct. The total charge of an atom is calculated by the difference of the number of protons and electrons: $5 - 7 = -2$.

ELECTRON CONFIGURATION

The atom consists of a nucleus of protons and neutrons surrounded by orbiting electrons. The nucleus is very dense and contains the majority of mass in the atom. The actual size of the atom, due to the large orbits of the electrons, is much larger than the nucleus.

ELECTRON CONFIGURATION refers to the location of an atom's electrons. Electrons surround the nucleus in clouds called ORBITALS, each of which holds two electrons. These orbitals are grouped into SUBSHELLS, each of which has a particular shape and holds a specific number of electrons. There are four orbital shapes:

- s has 1 orbital and holds $1 \times 2 = 2$ electrons
- p has 3 orbitals and holds $3 \times 2 = 6$ electrons
- d has 5 orbitals and holds $5 \times 2 = 10$ electrons
- f has 7 orbitals and holds $7 \times 2 = 14$ electrons

Subshells are grouped into SHELLS identified by integers (1, 2, 3, …). Shells with smaller integers are smaller and are located close to the nucleus; shells with larger numbers are larger and are located farther from the nucleus.

The location of an electron can be described by its shell number and subshell letter. For example, the single electron in hydrogen is in orbital $1s$. The number of electrons in each orbital is written as a superscript, so the full electron configuration for hydrogen is $1s^1$. The notation for the first four shells is shown in Table 9.1.

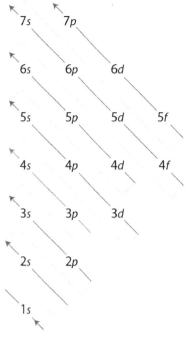

increasing energy
→
1s 2s 2p 3s 3p 4s 3d 4p 5s 4d 5p 6s …

Figure 9.2. Filling Electron Orbitals

Table 9.1. Electron Configuration Notation

SHELL	SUBSHELL	NO. OF ORBITALS	NO. OF ELECTRONS IN SUBSHELL	NOTATION FOR FULL SUBSHELL
1	s	1	2	$1s^2$
2	s	1	2	$2s^2$
	p	3	6	$2p^6$
3	s	1	2	$3s^2$
	p	3	6	$3p^6$
	d	5	10	$3d^{10}$
4	s	1	2	$4s^2$
	p	3	6	$4p^6$
	d	5	10	$4d^{10}$
	f	7	14	$4f^{14}$

Electrons fill orbitals in a specific order, starting with low-energy orbitals and then filling in higher-energy orbitals. The general order in which electrons are filled is shown in Figure 0.2. Note that not all elements follow this order: large elements that have electrons in d and f orbitals will often fill orbitals in unpredictable ways.

The reactivity of each individual atom is determined by the number of electrons in its outermost, or VALENCE, shell. Typically, the closer an atom is to reaching a full valence shell, the more reactive it is. Elements that have a single electron in a shell (such as sodium: last orbital $3s^1$) or that need only a single electron to fill a shell (such as chlorine: last orbital $3p^5$) are the most reactive.

There are some elements that are not reactive at all. These are the noble gases, which possess a full valence shell. Thus, they have no free electrons with which to react. In chemistry, there are no common reactions that occur with a noble gas.

Example

Which of the following is the electron configuration for phosphorus?

A) $1s^2 2s^2 2p^6 3s^2 3p^3$

B) $1s^2 2s^2 2p^6 3s^2 3p^6$

C) $1s^2 2p^6 3s^2 3p^3$

D) $1s^2 2s^2 2p^2 3s^2 3p^3 4s^2 4p^3$

Answer:

A) is correct. Phosphorus has fifteen electrons. Filling the orbitals from lowest to highest energy (as shown in Figure 9.2.) gives the electron configuration $1s^2 2s^2 2p^6 3s^2 3p^3$.

THE PERIODIC TABLE OF ELEMENTS

The **PERIODIC TABLE** is a table used to organize and characterize the various elements. The table was first proposed by Dmitri Mendeleev in 1869, and a similar organization system is still used today. In the table, each column is called a **GROUP**, and each row is called a **PERIOD**. Elements in the same column have similar electron configurations and the same number of electrons in their valence shells.

Reading the Periodic Table

Each cell in the table includes the symbol for the element, which is a letter or set of letters; for example, C for carbon and Fe for iron. The number at the top of each cell in the table is the **ATOMIC NUMBER**. This represents the number of protons in the element. The number below the element symbol is the **ATOMIC MASS**, which represents the total mass of the element (atomic mass – atomic number = # of neutrons).

Because atoms of the same element can have different numbers of neutrons, elements have no single standard atomic mass. Instead, the atomic mass is the weighted average of all commonly found species of the element. For this reason, it is almost never a whole number. For example, a small amount of carbon actually has an atomic mass of 13, possessing seven neutrons instead of the usual six, giving carbon an atomic mass of 12.011. Atoms of the same element with different numbers of neutrons are called **ISOTOPES**.

> Many elemental symbols are derived from the Latin names for elements. For example, the symbol for gold is Au, from its Latin name, *Aurum*.

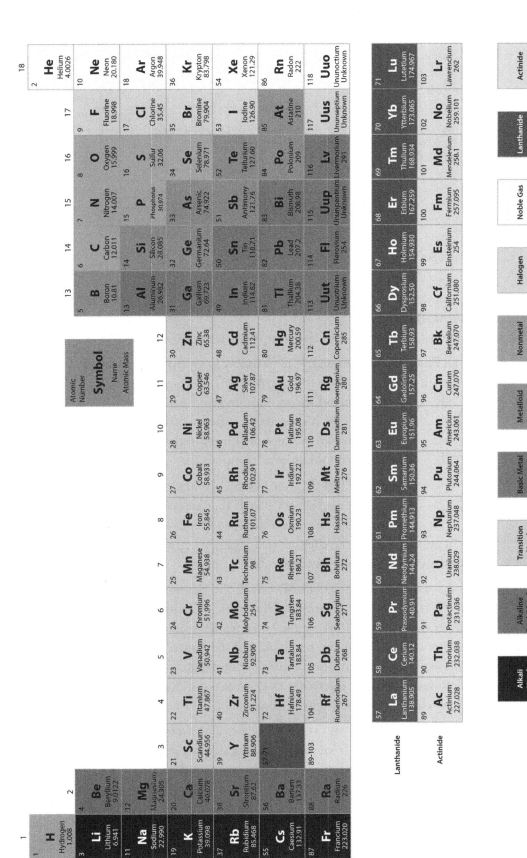

Figure 9.3. The Periodic Table of the Elements

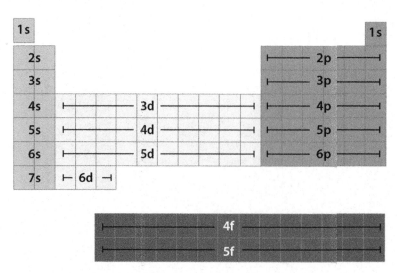

Figure 9.4. Reading the Periodic Table

Groups of Elements

Below are the important properties of the groups in the periodic table of elements.

GROUP 1 (THE ALKALI METALS): The elements in group 1 are all silvery metals that are soft and can be easily crushed or cut. They all possess a single valence electron, meaning they easily form +1 cations and are highly reactive. Because these metals are so reactive, they are not usually found in their pure form but instead are found as ionic compounds.

GROUP 2 (THE ALKALI EARTH METALS): The elements in group 2 are also silvery metals that are soft. These metals contain two valence electrons, so they are not as reactive as those in group 1. However, they are still highly reactive: they form +2 cations and are found in ionic compounds.

GROUPS 3 – 12 (THE TRANSITION METALS): The elements from groups 3 to 12 are the transition metals and are all capable of conducting electricity (some better than others). Because their valence electrons are in *d* orbitals, their electron configurations are complex, and they form many different compounds and bonds. Transition metals are moderately reactive and malleable and can conduct electricity due to the capability of gaining and losing many electrons in their outer electron shell.

GROUPS 13 AND 14 (SEMI-METALLIC): The elements in groups 13 and 14 are semi-metallic. They have moderate conductivity and are very soft. Elements in group 13 have three valence electrons, and elements in group 14 have four, allowing for five and four bonds, respectively.

GROUP 15: This group is characterized by a shift from the top of this group (gases) to the bottom (semi-metallic). This group has five valence electrons and can form three bonds. The semi-metallic elements, such as arsenic and antimony, can react in specific circumstances but are generally not considered reactive.

Group 16: This group is also characterized by a shift from gases at the top of the group to semi-metallic at the bottom. This group has six valence electrons and is quite reactive. The need to obtain only two more electrons to fill the valence shell means that these elements are electronegative and typically form an anion with a charge of –2. As a result, these elements are reactive and tend to bond with the alkali or alkali earth metals.

Group 17 (Halogens): The halogens are all gases, and all contain seven electrons in their valence shell. They are extremely reactive, much like the alkali metals. Due to their reactivity and gaseous form at room temperature, they are often hazardous to humans. Inhaling chlorine or fluorine, for example, is usually deadly. The halogens will react in order to obtain a single additional electron to fill their valence shell and typically have a charge of –1.

Group 18 (The Noble Gases): The noble gases have a full valence shell. Because their electron orbitals are already full, the noble gases are largely unreactive, except for a few rare exceptions. The heavier noble gases (xenon and radon) can sometimes react with other species under high temperature and pressure conditions.

Trends in the Periodic Table

Some element properties can be predicted based on the placement of the element on the periodic table.

- **Atomic radius**, the distance from the center of the atom to its outermost electron shell, increases from right to left and top to bottom on the periodic table.

- **Electronegativity** measures how strongly an atom attracts electrons. In general, electronegativity increases from left to right and bottom to top on the periodic table with fluorine being the most electronegative element.

- **Ionization energy**, a measure of how much energy is required to remove an electron from an atom, increases from lower left to top right.

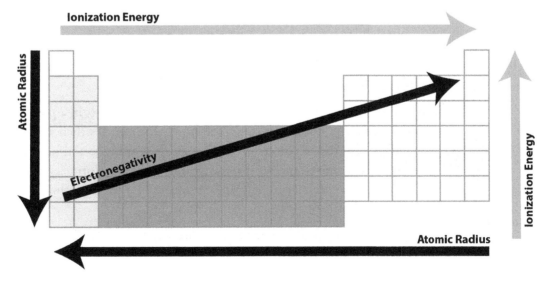

Figure 9.5. Trends in the Periodic Table

Examples

1. Which of the following elements is an alkali metal?

   A) sodium

   B) oxygen

   C) neon

   D) iron

   Answer:

   A) is correct. Sodium (Na) is in group 1, the alkali metals.

2. Which of the following lists the elements carbon, fluorine, oxygen, and nitrogen in order of increasing electronegativity?

   A) $C < N < O < F$

   B) $F < N < O < C$

   C) $F < O < N < C$

   D) $C < N < F < O$

   Answer:

   A) is correct. Electronegativity increases across a period (row). From left to right, the order of the elements is $C < N < O < F$.

CHEMICAL BONDING

Molecules and Compounds

Atoms can exist on their own or bound together. When two or more atoms are held together by chemical bonds, they form a MOLECULE. If the molecule contains more than one type of atom, it is a COMPOUND. Molecules and compounds form the smallest unit of a substance—for example, if water (H_2O) is broken down into hydrogen and oxygen atoms, it no longer has the unique properties of water. Molecules and compounds always have the same ratio of elements. Water, for example, always has two hydrogens for every one oxygen.

Intramolecular Forces

A chemical bond is a force that holds two atoms together. There are three primary types of bonds: ionic, covalent, and metallic.

In an IONIC BOND, one atom has lost electrons to the other, which results in a positive charge on one atom and a negative charge on the other atom. The bond is then a result of the electrostatic interaction between these positive and negative charges. For example, in the compound sodium chloride, sodium has lost an electron to chlorine, resulting in a positive charge on sodium and a negative charge on chlorine.

In a COVALENT BOND, electrons are shared between two atoms; neither atom completely loses or gains an electron. This can be in the form of one pair of shared electrons (a single bond), two pairs (a double bond), or three pairs of electrons shared (triple bond). In

> Water is often called the universal solvent because its strong dipole allows it to dissolve most polar and ionic compounds. Nonpolar substances, such as oil, will not dissolve in water because they have no charge to interact with water's dipole.

diatomic oxygen gas, for example, the two oxygen molecules share two sets of electrons.

Covalent bonds are often depicted using Lewis diagrams, in which an electron is represented by a dot, and a shared pair of electrons is represented by a line.

Electrons within a covalent bond are not always shared equally. More electronegative atoms, which exert a strong pull on the electrons, will hold onto the electrons longer than less electronegative atoms. For example, oxygen is more electronegative than hydrogen, so in H_2O (water), both oxygens have a slight negative charge, and the hydrogen has a slight positive charge. This imbalance is called POLARITY, and the small charge, a DIPOLE.

Note that there is a commonality between these two types of bonding. In both ionic and covalent bonding types, the bond results in each atom having a full valence shell of electrons. When bonding, atoms seek to find the most stable electron configuration. In the majority of cases, this means filling the valence shell of the atom either through the addition or removal of electrons.

METALLIC BONDS are created when metals form tightly packed arrays. Valence electrons are not attached to a particular atom and instead float freely among the positive metallic cations. This "sea" of electrons creates a strong bond that has high electrical and thermal conductivity.

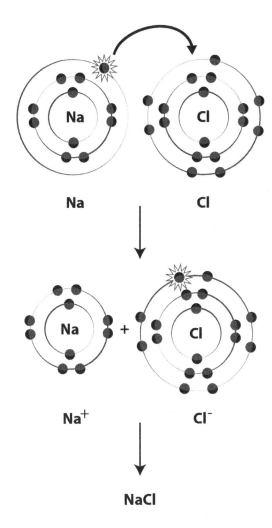

Figure 9.6. The Ionic Bond in Table Salt (NaCl)

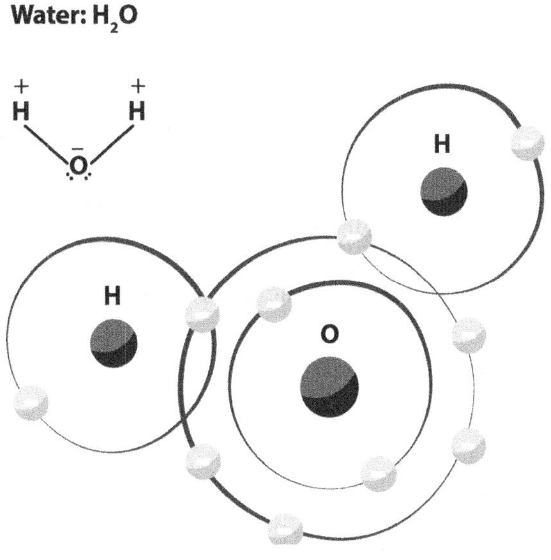

Water: H₂O

Figure 9.7. The Covalent Bond in Water (H_2O)

Intermolecular Forces

What causes water to stick together, forming a liquid at room temperature but a solid at lower temperatures? Why do we need more heat and energy to increase the temperature of water compared to other substances? The answer is **INTERMOLECULAR FORCES**: attractive or repulsive forces that occur between molecules. These are different from ionic and covalent bonds, which occur within a molecule.

The force of attraction between hydrogen and an extremely electronegative atom, such as oxygen or nitrogen, is known as a **HYDROGEN BOND**. For example, in water (H_2O), oxygen atoms are attracted to the hydrogen atoms in nearby molecules, creating hydrogen bonds. These bonds are significantly weaker than the chemical bonds that involve sharing or transfer of electrons, and they have only 5 to 10 percent of the strength of a covalent bond.

Despite its relative weakness, hydrogen bonding is quite important in the natural world; it has major effects on the properties of water and ice and is important biologically with regard to proteins and nucleic acids as well as the DNA double-helix structure.

VAN DER WAALS FORCES are electrical interactions between two or more molecules or atoms. They are the weakest type of intermolecular attraction, but their net effect can be quite strong. There are two major types of van der Waals forces. The **LONDON DISPERSION FORCE** is a temporary force that occurs when electrons in two adjacent atoms form spontaneous, temporary dipoles due to the positions the atoms are occupying. This is the weakest intermolecular force, and it does not exert a force over long distances.

The second type of van der Waals force is **DIPOLE-DIPOLE INTERACTIONS**, which are the result of two dipolar molecules interacting with each other. This interaction occurs when the partial positive dipole in one molecule is attracted to the partial negative dipole in the other molecule.

Examples

1. Which of the following bonds is the most polar?

A) H—C

B) H—O

C) H—F

D) H—N

Answer:

C) is correct. Fluorine is more electronegative than carbon (C), oxygen (O), or nitrogen (N). In the bond with hydrogen, it will pull the shared electrons more strongly, creating the bond with the highest polarity.

2. Which of the following elements is most likely to form an ionic bond?

A) argon

B) calcium

C) copper

D) nitrogen

Answer:

B) is correct. Calcium is an alkaline earth metal and easily forms a +2 cation, which in turn forms an ionic bond with an anion. Argon is a noble gas and does not form bonds, and copper is a metal that forms metallic bonds. Nitrogen most often forms covalent bonds.

PHYSICAL AND CHEMICAL PROPERTIES

Substances, whether they are composed of individual atoms or molecules, all have unique properties that are grouped into two categories: physical and chemical. A change in a **PHYSICAL PROPERTY** (called a physical change) results only in a change of the physical structure, not in the chemical composition of a reactant. For example, a change of state is a physical reaction. A physical property may be identified just by observing, touching, or measuring the substance in some way.

A change in a **CHEMICAL PROPERTY** is one in which the molecular structure or composition of the compound has been changed. Chemical properties cannot be identified simply by observing a material. Rather, the material must be engaged in a chemical reaction in order to identify its chemical properties.

Physical and chemical properties are often influenced by intramolecular and intermolecular forces. For example, substances with strong hydrogen bonds will have higher boiling points.

Table 9.2. Physical and Chemical Properties

PHYSICAL PROPERTIES	CHEMICAL PROPERTIES
temperature	heat of combustion
color	flammability
mass	toxicity
viscosity	chemical stability
density	enthalpy of formation

Example

Which of the following describes a physical change?

A) Water becomes ice.

B) Batter is baked into a cake.

C) A firecracker explodes.

D) An acid is neutralized with a base.

Answer:

A) is correct. When water changes states, its chemical composition does not change. Once water becomes ice, the ice can easily turn back into water.

STATES OF MATTER

A **STATE** (also called a phase) is a description of the physical characteristics of a material. There are four states: solid, liquid, gas, and plasma.

- A **SOLID** is a dense phase characterized by close bonds between all molecules in the solid; solids have a definite shape and volume.
- A **LIQUID** is a fluid phase characterized by loose bonds between molecules in the liquid; liquids have an indefinite shape but a definite volume.
- A **GAS** is a very disperse phase characterized by the lack of, or very weak, bonds between molecules; gases have both an indefinite shape and volume.
- The **PLASMA** phase occurs when a substance has been heated and pressurized past its critical point, resulting in a new phase that has liquid and gas properties.

A substance will change phase depending on the temperature and pressure. As temperature increases, the phase will progress from solid to liquid to gas. As pressure increases, the opposite is true, and the phase will progress from gas to liquid to solid.

> The "smoke" released from dry ice is solid CO_2 sublimating into a gas. Can you think of other everyday examples of phase changes?

These phase changes have specific names, as shown below. Note that reciprocal changes will involve the same amount of energy; however, moving from a less to a more energetic state uses energy, while moving from a more to a less energetic state will release energy.

Table 9.3. Phase Changes

NAME	FROM	TO	OCCURS AT	ENERGY CHANGE
evaporation	liquid	gas	boiling point	uses energy
condensation	gas	liquid	boiling point	releases energy
melting	solid	liquid	freezing point	uses energy
freezing	liquid	solid	freezing point	releases energy
sublimation	solid	gas	---	uses energy
deposition	gas	solid	---	releases energy

PHASE DIAGRAMS are used to show the relationships between phases, temperature, and pressure for a particular substance. In the phase diagram, there are two points that are interesting to note. At the **TRIPLE POINT**, all three phases exist together, and at the **CRITICAL POINT**, the substance enters the plasma phase.

The boiling point and freezing point of a molecule are related to its structure. There are three important factors that contribute to boiling and freezing points:

1. Strength of intermolecular forces: the greater the intermolecular force, the greater the boiling point of the substance will be.
2. Molecule size: as the molecule becomes larger, the boiling point of the molecule typically increases.
3. Molecule branching: as more branch points are present in the molecule, the molecule's boiling point will decrease.

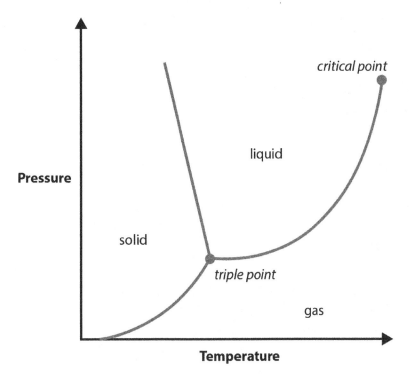

Figure 9.8. Phase Diagram

Methane has a molecular weight of 16 grams per mole, and water has a molecular weight of 18 grams per mole. Neither molecule is branched. As a result, factors 2 and 3 (as listed above), are not relevant. However, water has a boiling point of 100°C, while methane has a boiling point of –164°C.

This large difference is a result of intermolecular forces. Water is a highly polar molecule that has strong intermolecular forces. On the other hand, methane is an uncharged, nonpolar molecule with next to no intermolecular forces. Thus, the energy required to break the bonds between water molecules, and cause the phase change from liquid to vapor, is much greater than that for the methane molecule.

Examples

1. Which of the following is likely to have the highest number of molecules?

A) 1 liter of gaseous CO_2

B) 1 liter of liquid CO_2

C) 1 liter of solid CO_2

D) 1 liter of a mix of solid and gaseous CO_2

Answer:

C) is correct. Molecules are more closely packed together in a solid than in a liquid or gas. So, 1 L of solid CO_2 would have more molecules than 1 L of gaseous or liquid CO_2.

2. Which of the following terms describes the phase change from liquid to solid?

A) evaporation

B) deposition

C) melting

D) freezing

Answer:

D) is correct. Freezing is the change from liquid to solid, as when liquid water freezes to form solid ice.

ACIDS AND BASES

The Definition of Acids and Bases

In general, an ACID can be defined as a substance that produces hydrogen ions (H^+) in solution, while a BASE produces hydroxide ions (OH^-). Acidic solutions, which include common liquids like orange juice and vinegar, share a set of distinct characteristics: they have a sour taste and react strongly with metals. Bases, such as bleach and detergents, will taste bitter and have a slippery texture.

> What acidic and basic solutions do you handle on a daily basis?

There are a number of different technical definitions for acids and bases, including the Arrhenius, Brønsted-Lowry, and Lewis acid definitions.

- The **ARRHENIUS** definition: An acid is a substance that produces H^+ hydrogen ions in aqueous solution. A base is a substance that produces hydroxide ions OH^- in aqueous solution.

- The **BRØNSTED-LOWRY** definition: An acid is anything that donates a proton H^+, and a base is anything that accepts a proton H^+.

- The **LEWIS** definition: An acid is anything able to accept a pair of electrons, and a base is anything that can donate a pair of electrons.

Measuring the Strength of Acids and Bases

The **pH** of a solution is a measure of the acidity or basicity of the solution. It is found by taking the negative log of the concentration of hydrogen ions, making pH an exponential scale:

$$pH = -\log[H^+]$$

The pH scale runs from 0 to 14 with a low pH being more acidic and a high pH being more basic. A pH of 7 is that of water with no dissolved ions and is considered neutral.

Strong acids and bases will dissolve completely in solution, while weak acids and bases will only partially dissolve. Thus, strong acids and bases will have high or low pH values, respectively, and weak acids and bases will have pH values closer to 7.

pH scale

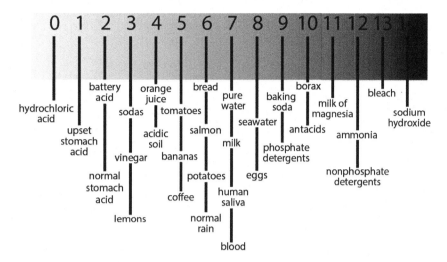

Figure 9.9. pH Scale

Table 9.4. Strong Acids and Bases

Strong acids	HCl	Hydrochloric acid
	HNO_3	Nitric acid
	H_2SO_4	Sulfuric acid
	$HClO_4$	Perchloric acid
	HBr	Hydrobromic acid
	HI	Hydroiodic acid
Strong bases	LiOH	Lithium hydroxide
	NaOH	Sodium hydroxide
	KOH	Potassium hydroxide
	$Ca(OH)_2$	Calcium hydroxide
	$Ba(OH)_2$	Barium hydroxide
	$Sr(OH)_2$	Strontium hydroxide

Acid Base Reactions

Acids and bases react with each other in solution to produce a salt and water: a process called **NEUTRALIZATION**. As a result of this reaction, if an equal amount of strong acid is mixed with an equal amount of strong base, the pH will remain at 7. For example, mixing hydrochloric acid and sodium hydroxide yields sodium chloride (a salt) and water, as shown below:

$$HCl + Na(OH) \rightarrow H_2O + NaCl$$

Examples

1. Which of the following acids is a strong acid?

   A) HClO

   B) HBr

   C) HF

   D) HN_3

   Answer:

   B) is correct. Hydrobromic acid (HBr) is one of the strong acids.

2. Which of the following best describes a substance with a pH of 12?

   A) very acidic

   B) slightly acidic

   C) neutral

   D) very basic

   Answer:

   D) is correct. Substances with a pH higher than 7 are basic. The pH scale goes up to 14, meaning a pH of 12 is very basic.

SOLUTIONS

In chemistry, the term MIXTURE describes a set of two or more substances that have been mixed together but are not chemically joined together. In a HOMOGENOUS mixture, the substances are evenly distributed; in a HETEROGENEOUS mixture, the substances are not evenly distributed.

Are the following mixtures homogenous or heterogeneous? lemonade, concrete, air, trail mix, salt water

A SOLUTION is a specific type of homogenous mixture in which all substances share the same basic properties and generally act as a single substance. In a solution, a SOLUTE is dissolved in a SOLVENT. For example, in salt water, salt is the solute and water is the solvent. The opposite process, in which a compound comes out of the solution, is called PRECIPITATION.

The CONCENTRATION of a solution—the amount of solute versus the amount of solvent—can be measured in a number of ways. Usually it is given as a ratio of solute to solvent in the relevant units. Some of these include:

- moles per volume (e.g., moles per liter)—also called MOLARITY
- moles per mass (e.g., moles per kilogram)—also called MOLALITY
- mass per volume (e.g., grams per liter)
- volume per volume (e.g., milliliter per liter)
- mass per mass (e.g., milligrams per gram)

Solubility

Solubility is a measure of how much solute will dissolve into a solvent. When a solution contains the maximum amount of solute possible, it is called a SATURATED SOLUTION. A solution with less solute is UNSATURATED, and a solution with more solute than can normally be dissolved in that solvent is SUPERSATURATED.

There are many factors that can affect the solubility of a compound, including temperature and pressure. Generally, solubility increases with temperature (although there are some compounds whose solubility will decrease with an increase in temperature). The relationship between solubility and temperature is shown in a solubility curve.

Another factor affecting solubility is the COMMON ION EFFECT, which occurs in solutions with two compounds that share a common ion. When the two compounds are mixed into a solvent, the presence of the common ion reduces the solubility of each compound. For example, NaCl and $MgCl_2$ share the common ion of chlorine. When they are mixed in a solution, the maximum saturation of the chlorine ion in water will be reached before the saturation of either sodium or magnesium is reached. This causes a reduction in the overall solubility.

Decompression sickness, also called the bends, is an ailment that afflicts divers who come to the surface too quickly. The high pressure deep in the ocean allows more gas to be dissolved in the fluid inside the diver's body. A quick drop in pressure (rising to the surface quickly) will lower the solubility of the gas, causing the gas to come out of solution and form bubbles inside the diver's body.

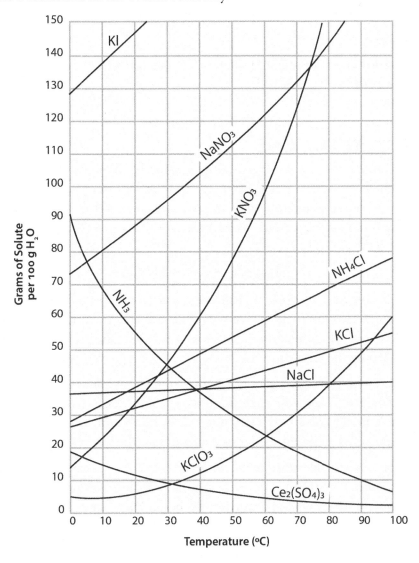

Figure 9.10. Solubility Curve

Examples

1. In a carbonated soda, carbon dioxide is dissolved in water. Which of the following terms describes the water in this mixture?

   A) common ion

   B) solvent

   C) solute

   D) precipitant

   Answer:

   B) is correct. The water is the solvent in which the solute (carbon dioxide) is dissolved.

2. Which of the following terms describes a solution in which more solvent can be dissolved?

   A) unsaturated

   B) saturated

   C) supersaturated

   D) homogenous

   Answer:

   A) is correct. An unsaturated solution has less solute than can be dissolved in the given amount of solvent.

CHEMICAL REACTIONS

In a CHEMICAL REACTION, one set of chemical substances, called the REACTANTS, is transformed into another set of chemical substances, called the PRODUCTS. This transformation is described in a chemical equation with the reactants on the left and products on the right. In the equation below, methane (CH_4) reacts with oxygen (O_2) to produce carbon dioxide (CO_2) and water (H_2O).

$$CH_4 + 2O_2 \rightarrow CO_2 + 2H_2O$$

When a reaction runs to COMPLETION, all the reactants have been used up in the reaction. If one reactant limits the use of the other reactants (i.e., if one reactant is used up before the others), it is called the LIMITING REACTANT. The YIELD is the amount of product produced by the reaction.

A chemical reaction that uses energy is ENDOTHERMIC, while a reaction that releases energy is EXOTHERMIC. Generally, creating bonds requires energy, and breaking bonds releases energy. Whether a reaction is endothermic or exothermic depends on the specific energy requirements of the bonds being broken and made in the reaction.

Processes can also be described as being endothermic or exothermic. For example, boiling water to form vapor is an endothermic process because it requires energy. Freezing liquid water to form ice is an exothermic process because it releases energy.

Balancing Equations

The integer values placed before the chemical symbols are the COEFFICIENTS that describe how many molecules of that substance are involved in the reaction. These values are important because in a chemical reaction, there is a conservation of mass. The inputs, or reactant mass, must equal the outputs, or products.

In order to BALANCE AN EQUATION, you'll need to add the coefficients necessary to match the atoms of each element on both sides. In the reaction below, the numbers of bromine (Br) and nitrate ions (NO_3^-) do not match up:

> Always balance H and O last when balancing chemical equations.

$$CaBr_2 + NaNO_3 \rightarrow Ca(NO_3)_2 + NaBr$$

To balance the equation, start by adding a coefficient of 2 to the products to balance the bromine:

$$CaBr_2 + NaNO_3 \rightarrow Ca(NO_3)_2 + 2NaBr$$

There are now 2 sodium ions on the right, so another 2 need to be added on the left to balance it:

$$CaBr_2 + 2NaNO_3 \rightarrow Ca(NO_3)_2 + 2NaBr$$

Notice that adding this 2 also balances the nitrate ions, so the equation is now complete.

Types of Reactions

There are five main types of chemical reactions. In a SYNTHESIS REACTION, two reactants combine to form a single product. A DECOMPOSITION REACTION is the opposite of a synthesis reaction and involves a single reactant breaking down into several products.

In a displacement reaction, one ion takes the place of another in a compound. SINGLE-DISPLACEMENT reactions include a free ion taking the place of the ion in a compound. In a DOUBLE-DISPLACEMENT reaction, ions in two different compounds switch places.

Finally, in a COMBUSTION REACTION, a fuel (usually an alkane or carbohydrate) will react with oxygen to form carbon dioxide and water. Combustion reactions also produce heat.

The five types of chemical reactions are summarized in Table 9.5.

Table 9.5. Types of Reactions

TYPE OF REACTION	GENERAL FORMULA	EXAMPLE REACTION
Synthesis	$A + B \rightarrow C$	$2H_2 + O_2 \rightarrow 2H_2O$
Decomposition	$A \rightarrow B + C$	$2H_2O_2 \rightarrow 2H_2O + O_2$
Single displacement	$AB + C \rightarrow A + BC$	$CH_4 + Cl_2 \rightarrow CH_3Cl + HCl$
Double displacement	$AB + CD \rightarrow AC + BD$	$CuCl_2 + 2AgNo_3 \rightarrow Cu(NO_3)_2 + 2AgCl$
Combustion	$C_xH_yO_z + O_2 \rightarrow CO_2 + H_2O$	$2C_8H_{18} + 25O_2 \rightarrow 16CO_2 + 18H_2O$

Oxidation and Reduction Reactions

An oxidation and reduction reaction (often called a redox reaction) is one in which there is an exchange of electrons. The species that loses electrons is OXIDIZED, and the species that gains electrons is REDUCED. The species that loses electrons is also called the REDUCING AGENT, and the species that gains electrons is the OXIDIZING AGENT.

The movement of electrons in a redox reaction is analyzed by assigning each atom in the reaction an OXIDATION NUMBER (or state) that corresponds roughly to that atom's charge. (The actual meaning of the oxidation number is much more complicated.) Once all the atoms in a reaction have been assigned an oxidation number, it is possible to see which elements have gained electrons and which elements have lost electrons. The basic rules for assigning oxidation numbers are given in the table below.

Table 9.6. Assigning Oxidation Numbers

SPECIES	EXAMPLE	OXIDATION NUMBER
Elements in their free state and naturally occurring diatomic elements	$Zn(s)$, O_2	0
Monoatomic ions	Cl^-	-1
Oxygen in compounds	H_2O	-2
Hydrogen in compounds	HCl	$+1$
Alkali metals in a compound	Na	$+1$
Alkaline earth metals in a compound	Mg	$+2$

RULES

The oxidation numbers on the atoms in a neutral compound sum to zero.	$NaOH$	Na: +1; O: -2; H: +1 $1 + -2 + 1 = 0$
The oxidation numbers of the atoms in an ion sum to the charge on that ion.	SO_3^{-2}	S: +4; O: -2 $4 + (-2)(3) = -2$

Examples

1. Which of the following types of reactions is shown below?

   $Pb(NO_3)_2 + K_2CrO_4 \rightarrow PbCrO_4 + 2\ KNO_3$

   A) combustion

   B) decomposition

   C) double displacement

   D) single replacement

   Answer:

   C) is correct. In the reaction, the Pb and K exchange their anions in a double-displacement reaction.

2. Which of the following equations is a balanced equation?

   A) $2KClO_3 \rightarrow KCl + 3O_2$

   B) $KClO_3 \rightarrow KCl + 3O_2$

   C) $2KClO_3 \rightarrow 2KCl + 3O_2$

   D) $6KClO_3 \rightarrow 6KCl + 3O_2$

Answer:

C) is correct. In this equation, there are equal numbers of each type of atom on both sides (2 K atoms, 2 Cl atoms, and 6 O atoms).

3. Which of the following substances is reduced in the reaction shown below?

$$Fe_2O_3 + 3CO \rightarrow 2Fe + 3CO_2$$

A) Fe

B) O

C) CO

D) CO_2

Answer:

A) is correct. Fe has an oxidation number of +3 in the compound Fe_2O_3 and an oxidation number of 0 on its own as Fe. Because Fe lost three electrons (to go from +3 to 0), it was reduced.

CHEMICAL KINETICS

Collision Theory and Reaction Rates

COLLISION THEORY refers to the idea that a chemical reaction cannot occur until two molecules that may react collide with one another. In a solid, although molecules are all touching one another, there is not much movement. As a result, chemical reactions in solid phase have a low reaction rate or none at all. A solid usually reacts only when its surface comes into contact with a liquid or gas.

In liquids or gases, molecules are able to move freely, which allows greater interaction and an increased chance that two capable molecules will react. For this reason, the majority of chemical reactions occur in the liquid phase or the gas phase. However, even if two molecules collide that could react, most of the time they do not. In order for a reaction to take place, the reaction must have a minimum amount of energy, a quantity known as the reaction's ACTIVATION ENERGY.

Different reactions will occur at different rates. This REACTION RATE is determined by a number of factors, including the concentration of reactants, particle surface area, and temperature. Generally, increasing any of these variables will increase the reaction rate by providing more opportunities for particles to collide.

- Increasing the concentration of reactants introduces more particles to the system, meaning they are more likely to collide.
- Increasing particle surface area makes it more likely particles will come in contact with each other.
- Increasing the temperature increases the velocity of the particles, making them more likely to collide.

Catalysts

Substances called CATALYSTS increase reaction rates by providing an alternative pathway with a lower activation energy. Catalysts themselves are unchanged during the chemical reaction. A chemical catalyst is commonly a metal or other elemental compound with many electrons in its valence shell; catalysts assist in the stabilization of reaction intermediates. Common chemical catalysts include platinum, palladium, nickel, and cobalt.

A biological catalyst is known as an ENZYME. Common enzymes include cellulase, amylase, or DNA polymerase. Biological catalysts typically function by bringing two reactants close together and are usually designed to catalyze a specific reaction. This specificity is referred to as the LOCK AND KEY MODEL: most keys can only open specific locks. Similarly, the shape of any one enzyme only matches the shape of the molecule it reacts with, called a SUBSTRATE. The ACTIVE SITE is the place on the enzyme that directly contacts the substrate, or the place where the two "puzzle pieces" fit together, facilitating the actual reaction.

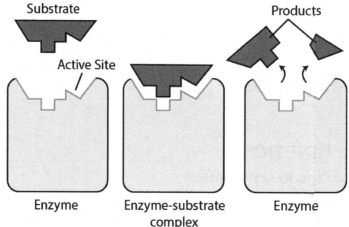

Figure 9.11. Enzyme Function

There are two types of catalysts subdivided by their phase: homogenous and heterogeneous. A HOMOGENOUS CATALYST is in the same phase as the reactants. Most enzymes are homogenous and are soluble in the same phase as the reactants.

A HETEROGENEOUS CATALYST is not in the same phase as the reactants. An example of a heterogeneous catalyst is the platinum found in the catalytic converter in the exhaust stream of cars. The catalyst is in the solid phase, and the reactants are in the gas phase.

Examples

1. Which of the following describes the effect of increasing the concentration of the reactants in a reaction?

   A) The reaction rate will increase.

   B) The reaction rate will decrease.

   C) The change in the reaction rate will depend on the temperature of the reaction.

   D) The change in the reaction rate will depend on the pressure of the reaction.

   Answer:

   A) is correct. A higher concentration of reactants increases the rate of reaction by increasing the number of collisions between reactant molecules.

2. Which of the following best describes the role of a catalyst in a reaction?

A) A catalyst increases the activation energy required for a reaction to take place.

B) A catalyst increases the rate at which reactants become products.

C) A catalyst shifts the reaction toward the reactants.

D) A catalyst increases the amount of product produced.

Answer:

B) is correct. A catalyst increases the rate of a reaction by providing an alternative path for the reaction that has a lower activation energy.

10

SCIENTIFIC REASONING

SYSTEMS

A **SYSTEM** is a set of interacting parts that work together to form an integrated whole. Many scientific disciplines study systems: doctors, for example, study organ systems like the respiratory system, which is made up of interacting parts that allow animals to breathe. Similarly, ecologists might look at all the plants and animals that interact in a specific area, and chemists might look at a set of chemicals interacting in a beaker. While obviously different, all these systems share some common traits.

Table 10.1. Characteristics of Systems

CHARACTERISTIC	EXAMPLE (RESPIRATORY SYSTEM)
All systems have a structure.	The respiratory system is highly organized.
All systems perform an action.	The respiratory system allows animals to breathe.
All systems have interacting parts.	The respiratory system is made up of many interacting parts, including the lungs, blood vessels, and bronchial tubes.
All systems have boundaries.	We can separate structures that are part of the respiratory system from those that are not.
Systems may receive input and produce output.	The respiratory system brings oxygen into the body and gets rid of carbon dioxide.
The processes in a system may be controlled by feedback.	The action of breathing is controlled in part by how much oxygen and carbon dioxide are in the body.

Sometimes larger systems are made of smaller, independent systems called **SUBSYSTEMS**. For example, a cell is made of many organelles. These organelles each perform their own tasks, which together support the system of the cell.

SCIENTIFIC INVESTIGATIONS

Although science can never definitively "prove" something, it does provide a means to answering many questions about our natural world. Scientists use different types of investigations, each providing different types of results, based upon what they are trying to find. There are three main types of scientific investigations: experimental, descriptive, and comparative.

A hypothesis is more than an educated guess; it is a testable proposition: an idea that cannot be tested scientifically is not a hypothesis.

EXPERIMENTAL INVESTIGATIONS are designed to test a HYPOTHESIS, which is a proposed explanation for a phenomenon based on observations or previous research. In an experimental investigation, an INDEPENDENT VARIABLE is manipulated, and the DEPENDENT VARIABLE is measured. Other factors that might affect the dependent variable, called CONTROL VARIABLES, are held constant throughout the experiment.

Table 10.2. Parts of an Experimental Investigation

PART	WHAT IS IT?	EXAMPLE
hypothesis	a proposed explanation for a phenomenon	People who increase the amount of cardiovascular exercise they receive will lose weight.
independent variable	the variable being manipulated	amount of cardiovascular exercise
dependent variable	the variable being measured	weight
control variables	variables that may affect the dependent variable that are held constant	diet of subjects type of cardiovascular exercise initial weight of subjects

DESCRIPTIVE INVESTIGATIONS start with observations. A model is then constructed to provide a visual of what was seen: a description. Descriptive investigations do not generally require hypotheses, as they usually just attempt to find more information about a relatively unknown topic.

Lastly, COMPARATIVE INVESTIGATIONS involve manipulating different groups in order to compare them with each other. There is no control during comparative investigations.

Once a hypothesis has been thoroughly tested and is generally accepted to be true in the scientific community, it can be incorporated into the existing body of scientific knowledge. This body of knowledge includes facts, laws, and theories. A FACT is simply an observation that is accepted as "true" by the scientific community. A LAW is a statement that describes how aspects of the natural world behave under specific circumstances. Finally, a THEORY is an accepted explanation for a natural phenomenon.

Table 10.3. Types of Scientific Knowledge

	WHAT IS IT?	EXAMPLE
fact	an observation that is accepted as true	Genes code for proteins.
law	a statement that describes how nature behaves	Mendel's law of independent assortment
theory	an accepted explanation for a natural phenomenon	theory of evolution

THE SCIENTIFIC METHOD

In order to ensure that experimental and comparative investigations are thorough and accurate, scientists use the scientific method, which has five main steps:

1. **Observe and ask questions:** look at the natural world to observe and ask questions about patterns and anomalies you see.

2. **Gather information:** look at what other scientists have done to see where your questions fit in with current research.

3. **Construct a hypothesis:** make a proposal that explains why or how something happens.

4. **Experiment and test your hypothesis:** set up an experimental investigation that allows you to test your hypothesis.

5. **Analyze results and draw conclusions:** examine your results and see whether they disprove your hypothesis. Note that you can't actually *prove* a hypothesis; you can only provide evidence to support it.

Examples

1. Which of the following BEST defines a hypothesis?

   A) an educated guess

   B) a study of the natural world

   C) an explanation of a natural phenomenon

   D) a testable proposed scientific explanation

   Answer:

   D) is correct. A hypothesis must be testable and propose an explanation of observed natural phenomena.

2. A student wants to find out if the time of day she takes an exam affects the score she receives. She gathers together all the tests she took in her algebra, biology, and world history classes during the last year and records the time she took the exam and the score she received. Which of the following is the dependent variable in her investigation?

   A) the time she took an exam

   B) the subject of the exam

   C) the score she received on an exam

   D) the number of exams she took

   Answer:

   C) is correct. She wants to see if time of day (the independent variable) affects her exam scores (the dependent variable).

PART IV: ENGLISH AND LANGUAGE USAGE

The English and Language Usage section will test your understanding of the basic rules of grammar. The good news is that you have been using these rules since you first began to speak. Even if you do not know a lot of the technical terms, many of these rules will be familiar to you. Some of the topics you might see include:

- matching pronouns with their antecedents
- matching verbs with their subjects
- ensuring that verbs are in the correct tense
- spelling irregular, hyphenated, and commonly misspelled words
- using correct capitalization
- distinguishing between types of sentences
- correcting sentence structure

11

GRAMMAR AND VOCABULARY

NOUNS AND PRONOUNS

NOUNS are people, places, or things. The subject of a sentence is typically a noun. For example, in the sentence *The hospital was very clean*, the subject, *hospital*, is a noun; it is a place. **PRONOUNS** stand in for nouns and can be used to make sentences sound less repetitive. Take the sentence, "Sam stayed home from school because Sam was not feeling well." The word *Sam* appears twice in the same sentence. Instead, you can use the pronoun *he* to stand in for *Sam* and say, "Sam stayed home from school because he was not feeling well."

Singular Pronouns
- I, me, my, mine
- you, your, yours
- he, him, his
- she, her, hers
- it, its

Plural Pronouns
- we, us, our, ours
- they, them, their, theirs

Because pronouns take the place of nouns, they need to agree both in number and gender with the noun they replace. So, a plural noun needs a plural pronoun, and a noun referring to something feminine needs a feminine pronoun. In the first sentence in this paragraph, for example, the plural pronoun *they* replaced the plural noun *pronouns*. There will usually be several questions on the English and Language Usage section that cover pronoun agreement, so it's good to get comfortable spotting pronouns.

> Wrong: If a student forgets their homework, they will not receive a grade.
>
> Correct: If a student forgets his or her homework, he or she will not receive a grade.

Student is a singular noun, but *their* and *they* are plural pronouns. So, the first sentence is incorrect. To correct it, use the singular pronoun *his* or *her*, or *he* or *she*.

> Wrong: Everybody will receive their paychecks promptly.
>
> Correct: Everybody will receive his or her paycheck promptly.

Everybody is a singular noun, but *their* is a plural pronoun. So, this sentence is incorrect. To correct it, use the singular pronoun *his* or *her*.

> Wrong: When nurses scrub in to surgery, you should wash your hands.
>
> Correct: When nurses scrub in to surgery, they should wash their hands.

This sentence begins in third-person perspective and then switches to second-person perspective. So, this sentence is incorrect. To correct it, use a third-person pronoun in the second clause.

> Wrong: After the teacher spoke to the student, she realized her mistake.
>
> Correct: After Mr. White spoke to his student, she realized her mistake.
> (*She* and *her* refer to the student.)
>
> Correct: After speaking to the student, the teacher realized her own mistake.
> (*Her* refers to the teacher.)

This sentence refers to a teacher and a student. But whom does *she* refer to, the teacher or the student? To eliminate the ambiguity, use specific names or state more specifically who made the mistake.

Examples

I have lived in Minnesota since August, but I still don't own a warm coat or gloves.

1. Which of the following lists includes all the nouns in the sentence?
   A) coat, gloves
   B) I, coat, gloves
   C) Minnesota, August, coat, gloves
   D) I, Minnesota, August, warm, coat, gloves

   Answer:

   C) is correct. *Minnesota* and *August* are proper nouns, and *coat* and *gloves* are common nouns. *I* is a pronoun, and *warm* is an adjective that modifies *coat*.

2. In which of the following sentences do the nouns and pronouns NOT agree?
   A) After we walked inside, we took off our hats and shoes and hung them in the closet.
   B) The members of the band should leave her instruments in the rehearsal room.
   C) The janitor on duty should rinse out his or her mop before leaving for the day.
   D) When you see someone in trouble, you should always try to help them.

   Answer:

   B) is correct. *The members of the band* is plural, so it should be replaced by the plural pronoun *their* instead of the singular *her*.

VERBS

A **VERB** is the action of a sentence: it describes what the subject of the sentence is or is doing. Verbs must match the subject of the sentence in person and number, and must be in the proper tense—past, present, or future.

Person describes the relationship of the speaker to the subject of the sentence: first (I, we), second (you), and third (he, she, it, they). *Number* refers to whether the subject of the sentence is singular or plural. Verbs are conjugated to match the person and number of the subject.

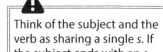 Think of the subject and the verb as sharing a single *s*. If the subject ends with an *s*, the verb should not, and vice versa.

Table 11.1. Conjugating Verbs for Person

PERSON	SINGULAR	PLURAL
First	I jump	we jump
Second	you jump	you jump
Third	he/she/it jumps	they jump

> Wrong: The cat chase the ball while the dogs runs in the yard.
>
> Correct: The cat chases the ball while the dogs run in the yard.

Cat is singular, so it takes a singular verb (which confusingly ends with an *s*); *dogs* is plural, so it needs a plural verb.

> Wrong: The cars that had been recalled by the manufacturer was returned within a few months.
>
> Correct: The cars that had been recalled by the manufacturer were returned within a few months.

Sometimes, the subject and verb are separated by clauses or phrases. Here, the subject *cars* is separated from the verb by the relatively long phrase "that had been recalled by the manufacturer," making it more difficult to determine how to correctly conjugate the verb.

> Correct: The doctor and nurse work in the hospital.
>
> Correct: Neither the nurse nor her boss was scheduled to take a vacation.
>
> Correct: Either the patient or her parents need to sign the release forms.

When the subject contains two or more nouns connected by *and*, that subject becomes plural and requires a plural verb. Singular subjects joined by *either/or*, *neither/nor*, or *not only/but also* remain singular; when these words join plural and singular subjects, the verb should match the closest subject.

Finally, verbs must be conjugated for tense, which shows when the action happened. Some conjugations include helping verbs like *was*, *have*, *have been*, and *will have been*.

If the subject is separated from the verb, cross out the phrases between them to make conjugation easier.

Table 11.2. Verb Tenses

TENSE	PAST	PRESENT	FUTURE
Simple	I <u>gave</u> her a gift yesterday.	I <u>give</u> her a gift every day.	I <u>will give</u> her a gift on her birthday.
Continuous	I <u>was giving</u> her a gift when you got here.	I <u>am giving</u> her a gift; come in!	I <u>will be giving</u> her a gift at dinner.

Table 11.2. Verb Tenses (continued)

TENSE	PAST	PRESENT	FUTURE
Perfect	I <u>had given</u> her a gift before you got there.	I <u>have given</u> her a gift already.	I <u>will have given</u> her a gift by midnight.
Perfect continuous	Her friends <u>had been giving</u> her gifts all night when I arrived.	I <u>have been giving</u> her gifts every year for nine years.	I <u>will have been giving</u> her gifts on holidays for ten years next year.

Tense must also be consistent throughout the sentence and the passage. For example, the sentence *I was baking cookies and eat some dough* sounds strange. That is because the two verbs, *was baking* and *eat*, are in different tenses. *Was baking* occurred in the past; *eat*, on the other hand, occurs in the present. To make them consistent, change *eat* to *ate*.

> Wrong: Because it will rain during the party last night, we had to move the tables inside.
>
> Correct: Because it rained during the party last night, we had to move the tables inside.

All the verb tenses in a sentence need to agree both with each other and with the other information in the sentence. In the first sentence above, the tense does not match the other information in the sentence: *last night* indicates the past (*rained*), not the future (*will rain*).

Examples

1. Which of the following sentences contains an incorrectly conjugated verb?

   A) The brother and sister runs very fast.

   B) Neither Anne nor Suzy likes the soup.

   C) The mother and father love their new baby.

   D) Either Jack or Jill will pick up the pizza.

   Answer:

   A) is correct. Choice A should read "The brother and sister run very fast." When the subject contains two or more nouns connected by *and*, the subject is plural and requires a plural verb.

2. Which of the following sentences contains an incorrect verb tense?

   A) After the show ended, we drove to the restaurant for dinner.

   B) Anne went to the mall before she headed home.

   C) Johnny went to the movies after he cleans the kitchen.

   D) Before the alarm sounded, smoke filled the cafeteria.

   Answer:

   C) is correct. Choice C should read "Johnny will go to the movies after he cleans the kitchen." It does not make sense to say that Johnny does something in the past (*went to the movies*) after doing something in the present (*after he cleans*).

ADJECTIVES AND ADVERBS

ADJECTIVES provide more information about a noun in a sentence. Take the sentence, "The boy hit the ball." If you want your readers to know more about the noun *boy*, you could use an adjective to describe him: *the little boy, the young boy, the tall boy.*

ADVERBS and adjectives are similar because they provide more information about a part of a sentence. However, adverbs do not describe nouns—that's an adjective's job. Instead, adverbs describe verbs, adjectives, and even other adverbs. For example, in the sentence "The doctor had recently hired a new employee," the adverb *recently* tells us more about how the action *hired* took place.

Adjectives, adverbs, and **MODIFYING PHRASES** (groups of words that together modify another word) should be placed as close as possible to the word they modify. Separating words from their modifiers can create incorrect or confusing sentences.

> Wrong: Running through the hall, the bell rang and the student knew she was late.
>
> Correct: Running through the hall, the student heard the bell ring and knew she was late.

The phrase *running through the hall* should be placed next to *student*, the noun it modifies.

The suffixes *–er* and *–est* are often used to modify adjectives when a sentence is making a comparison. The suffix *–er* is used when comparing two things, and the suffix *–est* is used when comparing more than two.

> Anne is taller than Steve, but Steve is more coordinated.
>
> Of the five brothers, Billy is the funniest, and Alex is the most intelligent.

Adjectives longer than two syllables are compared using *more* (for two things) or *most* (for three or more things).

> Wrong: Of my two friends, Clara is the smartest.
>
> Correct: Of my two friends, Clara is smarter.

More and *most* should not be used in conjunction with *–er* and *–est* endings.

> Wrong: My most warmest sweater is made of wool.
>
> Correct: My warmest sweater is made of wool.

Examples

The new chef carefully stirred the boiling soup and then lowered the heat.

1. Which of the following lists includes all the adjectives in the sentence?

   A) new, boiling

   B) new, carefully, boiling

   C) new, carefully, boiling, heat

   D) new, carefully, boiling, lowered, heat

Answer:

A) is correct. *New* modifies the noun *chef*, and *boiling* modifies the noun *soup*. *Carefully* is an adverb modifying the verb *stirred*. *Lowered* is a verb, and *heat* is a noun.

2. Which of the following sentences contains an adjective error?

   A) The new red car was faster than the old blue car.

   B) Reggie's apartment is in the tallest building on the block.

   C) The slice of cake was tastier than the brownie.

   D) Of the four speeches, Jerry's was the most long.

Answer:

D) is correct. Choice D should read, "Of the four speeches, Jerry's was the longest." The word *long* has only one syllable, so it should be modified with the suffix *–est*, not the word *most*.

OTHER PARTS OF SPEECH

PREPOSITIONS express the location of a noun or pronoun in relation to other words and phrases described in a sentence. For example, in the sentence "The nurse parked her car in a parking garage," the preposition *in* describes the position of the car in relation to the garage. Together, the preposition and the noun that follow it are called a **PREPOSITIONAL PHRASE**. In this example, the prepositional phrase is *in a parking garage*.

> An independent (or main) clause can stand alone as its own sentence. A dependent (or subordinate) clause must be attached to an independent clause to make a complete sentence.

CONJUNCTIONS connect words, phrases, and clauses. The conjunctions summarized in the acronym FANBOYS—For, And, Nor, But, Or, Yet, So—are called **COORDINATING CONJUNCTIONS** and are used to join **INDEPENDENT CLAUSES** (clauses that can stand alone as a complete sentence). For example, in the following sentence, the conjunction *and* joins together two independent clauses:

> The nurse prepared the patient for surgery, and the doctor performed the surgery.

Other conjunctions, like *although*, *because*, and *if*, join together an independent and **DEPENDENT CLAUSE** (which cannot stand on its own). Take the following sentence:

> She had to ride the subway because her car was broken.

The clause *because her car was broken* cannot stand on its own.

INTERJECTIONS, like *wow* and *hey*, express emotion and are most commonly used in conversation and casual writing.

Examples

Choose the word that best completes the sentence.

1. Her love _____ blueberry muffins kept her coming back to the bakery every week.

   A) to

   B) with

   C) of

   D) about

   Answer:

   C) is correct. The correct preposition is *of*.

2. Christine left her house early on Monday morning, _____ she was still late for work.

   A) but

   B) and

   C) for

   D) or

   Answer:

   A) is correct. In this sentence, the conjunction is joining together two contrasting ideas, so the correct answer is *but*.

CAPITALIZATION

Capitalization questions on the TEAS will ask you to spot errors in capitalization within a phrase or sentence. Below are the most important rules for capitalization you are likely to see on the test.

The first word of a sentence is always capitalized.

> We will be having dinner at a new restaurant tonight.

The first letter of a proper noun is always capitalized.

> We're going to Chicago on Wednesday.

Titles are capitalized if they precede the name they modify.

> Joe Biden, the vice president, met with President Obama.

Months are capitalized, but not the names of the seasons.

> Snow fell in March even though winter was over.

The names of major holidays should be capitalized. The word *day* is only capitalized if it is part of the holiday's name.

> We always go to a parade on Memorial Day, but Christmas day we stay home.

The names of specific places should always be capitalized. General location terms are not capitalized.

> We're going to San Francisco next weekend so I can see the ocean.

Titles for relatives should be capitalized when they precede a name, but not when they stand alone.

> Fred, my uncle, will make fried chicken, and Aunt Betty is going to make spaghetti.

Example

Which of the following sentences contains an error in capitalization?

A) My two brothers are going to New Orleans for Mardi Gras.

B) On Friday we voted to elect a new class president.

C) Janet wants to go to Mexico this Spring.

D) Peter complimented the chef on his cooking.

Answer:

C) is correct. *Spring* is the name of a season and should not be capitalized.

HOMOPHONES AND SPELLING

Homophones

The TEAS will include questions that ask you to choose between **HOMOPHONES**, words that are pronounced the same but have different meanings. *Bawl* and *ball*, for example, are homophones: they sound the same, but the first means to cry, and the second is a round toy.

Common homophones include:

- bare/bear
- brake/break
- die/dye
- effect/affect
- flour/flower
- heal/heel
- insure/ensure
- morning/mourning
- peace/piece
- poor/pour
- principal/principle
- sole/soul
- stair/stare
- suite/sweet
- their/there/they're
- wear/where

Spelling Rules

You will also be tested on spelling, so it is good to familiarize yourself with commonly misspelled words and special spelling rules. The test questions will ask you to either find a misspelled word in a sentence or identify words that don't follow standard spelling rules.

Double a final consonant when adding suffixes if the consonant is preceded by a single vowel.

> run → running
>
> admit → admittance

Drop the final vowel when adding a suffix.

sue → suing

observe → observance

Change the final *y* to an *i* when adding a suffix.

lazy → laziest

tidy → tidily

Regular nouns are made plural by adding *s*. Irregular nouns can follow many different rules for pluralization, which are summarized in the table below.

Table 11.3. Irregular Plural Nouns

ENDS WITH . . .	MAKE IT PLURAL BY . . .	EXAMPLE
y	changing *y* to *i* and adding *–es*	baby → babies
f	changing *f* to *v* and adding *–es*	leaf → leaves
fe	changing *f* to *v* and adding *–s*	knife → knives
o	adding *–es*	potato → potatoes
us	changing *–us* to *–i*	nucleus → nuclei

Always the same	Doesn't follow the rules
sheep	man → men
deer	child → children
fish	person → people
moose	tooth → teeth
pants	goose → geese
binoculars	mouse → mice
scissors	ox → oxen

Commonly Misspelled Words

- accommodate
- across
- argument
- believe
- committee
- completely
- conscious
- discipline
- experience
- foreign
- government
- guarantee
- height
- immediately
- intelligence
- judgment
- knowledge
- license
- lightning
- lose
- maneuver
- misspell
- noticeable
- occasionally
- occurred
- opinion
- personnel
- piece
- possession
- receive
- separate
- successful
- technique
- tendency
- unanimous
- until
- usually
- vacuum
- whether
- which

→

CONTINUE

Examples

1. Which of the following sentences contains a spelling error?

   A) It was unusually warm that winter, so we didn't need to use our fireplace.

   B) Our garden includes tomatos, squash, and carrots.

   C) The local zoo will be opening a new exhibit that includes African elephants.

   D) My sister is learning to speak a foreign language so she can travel abroad.

   Answer:

   B) is correct. *Tomatos* should be spelled *tomatoes*.

The nurse has three _____ to see before lunch.

2. Which of the following words correctly completes the sentence?

   A) patents

   B) patience

   C) patients

   D) patience

   Answer:

   C) is correct. *Patients* is the correct spelling and the correct homophone. *Patients* are people in a hospital and *patience* is the ability to avoid getting upset in negative situations.

12

SENTENCE STRUCTURE

PHRASES

To understand what a phrase is, you have to know about subjects and predicates. The **SUBJECT** is what the sentence is about; the **PREDICATE** contains the verb and its modifiers.

> The nurse at the front desk will answer any questions you have.

The subject is *the nurse at the front desk*, and the predicate is *will answer any questions you have*.

A **PHRASE** is a group of words that communicates only part of an idea because it lacks either a subject or a predicate. Phrases are categorized based on the main word in the phrase. A **PREPOSITIONAL PHRASE** begins with a preposition and ends with an object of the preposition, a **VERB PHRASE** is composed of the main verb along with any helping verbs, and a **NOUN PHRASE** consists of a noun and its modifiers.

> Prepositional phrase: The dog is hiding <u>under the porch</u>.
>
> Verb phrase: The chef <u>wanted to cook</u> a different dish.
>
> Noun phrase: <u>The big red barn</u> rests beside <u>the vacant chicken house</u>.

Example

Identify the type of phrase underlined in the following sentence.

The new patient was assigned to the nurse <u>with the most experience</u>.

A) prepositional phrase

B) noun phrase

C) verb phrase

D) verbal phrase

Answer:

A) is correct. The underlined section of the sentence is a prepositional phrase beginning with the preposition *with*.

CLAUSES

CLAUSES contain both a subject and a predicate. They can be either independent or dependent. An INDEPENDENT (or main) CLAUSE can stand alone as its own sentence.

> The dog ate her homework.

Dependent (or subordinate) clauses cannot stand alone as their own sentences. They start with a subordinating conjunction, relative pronoun, or relative adjective, which will make them sound incomplete.

> <u>Because</u> the dog ate her homework

A sentence can be classified as simple, compound, complex, or compound-complex based on the type and number of clauses it has.

Table 12.1. Types of Clauses

SENTENCE TYPE	NUMBER OF INDEPENDENT CLAUSES	NUMBER OF DEPENDENT CLAUSES
simple	1	0
compound	2 or more	0
complex	1	1 or more
compound-complex	2 or more	1 or more

A SIMPLE SENTENCE consists of one independent clause. Because there are no dependent clauses in a simple sentence, it can be a two-word sentence, with one word being the subject and the other word being the verb, such as *I ran*. However, a simple sentence can also contain prepositions, adjectives, and adverbs. Even though these additions can extend the length of a simple sentence, it is still considered a simple sentence as long as it does not contain any dependent clauses.

> Simple: San Francisco in the springtime is one of my favorite places to visit.

Although the sentence is lengthy, it is simple because it contains only one subject and one verb (*San Francisco* and *is*), modified by additional phrases.

On the test you will have to both identify and construct different kinds of sentences.

COMPOUND SENTENCES have two or more independent clauses and no dependent clauses. Usually a comma and a coordinating conjunction (the FANBOYS: For, And, Nor, But, Or, Yet, and So) join the independent clauses, though semicolons can be used as well.

> Compound: The game was canceled, but we will still practice on Saturday.

This sentence is made up of two independent clauses joined by a conjunction (*but*), so it is compound.

COMPLEX SENTENCES have one independent clause and at least one dependent clause. The two clauses will be joined by a subordinating conjunction.

> Complex: I love listening to the radio in the car because I can sing along.

The sentence has one independent clause (*I love...car*) and one dependent (*because I...along*), so it is complex.

Can you write a simple, compound, complex, and compound-complex sentence using the same independent clause?

COMPOUND-COMPLEX SENTENCES have two or more independent clauses and at least one dependent clause. Compound-complex sentences will have both a coordinating and a subordinating conjunction.

> I wanted to get a dog, but I have a fish because my roommate is allergic to pet dander.

This sentence has three clauses: two independent (*I wanted...dog* and *I have a fish*) and one dependent (*because my...dander*), so it is compound-complex.

Examples

1. Which of the following choices is a simple sentence?

   A) Elsa drove while Erica navigated.

   B) Betty ordered a fruit salad, and Sue ordered eggs.

   C) Because she was late, Jenny ran down the hall.

   D) John ate breakfast with his mother, brother, and father.

   Answer:

   D) is correct. Choice D contains one independent clause with one subject and one verb. Choices A and C are complex sentences because they each contain both a dependent and independent clause. Choice B contains two independent clauses joined by a conjunction and is therefore a compound sentence.

2. Which of the following sentences is a compound-complex sentence?

   A) While they were at the game, Anne cheered for the home team, but Harvey rooted for the underdogs.

   B) The rain flooded all of the driveway, some of the yard, and even part of the sidewalk across the street.

   C) After everyone finished the test, Mr. Brown passed a bowl of candy around the classroom.

   D) All the flowers in the front yard are in bloom, and the trees around the house are lush and green.

   Answer:

   A) is correct. Choice A is a compound-complex sentence because it contains two independent clauses and one dependent clause. Despite its length, choice B is a simple sentence because it contains only one independent clause. Choice C is a complex sentence because it contains one dependent clause and one independent clause. Choice D is a compound sentence; it contains two independent clauses.

PUNCTUATION

The basic rules for using the major punctuation marks are given in Table 12.2.

Table 12.2. How to Use Punctuation

PUNCTUATION	USED FOR	EXAMPLE
period	ending sentences	Periods go at the end of complete sentences.
question mark	ending questions	What's the best way to end a sentence?
exclamation point	ending sentences that show extreme emotion	I'll never understand how to use commas!
comma	joining two independent clauses (always with a coordinating conjunction)	Commas can be used to join clauses, but they must always be followed by a coordinating conjunction.
	setting apart introductory and nonessential words and phrases	Commas, when used properly, set apart extra information in a sentence.
	separating items in a list	My favorite punctuation marks include the colon, semicolon, and period.
semicolon	joining together two independent clauses (never used with a conjunction)	I love exclamation points; they make sentences seem so exciting!
colon	introducing a list, explanation, or definition	When I see a colon I know what to expect: more information.
apostrophe	forming contractions	It's amazing how many people can't use apostrophes correctly.
	showing possession	Parentheses are my sister's favorite punctuation; she finds commas' rules confusing.
quotation marks	indicating a direct quote	I said to her, "Tell me more about parentheses."

Examples

1. Which of the following sentences contains an error in punctuation?

    A) I love apple pie! John exclaimed with a smile.

    B) Jennifer loves Adam's new haircut.

    C) Billy went to the store; he bought bread, milk, and cheese.

    D) Alexandra hates raisins, but she loves chocolate chips.

    Answer:

    A) is correct. Choice A should use quotation marks to set off a direct quote: *"I love apple pie!" John exclaimed with a smile.*

2. Which punctuation mark correctly completes the sentence?

    Sam, why don't you come with us for dinner_

    A) .

    B) ;

    C) ?

    D) :

    Answer:

    C) is correct. The sentence is a question, so it should end with a question mark.

PART V: TEST YOUR KNOWLEDGE

13

PRACTICE TEST

READING

The next five questions are based on the following passage.

In recent decades, jazz has been associated with New Orleans and festivals like Mardi Gras, but in the 1920s jazz was a booming trend whose influence reached into many aspects of American culture. In fact, the years between World War I and the Great Depression were known as the Jazz Age, a term coined by F. Scott Fitzgerald in his famous novel *The Great Gatsby*. Sometimes also called the Roaring Twenties, this time period saw major urban centers experience new economic, cultural, and artistic vitality. In the United States, musicians flocked to cities like New York and Chicago, which would become famous hubs for jazz musicians. Ella Fitzgerald, for example, moved from Virginia to New York City to begin her much-lauded singing career, and jazz pioneer Louis Armstrong got his big break in Chicago.

Jazz music was played by and for a more expressive and free populace than the United States had previously seen. Women gained the right to vote and were openly seen drinking and wearing revealing clothing. This period marked the emergence of the flapper, a woman determined to make a statement about her new role in society. Jazz music also provided the soundtrack for the explosion of African American art and culture now known as the Harlem Renaissance. In addition to Fitzgerald and Armstrong, numerous musicians, including Duke Ellington, Fats Waller, and Bessie Smith, promoted their distinctive and complex music as an integral part of the emerging African American culture.

1. Which of the following is the author's main purpose for writing this passage?

   A) to explain the role jazz musicians played in the Harlem Renaissance

   B) to inform the reader about the many important musicians playing jazz in the 1920s

   C) to discuss how jazz influenced important cultural movements in the 1920s

   D) to provide a history of jazz music in the 20th century

2. *Jazz music also provided the soundtrack for the explosion of African American art and culture now known as the Harlem Renaissance.*

   The sentence above appears in the second paragraph of the passage. This sentence is best described as which of the following?

   A) theme

   B) topic

   C) main idea

   D) supporting idea

3. The passage is reflective of which of the following types of writing?

    A) technical

    B) expository

    C) persuasive

    D) narrative

4. Which of the following conclusions may be drawn directly from the second paragraph of the passage?

    A) Jazz music was important to minority groups struggling for social equality in the 1920s.

    B) Duke Ellington, Fats Waller, and Bessie Smith were the most important jazz musicians of the Harlem Renaissance.

    C) Women were able to gain the right to vote with the help of jazz musicians.

    D) Duke Ellington, Fats Waller, and Bessie Smith all supported women's right to vote.

5. Which of the following is the topic sentence for the whole passage?

    A) In recent decades, jazz has been associated with New Orleans and festivals like Mardi Gras, but in the 1920s jazz was a booming trend whose influence was reaching into many aspects of American culture.

    B) Sometimes also called the Roaring Twenties, this time period saw major urban centers experiencing new economic, cultural, and artistic vitality.

    C) The Jazz Age brought along with it a more expressive and free populace.

    D) Jazz music also provided the soundtrack for the explosion of African American art and culture now known as the Harlem Renaissance.

The next six questions are based on the passage below.

Popcorn is often associated with fun and festivities, both in and out of the home. It's eaten in theaters, usually after being salted and smothered in butter, and in homes, fresh from the microwave. But popcorn isn't just for fun—it's also a multi-million dollar industry with a long and fascinating history.

While popcorn might seem like a modern invention, its history actually dates back thousands of years, making it one of the oldest snack foods enjoyed around the world. Popping is believed by food historians to be one of the earliest uses of cultivated corn. In 1948, Herbert Dick and Earle Smith discovered old popcorn dating back 4,000 years in the New Mexico Bat Cave. For the Aztec Indians that called the caves home, popcorn (or *momochitl*) played an important role in society, both as a food staple and in ceremonies. The Aztecs cooked popcorn by heating sand in a fire; when it was heated, kernels were added and would pop when exposed to the heat of the sand.

The American love affair with popcorn began in 1912, when popcorn was first sold in theaters. The popcorn industry flourished during the Great Depression by advertising popcorn as a wholesome and economical food. Selling for 5 to 10 cents a bag, it was a luxury that the downtrodden could afford. With the introduction of mobile popcorn machines at the World's Columbian Exposition in the late 1800s, popcorn moved from the theater into fairs and parks. Popcorn continued to rule the snack food kingdom until the rise in popularity of home televisions during the 1950s.

The popcorn industry reacted to their decline in sales quickly by introducing pre-popped and un-popped popcorn for home consumption. However, it wasn't until microwave popcorn became commercially available in 1981 that at-home popcorn consumption began to grow exponentially. With the wide availability of microwaves in the United States, popcorn also began popping up in offices and hotel rooms. The home still remains the most popular popcorn eating spot, though: today, 70 percent of the 16 billion quarts of popcorn consumed annually in the United States is eaten at home.

6. The author's description of the growth of the popcorn industry is reflective of which of the following types of text structure?

A) cause-effect

B) comparison-contrast

C) chronological

D) problem-solution

7. *Popcorn is often associated with fun and festivities, both in and out of the home.*

The sentence above appears as the first sentence of the passage. This sentence is best described as which of the following?

A) summary sentence

B) topic sentence

C) main idea

D) supporting idea

8. Which of the following conclusions may be drawn directly from the third paragraph of the passage?

A) People ate less popcorn in the 1950s than in previous decades because they went to the movies less.

B) Without mobile popcorn machines, people would not have been able to eat popcorn during the Great Depression.

C) People enjoyed popcorn during the Great Depression because it was a luxury food.

D) During the 1800s, people began abandoning theaters to go to fairs and festivals.

9. The author intends to do which of the following by using the words *The American love affair with popcorn began in 1912?*

A) entertain

B) express feelings

C) persuade

D) inform

10. Which of the following is the author's main purpose for writing this passage?

A) to explain how microwaves affected the popcorn industry

B) to show that popcorn is older than many people realize

C) to illustrate the history of popcorn from ancient cultures to modern times

D) to demonstrate the importance of popcorn in various cultures

11. Based on the passage, which of the following is the most likely inference?

A) Popcorn tastes better when it is cooked on heated sand.

B) The popcorn industry will continue to thrive in the United States.

C) If movie theaters go out of business, the popcorn industry will also fail.

D) Archaeologists would likely find other examples of ancient cultures eating popcorn if they looked hard enough.

The next three questions are based on the passage below.

Mason was one of those guys who just always seemed at home. Stick him on a bus, and he'd make three new friends; when he joined a team, it was only a matter of time before he was elected captain. This particular skill rested almost entirely in his eyes. These brown orbs seemed lit from within, and when Mason focused that fire, it was impossible not to feel its warmth. People sought out Mason for the feeling of comfort he so easily created, and anyone with a good joke would want to tell it to Mason. His laughter started with a spark in his eyes that traveled down to create his wide, open smile.

$\longrightarrow$

CONTINUE

12. Based on a prior knowledge of literature, the reader can infer that this passage was taken from which of the following?

A) a short-story collection

B) a science magazine

C) an academic journal

D) a history textbook

13. Which of the following is the author's intent in the passage?

A) entertain

B) express feelings

C) persuade

D) inform

14. Which of the following is a logical conclusion that can be drawn from this description?

A) Mason wishes people would tell him more jokes.

B) Mason is very good at sports.

C) Mason does not like when strangers approach him.

D) Mason has many friends.

The next two questions are based on the following memo.

The following memo was sent by the Human Resources Department to each department leader within the company.

MEMO

From: Human Resource Department

To: Department Leaders

Date: December 6, 2018

Subject: Personal Use of Computers

Management has been conducting standard monitoring of computer usage, and we are dismayed at the amount of personal use occurring during business hours. Employee computers are available for the sole purpose of completing company business and for nothing else. These rules must be respected. If employees are found to be using computers for personal use during work hours, disciplinary action will be taken. Personal use should occur in emergency situations only, and in these cases use should be limited to 30 minutes. Please communicate these requirements to all personnel in your department.

15. Which of the following is the main purpose of this email?

A) to notify employees that their computer use is being monitored

B) to inform a group of employees about disciplinary action that has been taken

C) to provide information about the computer usage policy to department leaders

D) to explain in which emergency situations it is appropriate for employees to use computers

16. Which of the following inferences may be logically drawn from the memo?

A) Department leaders will be punished if employees are found to be using computers inappropriately.

B) Employees will likely leave the company rather than stop using their computers for personal business.

C) Management will allow some flexibility about the rules for computer use for department leaders.

D) Management will not hesitate to initiate disciplinary action against employees who use computers inappropriately.

The next three questions are based on the following passage.

It could be said that the great battle between the North and South we call the Civil War was a battle for individual identity. The states of the South had their own culture, one based on farming, independence, and the rights of both man and state to determine their own paths. Similarly, the North had forged its own identity as a center of centralized commerce and manufacturing. This clash of lifestyles was bound to create tension, and this tension was bound to lead to war. But people who try to sell you this narrative are wrong. The Civil War was not a battle of cultural identities—it was a battle about slavery. All other explanations for the war are either a direct consequence of the South's desire for wealth at the expense of her fellow man or a fanciful invention to cover up this sad portion of our nation's history. And it cannot be denied that this time in our past was very sad indeed.

17. Which of the following describes this type of writing?

A) technical

B) expository

C) persuasive

D) narrative

18. Which of the following is a likely motive for the author?

A) to convince readers that slavery was the main cause of the Civil War

B) to illustrate the cultural differences between the North and the South before the Civil War

C) to persuade readers that the North deserved to win the Civil War

D) to demonstrate that the history of the Civil War is too complicated to be understood clearly

19. Which of the following statements best describes the author's point of view?

A) The Civil War was the result of cultural differences between the North and South.

B) The Civil War was caused by the South's reliance on slave labor.

C) The North's use of commerce and manufacturing allowed it to win the war.

D) The South's belief in the rights of man and state cost them the war.

The next two questions are based on the following passage.

Patients are to arrive at the hospital two hours before the scheduled start time for their surgery. All surgery patients must check in at the Hospital Admissions Desk before proceeding to the Third-Floor Surgery Admissions Desk. The admitting nurse will ensure that all required paperwork has been completed before the patient is taken to the Surgery Holding Room. Once admitted to the Holding Room, the patient will need permission from the head nurse to leave and reenter. One family member or friend may accompany the patient in the Holding Room. All other family and friends will be asked to remain in the Third-Floor Waiting Area.

20. Which of the following is the first place a patient entering the hospital would visit?

A) Surgery Admissions Desk

B) Hospital Admissions Desk

C) Surgery Holding Room

D) Third-Floor Waiting Area

21. A patient who has checked in at the Surgery Admissions Desk would go to which location next?

A) Surgery Admissions Desk

B) Hospital Admissions Desk

C) Surgery Holding Room

D) Third-Floor Waiting Area

22. Which of the following would be a primary source for an article on the Battle of Gettysburg?

   A) a letter written by a local farmer who witnessed the battle

   B) a documentary about the battle produced by a local TV station

   C) a novelization of the battle written by the great-grandson of a Union soldier

   D) a history textbook for a college-level course in American history

---

The next two questions are based on the following lists.

Tree Species by Ecosystem

Tropical Rain Forest: mahogany, Brazil nut, rubber tree, tualang, strangler figs

Tropical Dry Forest: palu, Ceylon ebony, governor's plum

Temperate Deciduous Forest: oak, maple, beech, elm, magnolia, sweet gum

Temperate Coniferous Forest: cedar, cypress, juniper, pine, spruce, redwood

23. According to the lists above, beech trees would be found in which ecosystem?

   A) tropical rain forest

   B) tropical dry forest

   C) temperate deciduous forest

   D) temperate coniferous forest

24. According to the lists above, which species of tree would be found in a temperate deciduous forest?

   A) tualang

   B) magnolia

   C) rubber tree

   D) juniper

25. Which of the following sentences indicates the end of a sequence?

   A) Unfortunately, the stock did not perform as well as we had hoped.

   B) The next day, we were able to find a band we liked that also fit our budget.

   C) Overall, my friends and I found the experience rewarding.

   D) Before we go to the restaurant, let's look at the menu.

26. Memory, types, 315 – 347
       autobiographical, 326
       explicit, 316 – 320
       implicit, 319 – 325
       long-term, 333 – 342
       short-term, 340 – 346

   According to the excerpt from the psychology textbook index above, which of the following pages should a reader check first for information on short-term memory?

   A) 316

   B) 319

   C) 333

   D) 340

The next two questions are based on the figure below.

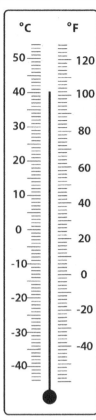

27. If the thermometer indicated a temperature of −40°F, what would the temperature be in degrees Celsius?

A) −40°C

B) −34°C

C) −6°C

D) 85°C

28. If the reading in the thermometer dropped 10°C, what would the temperature be in degrees Fahrenheit?

A) 82°F

B) 85°F

C) 92°F

D) 100°F

The next three questions are based on the figure showing the inventory at Gigi's Diner below.

29. Which food does Gigi's have the least of?

A) bacon slices

B) cheese slices

C) hamburger buns

D) hamburger patties

30. According to the graph above, how many more hamburger buns does Gigi's need in order to make 200 hamburgers?

A) 120

B) 161

C) 181

D) 200

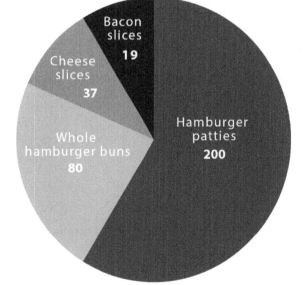

31. Which of the following is the number of hamburgers Gigi's could make if each burger includes 1 bacon slice and 2 cheese slices?

A) 18

B) 19

C) 39

D) 80

31. Which of the following is the number of hamburgers Gigi's could make if each burger includes 1 bacon slice and 2 cheese slices?

A) 18

B) 19

C) 39

D) 80

32. The president's speech was eloquent and touched many voters with its wit and flair.

Which of the following is the definition of the word *eloquent*?

A) long-winded

B) dispassionate

C) loud

D) well-spoken

The next three questions are based on the figure below.

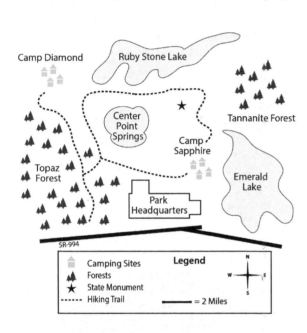

34. Approximately how many miles is Camp Diamond from Camp Sapphire?

A) 0.1 miles

B) 1.0 miles

C) 10 miles

D) 100 miles

35. Which location is directly south of Tannanite Forest?

A) Ruby Stone Lake

B) Camp Sapphire

C) Emerald Lake

D) Camp Diamond

33. Which direction is Topaz Forest in relation to Emerald Lake?

A) north

B) south

C) east

D) west

The next two questions are based on the table below.

Shoe Store Prices

RETAILER	BASE PRICE	SHIPPING & HANDLING	TAXES
Wholesale Footwear	$59.99	$10.95	$7.68
Bargain Sales	$65.99	$5.95	$5.38
Famous Shoes	$79.99	$0.00	$4.89
Fancy Shoes	$89.99	$2.95	$8.99

36. Dennis wants to buy shoes and has $80 to spend. Which retailer(s) can he afford to buy from if he has to pay shipping and handling and taxes?

A) Wholesale Footwear

B) Fancy Shoes

C) Wholesale Footwear and Bargain Sales

D) Wholesale Footwear, Bargain Sales, and Famous Shoes

37. If Dennis bought his shoes online and didn't have to pay any taxes, shoes from which retailer would cost the least?

A) Wholesale Footwear

B) Bargain Sales

C) Famous Shoes

D) Fancy Shoes

38. A student needs to find the definition of a word in her history textbook. Which of the following will be the most helpful?

A) preface

B) glossary

C) appendix

D) index

39. A student wants to look online to find unbiased information about organic foods. Analyze the following websites and their taglines to determine which site he should use.

A) www.dangerinthegrocerystore.com; "The truth about the toxic chemicals in your produce."

B) www.growbetter.com; "Your one-stop shop for agricultural pesticides and fertilizers."

C) www.betterfood.org; "A non-profit that provides nutritional support to needy families."

D) www.foodandnutrition.gov; "An official site of the United States Surgeon General."

40. According to the table of contents below, which of the following lists includes only subheadings?

Chapter 2: Early American History

1. Early Settlement
   A. Plymouth
   B. Jamestown
2. The American Revolution
   A. American Victories
   B. British Victories
3. A New Century
   A. The Constitutional Convention
   B. The Ratification Years

A) Plymouth, Jamestown, British Victories, and A New Century

B) American Victories, British Victories, A New Century, and The Ratification Years

C) American Victories, British Victories, The Constitutional Convention, and The Ratification Years

D) Early Settlement, The American Revolution, A New Century, and The Ratification Years

41. When connecting line A to port B, make sure that port C is **completely** closed. If port C is left open, fluid will leak as soon as line A is connected. Once line A and port B are **fully** connected, port C can be opened as needed.

The bold text in the directions above indicate which of the following?

A) brand names

B) emphasis

C) commands

D) proper nouns

42. Read and follow the directions below.

> 1. You start with $20 in your wallet.
> 2. You spend $5 on lunch.
> 3. You receive $20 for mowing your neighbor's yard.
> 4. You spend $10 on a new shirt.
> 5. You receive $10 for driving a friend to work.
> 6. You spend $30 on fuel for your vehicle.

How much money do you have left?

A) $0

B) $5

C) $10

D) $20

The next two questions are based on the table below.

Tee Shirt Prices

COMPANY	PRICES
Maximum Tees	$15.99 for the first 100 shirts; $12.99 for each additional shirt
Wholesale Tees	$16.50 per shirt
Total Tees	$19.99 for the first 50 shirts; $14.99 for each additional shirt
Classic Tees	$16.50 for the first 50 shirts; $11.50 for each additional shirt

43. An ecological protection group wants to buy 50 shirts. Which company will provide the least expensive order?

A) Maximum Tees

B) Wholesale Tees

C) Total Tees

D) Classic Tees

44. A sports team wants to place an order for 100 shirts. Ordering from which company will cost them the least amount of money?

A) Maximum Tees

B) Wholesale Tees

C) Total Tees

D) Classic Tees

45. After following the directions below, how much water is left?

> 1. You have 3 gallons of water.
> 2. You use 0.5 gallons to water your plant.
> 3. You use 1 gallon to refill your dog's water bowl.
> 4. You put 0.5 gallons in an ice tray to make ice cubes.

A) 0 gallons

B) 0.5 gallons

C) 1 gallon

D) 1.5 gallons

46. Elaine was feeling <u>lethargic</u> after a poor night's sleep, but she still managed to get to work on time.

Which of the following is the definition of the underlined word in the sentence above?

A) tired

B) confused

C) angry

D) rushed

47. Analyze the headings below. Which of the following headings is out of place?

Chapter 6: Art of the Middle Ages

I.   The Stories Behind Famous Paintings

II. Notable Sculpting Techniques

III. Recipes for Common Dishes

IV. Textiles and Tapestries

A) The Stories Behind Famous Paintings

B) Notable Sculpting Techniques

C) Recipes for Common Dishes

D) Textiles and Tapestries

48. Read and follow the directions below.

1. Start at the center of town.

2. Drive north 10 miles.

3. Turn left and drive west 5 miles.

4. Turn left and drive south 2 miles.

5. Turn right and drive west 1 mile.

Which of the following is now your distance from the center of town?

A) 12 miles north, 6 miles west

B) 8 miles north, 6 miles west

C) 12 miles north, 4 miles west

D) 8 miles north, 4 miles west

49. Miguel was concerned that his <u>laceration</u> would need stitches.

Which of the following is the definition of the underlined word in the sentence above?

A) deep cut

B) minor wound

C) broken bone

D) swollen joint

50. Examine the headings below. Based on the pattern, which of the following is a reasonable heading to insert in the blank spot?

Chapter 3: Planning Your Vacation

1. Getting There

   A. Air Travel

   B. Traveling by Train

   C. _____

   D. Taking the Bus

2. Accommodations

3. Dining

A) Choosing a Destination

B) Navigating the Airport

C) Finding a Hotel

D) Road Trips

51. Read and follow the directions below.

1. You start with one red marble and two green marbles in a pouch.

2. Remove one red marble.

3. Add one green marble.

4. Add one red marble.

5. Add one green marble.

6. Remove one red marble.

7. Remove one green marble.

8. Add three red marbles.

9. Add two green marbles.

Which of the following is the number of marbles now in the pouch?

A) five red, three green

B) three red, five green

C) four red, four green

D) six red, two green

52. The couple's "plan" was little more than just a desire to travel. They showed up at the airport with no tickets, no itinerary, and no destination in mind.

The use of quotes in the text above signifies which of the following?

A) foreign phrases

B) emphasized words

C) dialogue

D) words used ironically

53. The guide words at the top of a dictionary page are *lexicon* and *lipid*. Which of the following words is an entry on this page?

A) luminous

B) leper

C) license

D) livid

MATHEMATICS

1. In a theater, there are 4,500 lower-level seats and 2,000 upper-level seats. What is the ratio of lower-level seats to total seats?

   A) $\frac{4}{9}$

   B) $\frac{4}{13}$

   C) $\frac{9}{13}$

   D) $\frac{9}{4}$

2. Which of the following is NOT a rational number?

   A) −4

   B) $\frac{1}{5}$

   C) $0.8\overline{33}$

   D) $\sqrt{2}$

3. If a person reads 40 pages in 45 minutes, approximately how many minutes will it take her to read 265 pages?

   A) 202

   B) 236

   C) 265

   D) 298

4. If a student answers 42 out of 48 questions correctly on a quiz, what percentage of questions did she answer correctly?

   A) 82.5%

   B) 85%

   C) 87.5%

   D) 90%

5. What is 1230.932567 rounded to the nearest hundredth?

   A) 1200

   B) 1230.9326

   C) 1230.93

   D) 1230

6. Add 0.98 + 45.102 + 32.3333 + 31 + 0.00009.

   A) 368.573

   B) 210.536299

   C) 109.41539

   D) 99.9975

7. Melissa is ordering fencing to enclose a square area of 5625 square feet. How many feet of fencing does she need?

   A) 75

   B) 150

   C) 300

   D) 5,625

8. If a discount of 25% off the retail price of a desk saves Mark $45, what was the desk's original price?

   A) $135

   B) $160

   C) $180

   D) $210

9. What number is 5% of 2000?

   A) 50

   B) 100

   C) 150

   D) 200

10. Adam owns 4 times as many shirts as he has pairs of pants, and he has 5 pairs of pants for every 2 pairs of shoes. What is the ratio of Adam's shirts to Adam's shoes?

    A) 25 shirts: 1 pair shoes

    B) 10 shirts : 1 pair shoes

    C) 20 shirts : 1 pair shoes

    D) 15 shirts : 2 pairs shoes

11. Jane earns $15 per hour babysitting. If she starts out with $275 in her bank account, which of the following equations represents how many hours she will have to babysit for her account to reach $400?

   A) $-400 = 15h - 275$

   B) $400 = \frac{15}{h} + 275$

   C) $400 = 15h$

   D) $400 = 15h + 275$

12. Patrick is coming home from vacation in Costa Rica and wants to fill one of his suitcases with bags of Costa Rican coffee. The weight limit for his suitcase is 22 kilograms, and the suitcase itself weighs 3.2 kilograms. If each bag of coffee weighs 800 grams, how many bags can he bring in his suitcase without going over the limit?

   A) 2

   B) 4

   C) 23

   D) 27

13. A bag contains twice as many red marbles as blue marbles, and the number of blue marbles is 88% of the number of green marbles. If g represents the number of green marbles, which of the following expressions represents the total number of marbles in the bag?

   A) $3.88g$

   B) $3.64g$

   C) $2.64g$

   D) $2.32g$

14. Which of the following is listed in order from least to greatest?

   A. $-0.95, 0, \frac{2}{5}, 0.35, \frac{3}{4}$

   B. $-1, -\frac{1}{10}, -0.11, \frac{5}{6}, 0.75$

   C. $-\frac{3}{4}, -0.2, 0, \frac{2}{3}, 0.55$

   D. $-1.1, -\frac{4}{5}, -0.13, 0.7, \frac{9}{11}$

15. Which inequality is equivalent to $\frac{2x+7}{9} < 2$?

   A) $3x < \frac{21}{3}$

   B) $x > -3$

   C) $x < \frac{11}{2}$

   D) $2x > 1$

16. $\frac{2}{9} \times \frac{3}{25} \times \frac{125}{6} \times \frac{3}{10} =$

   A) $\frac{1}{5}$

   B) $\frac{1}{6}$

   C) 6

   D) $\frac{11}{30}$

17. $\left(\frac{3}{4} + \frac{1}{5}\right) - \left(\frac{2}{3} + \frac{3}{2}\right) =$

   A) $\frac{7}{8}$

   B) $\frac{-73}{60}$

   C) $\frac{73}{60}$

   D) $\frac{-26}{30}$

18. Which inequality is equivalent to $3x + 2 > 5$?

   A) $x < 1$

   B) $x > -1$

   C) $x > 1$

   D) $x > 3$

19. Michael is making cupcakes. He plans to give $\frac{1}{2}$ of the cupcakes to a friend and $\frac{1}{3}$ of the cupcakes to his coworkers. If he makes 48 cupcakes, how many will he have left over?

   A) 8

   B) 10

   C) 16

   D) 24

20. $\frac{2}{9} + \left(\frac{5}{6} - \frac{1}{2}\right) =$

A) $\frac{5}{12}$

B) $\frac{7}{9}$

C) $\frac{5}{9}$

D) $\frac{8}{45}$

Use the chart below to answer questions 21 and 22.

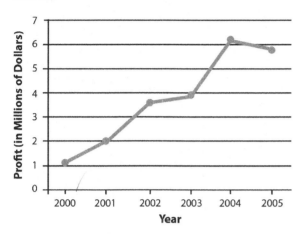

21. Referencing the line graph, approximately how much did profit increase from 2003 to 2004 in dollars?

A) 2.3 million

B) 6.2 million

C) 3.9 million

D) 3.2 million

22. Approximately how much more profit was earned in 2001 than in 2000?

A) 2.2 million

B) 1.0 million

C) 3.5 million

D) 6.1 million

23. Juan plans to spend 25% of his workday writing a report. If he is at work for 9 hours, how many hours will he spend writing the report?

A) 2.25

B) 2.50

C) 2.75

D) 4.00

24. Jessie leaves her home and rides her bike 12 miles south and then 16 miles east. She then takes the shortest possible route back home. What was the total distance she traveled?

A) 18 miles

B) 32 miles

C) 48 miles

D) 56 miles

25. An ice chest contains 24 sodas, some regular and some diet. The ratio of diet soda to regular soda is 1:3. How many regular sodas are there in the ice chest?

A) 1

B) 4

C) 18

D) 24

26. What is the area of the shape?

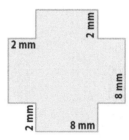

A. 6 mm²

B. 16 mm²

C. 64 mm²

D. 128 mm²

27. Which expression is equivalent to dividing 300 by 12?

A) $2(150 - 6)$

B) $(300 \div 4) \div 6$

C) $(120 \div 6) + (180 \div 6)$

D) $(120 \div 12) + (180 \div 12)$

28. Solve for x: $5x - 4 = 3(8 + 3x)$

A) -7

B) $-\frac{3}{4}$

C) $\frac{3}{4}$

D) 7

29. The pie graph below shows how a state's government plans to spend its annual budget of $3 billion. How much more money does the state plan to spend on infrastructure than education?

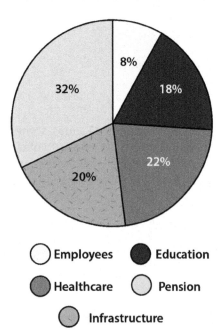

A. $60,000,000

B. $120,000,000

C. $300,000,000

D. $600,000,000

30. Out of 1560 students at Ward Middle School, 15% want to take French. Which expression represents how many students want to take French?

A) 1560 ÷ 15

B) 1560 × 15

C) 1560 × 0.15

D) 1560 ÷ 0.15

31. If a car uses 8 gallons of gas to travel 650 miles, how many miles can it travel using 12 gallons of gas?

A) 870 miles

B) 895 miles

C) 915 miles

D) 975 miles

32. A bike store is having a 30%-off sale, and one of the bikes is on sale for $385. What was the original price of this bike?

A) $253.00

B) $450.00

C) $500.50

D) $550.00

33. Justin has a summer lawn care business and earns $40 for each lawn he mows. He also pays $35 per week in business expenses. Which of the following expressions represents Justin's profit after x weeks if he mows m number of lawns?

A) $40m - 35x$

B) $40m + 35x$

C) $35x(40 + m)$

D) $35(40m + x)$

34. In a neighborhood, $\frac{2}{5}$ of the houses are painted yellow. If there are 24 houses that are NOT painted yellow, how many yellow houses are in the neighborhood?

A) 16

B) 9.6

C) 24

D) 40

35. 5 numbers have an average of 16. If the first 4 numbers have a sum of 68, what is the 5th number?

A) 12

B) 16

C) 52

D) 80

36. Adam is painting the outside walls of a 4-walled shed. The shed is 5 feet wide, 4 feet deep, and 7 feet high. How many square feet of paint will Adam need?

A) 46 square feet

B) 63 square feet

C) 126 square feet

D) 140 square feet

SCIENCE

1. Which of the following chambers of the heart pumps oxygenated blood to the rest of the body?

   A) left atrium

   B) right atrium

   C) left ventricle

   D) right ventricle

2. After air is inhaled through the mouth, nose, and throat, which of the following structures does it travel through?

   A) alveoli

   B) bronchi

   C) bronchioles

   D) trachea

3. Which of the following is NOT a function of the liver?

   A) digestive juice production

   B) bile production

   C) detoxification

   D) blood preparation

4. Which of the following cells are responsible for carrying oxygen?

   A) leukocytes

   B) thrombocytes

   C) erythrocytes

   D) plasma cells

5. Oxygen is exchanged between blood and tissues at which of the following areas?

   A) capillaries

   B) veins

   C) ventricles

   D) arteries

6. When exhaling, the diaphragm—

   A) relaxes, reducing the space available for the lungs

   B) relaxes, increasing the space available for the lungs

   C) contracts, reducing the space available for the lungs

   D) contracts, increasing the space available for the lungs

7. How many electrons are included in the double bond between the two oxygen atoms in O_2?

   A) 2

   B) 4

   C) 6

   D) 8

8. Which of the following is the anterior bone of the lower leg?

   A) ulna

   B) fibula

   C) tibia

   D) radius

9. Which of the following regions of the brain is the active link between the endocrine and nervous systems?

   A) cerebellum

   B) pons

   C) cerebrum

   D) hypothalamus

10. Which of the following joints is formed by the humerus and the ulna?

    A) ball-and-socket joint

    B) hinge joint

    C) saddle joint

    D) gliding joint

11. Which of the following is another name for the patella?

    A) breastbone

    B) kneecap

    C) finger bone

    D) funny bone

12. Which of the following is the part of a muscle that remains stationary during movement?

    A) insertion

    B) agonist

    C) origin

    D) antagonist

13. Which of the following is the process that produces a liquid from a gas?

    A) vaporization

    B) condensation

    C) sublimation

    D) melting

14. What is the primary function of the quadriceps muscle?

    A) extend the knee joint

    B) flex the knee joint

    C) extend the hip joint

    D) flex the hip joint

15. Which of the following parts of the brain is responsible for memory and language processing?

    A) pons

    B) cerebrum

    C) cerebellum

    D) medulla oblongata

16. How many thoracic spinal nerves are there in the human body?

    A) eight

    B) nine

    C) twelve

    D) fourteen

17. Which of the following is NOT a specialized sense?

    A) touch

    B) balance

    C) sight

    D) hearing

18. In which region of the small intestine are most of the nutrients absorbed?

    A) jejunum

    B) ileum

    C) duodenum

    D) colon

19. Which of the following macromolecules is broken down by trypsin?

    A) protein

    B) lipid

    C) nucleic acids

    D) carbohydrates

20. Which of the following supplies blood to the lower body?

    A) superior vena cava

    B) inferior vena cava

    C) iliac artery

    D) aortic arch

21. Which type of cell is responsible for the degradation of bone tissue?

    A) osteoclasts

    B) osteoblasts

    C) osteocytes

    D) lining cells

22. The elements in Group 1 have _____ valence electrons and are _____ reactive than the elements in Group 2.

    A) zero; more

    B) zero; less

    C) one; less

    D) one; more

23. One function of lymphocytes in the lymph nodes is to ingest invading bacteria and other harmful debris to keep our bodies healthy. Which of the following most likely carries out this process?

A) pinocytosis

B) facilitated transport

C) phagocytosis

D) exocytosis

24. Which of the following is NOT an example of the end result of a negative feedback loop?

A) release of oxytocin during childbirth

B) vasoconstriction during an incident of low blood pressure

C) stimulus of sweat glands in thermoregulation

D) insulin production and storage of glucose during digestion

25. Muscle tissues will often require quick bursts of energy. As a result, which of the following organelles would be most likely to be found in higher than normal amounts in muscle cells?

A) ribosomes

B) lysosomes

C) vacuoles

D) mitochondria

26. Consider a prokaryotic organism that typically lives in a 10 percent saline concentration environment. Which of the following environments would cause the organism to lose mass at the greatest rate due to osmosis?

A) a solution of pure water

B) a solution of 3 percent saline concentration

C) a solution of 10 percent saline concentration

D) a solution of 20 percent saline concentration

27. Which of the following is NOT a function of the respiratory system in humans?

A) to exchange gas

B) to produce sound and speech

C) to distribute oxygen to the rest of the body

D) to remove particles from the air

28. Which of the following elements is the most electronegative?

A) chlorine

B) iron

C) magnesium

D) silicon

29. Which of the following choices would contain the code for making a protein?

A) mRNA

B) tRNA

C) rRNA

D) DNA polymerase

30. Which of the salts on the solubility curve graph has the greatest solubility at 50°C?

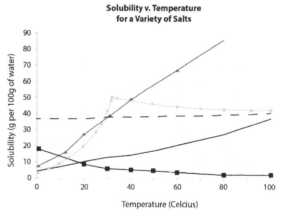

A) Na_2SO_4

B) NaCl

C) $Ba(NO_3)_2$

D) Na_2HAsO_4

31. Which of the following statements best defines a scientific model?

    A) a real-world example of a theory

    B) a simplification or metaphor for an observed phenomenon

    C) a proposed explanation for an observed phenomenon

    D) a statement about a fundamental aspect of the universe

32. A chemistry student is conducting an experiment in which she tests the relationship between reactant concentration and heat produced by a reaction. In her experiment, she alters the reactant concentration and measures heat produced. Which of the following is the independent variable in this experiment?

    A) reactant concentration

    B) reaction rate

    C) amount of heat produced by the reaction

    D) product concentration

33. Which of the following is NOT a homogeneous mixture?

    A) air

    B) sandy water

    C) brass

    D) salt dissolved in water

34. Alleles for brown eyes (B) are dominant over alleles for blue eyes (b). If two parents are both heterozygous for this gene, what is the percent chance that their offspring will have brown eyes?

    A) 100

    B) 75

    C) 66

    D) 50

35. How many neutrons are in an atom of the element $_{88}^{38}$Sr?

    A) 38

    B) 88

    C) 50

    D) 126

36. The graph shows the temperature of water as heat is added. Which of the following processes is occurring between points B and C?

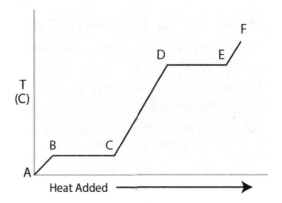

    A) boiling

    B) melting

    C) deposition

    D) sublimation

37. Which of the following is NOT present in an animal cell?

    A) nucleus

    B) mitochondria

    C) cytoplasm

    D) cell wall

38. Which of the following is a decomposition reaction?

    A) $2Na + Cl_2 \rightarrow 2NaCl$

    B) $Zn + 2HCl \rightarrow ZnCl_2 + H_2$

    C) $CH_4 + 2O_2 \rightarrow CO_2 + 2H_2O$

    D) $H_2CO_3 \rightarrow H_2O + CO_2$

39. Which ion has the greatest number of electrons?

   A) Ca^{2+}

   B) Cl^-

   C) Ca^+

   D) P^{3-}

40. Which of the following materials is the primary structural protein of the epidermis, nails, and skin?

   A) eponychium

   B) collagen

   C) keratin

   D) cartilage

41. Damage to the parathyroid would most likely affect which of the following?

   A) stress levels

   B) bone density

   C) secondary sex characteristics

   D) circadian rhythms

42. Which of the following does NOT correctly match the part of the cell and its primary function?

   A) mitochondria: production of ATP through oxidative phosphorylation

   B) nucleus: DNA replication and transcription

   C) smooth endoplasmic reticulum: translation of mRNA into proteins

   D) Golgi apparatus: packaging and transportation of proteins within and in/out of cells

43. Which of the following is the final vessel through which semen must pass before being expelled from the body?

   A) ejaculatory duct

   B) penile urethra

   C) membranous urethra

   D) vas deferens

44. Which of the following groups of bones are part of the axial skeleton?

   A) pectoral girdle

   B) rib cage

   C) arms and hands

   D) pelvic girdle

45. Which of the following is NOT a type of white blood cell?

   A) helper T-cell

   B) plasma cell

   C) antibody

   D) phagocyte

46. Which of the following initiates the breakdown of carbohydrates?

   A) salivary amylase

   B) stomach acid

   C) bile salts

   D) peristalsis

47. Which of the following is NOT a function of the pituitary gland?

   A) receive and interpret internal and external stimuli from sensory nerves

   B) release trophic hormones to trigger other glands to produce hormones

   C) store hormones from the hypothalamus and release as needed

   D) produce hormones and send to target cells via the bloodstream

48. Which of the following units is most appropriate for measuring the mass of an ant?

   A) meters

   B) grams

   C) liters

   D) kilograms

49. Which of the following cellular processes does NOT use ATP?

   A) facilitated diffusion

   B) DNA replication

   C) active transport through the cell membrane

   D) movement of the mot complex in a flagellum

50. Hemophilia is a hereditary genetic disorder that prevents blood from clotting correctly. The allele for hemophilia is recessive and carried on the X chromosome.

   A couple has two sons, one who has hemophilia and one who does not. Which of the following is true of the parents' genotypes?

   A) The mother is an asymptomatic carrier of the disorder.

   B) The father is an asymptomatic carrier of the disorder.

   C) The mother does not carry the gene for the disorder.

   D) The father does not carry the gene for the disorder.

51. Which of the following is NOT a hormone-producing gland of the endocrine system?

   A) prostate

   B) pituitary

   C) adrenal

   D) thyroid

52. Which of the following is the division of the nervous system primarily responsible for regulating all involuntary and subconscious muscle functions?

   A) somatic nervous system

   B) autonomic nervous system

   C) sympathetic nervous system

   D) peripheral nervous system

53. A scientist discovers a new species of snail that lives in the ocean. He tested the ability of this species to handle heat by measuring its growth rate as he increased the temperature of the water. He also tested two different concentrations of salt to determine which type of marine environment the snail would be best suited for.

   Which of the following is the dependent variable in the experiment described above?

   A) salt concentration

   B) temperature

   C) growth rate

   D) number of snails

ENGLISH AND LANGUAGE USAGE

1. She told them to _____ their room before they left for the party.

   Which of the following correctly completes the sentence?

   A) cleaned

   B) tidy

   C) clears

   D) neat

2. We left for the party, but my sister had to return home because _____ forgot her purse.

   Which of the following is the correct pronoun for the sentence above?

   A) he

   B) they

   C) we

   D) she

3. Which of the following is punctuated correctly?

   A) The dentist told her patient he needed to return later in the week because he had more cavities.

   B) The dentist told her patient he needed to return later in the week: because he had more cavities.

   C) The dentist told her patient he needed to return later in the week; because he had more cavities.

   D) The dentist told her patient he needed to return later in the week—because he had more cavities.

4. The invitation presented her with a dilemma: should she go the wedding or go out to diner with her sister?

   Which word is misspelled in the sentence?

   A) invitation

   B) dilemma

   C) wedding

   D) diner

5. In which of the following sentences does the verb agree with the subject?

   A) The head zookeeper, who has been with the zoo for over twenty years, have agreed to set up a new enclosure for the elephants.

   B) Of all the elephants owned by the zoo, only some has been approved to move to the new enclosure.

   C) The rest of the elephants has been given to a well-respected rescue organization.

   D) The rescue organization, which takes in animals from zoos across the country, has agreed not to sell the elephants to another zoo.

6. Which of the following is a simple sentence?

   A) He threw the ball across the field to his friend.

   B) He threw the ball to the dog, and the dog ran after it.

   C) He threw the ball across the field because he wanted to see if he could.

   D) He threw the ball across the field; it landed in a ditch.

7. I had worked a very long shift, _____ I still had to run errands after work.

   Which conjunction best completes the sentence?

   A) nor

   B) or

   C) but

   D) so

8. The customer was irate and shouted angrily at the staff before leaving.

   Which of the following is the meaning of *irate* in the sentence above?

   A) confused

   B) calculating

   C) furious

   D) frightened

9. We agreed that Chris would plan our mom's birthday party, he had already selected a restaurant, and I didn't have time to pick up a gift.

Which punctuation mark is used incorrectly in the sentence?

A) the apostrophe in the word *mom's*

B) the comma after the word *party*

C) the comma after the word *restaurant*

D) the apostrophe in the word *didn't*

10. He ran quickly while training hard for the race that weekend.

The word *quickly* serves as which of the following parts of speech in the sentence above?

A) verb

B) adjective

C) noun

D) adverb

11. Which sentence is irrelevant as part of a paragraph composed of these sentences?

A) My mom took me to see *The Lion King* on Broadway when I was six, and I knew that I belonged on the stage.

B) I used to perform for my parents in our living room, and I knew all the lines to "Circle of Life" by heart.

C) *The Lion King* is the third-longest-running show on Broadway and the highest grossing musical of all time.

D) Other people may spend a lifetime looking for the right career, but I've wanted to be an actor since I was a little kid.

12. The shiny new fire truck visited the local elementary school.

Which of the following is the complete subject of the sentence?

A) fire truck

B) the shiny new fire truck

C) elementary school

D) the local elementary school

13. My alarm clock didn't go off.

Fortunately, my boss was also running late.

I arrived at work late.

I didn't get in trouble.

Which option best uses grammar to combine the sentences for clarity and readability?

A) I arrived at work late because my alarm clock didn't go off. Fortunately, my boss was also running late, so I didn't get in trouble.

B) My alarm didn't go off, but I didn't get in trouble because fortunately my boss was also running late even though I arrived at work late.

C) I didn't get in trouble because I arrived at work late. My alarm clock didn't go off, and I arrived at work late.

D) I arrived at work late. Fortunately, my boss was also running late. My alarm clock didn't go off, but I didn't get in trouble.

14. Which of the following is a complex sentence?

A) I forgot my homework because I was in such a hurry to get to the bus stop.

B) I forgot my homework, but my teacher said I can turn it in tomorrow.

C) I forgot my homework on the dining room table next to my backpack and my lunch.

D) I forgot my homework, but I can turn it in tomorrow if I ask my teacher for permission.

15. Which of the following sentences is written in the third person?

A) You need to check on the patient in room 302.

B) Check on the patient in room 302.

C) He checked on the patient in room 302.

D) I will check on the patient in room 302.

16. The boss's perfunctory apology left her employees feeling that she wasn't taking their complaints seriously.

Which word best captures the meaning of *perfunctory* as used in the sentence?

A) timid

B) complicated

C) bitter

D) disinterested

17. Which of the following sentences is punctuated correctly?

A) You need to call the lab, check the test results, and contact the patient's doctors.

B) You need to call the lab check the test results, and contact the patients doctors.

C) You need to: call the lab, check the test results, and contact the patient's doctors.

D) You need to—call the lab, check the test results and contact the patients doctors.

18. Which sentence makes the best topic sentence?

A) Giant pandas live solitary lives and roam large tracks of land looking for food.

B) Many zoos are working to provide natural, more authentic housing for animals.

C) Natural borders, such as moats and rock walls, can help make animals feel at home.

D) Sadly, it seems many zoos do not have the funding to build these large habitats.

19. The letters were quite _____ and contained intimate details.

Which of the following correctly completes the sentence above?

A) personal

B) personnal

C) personnel

D) personel

20. He waited _____

Which of the following if inserted in the blank would create a simple sentence?

A) for the bus.

B) for the bus, but it was running late.

C) for the bus, so he could get to work on time.

D) for the bus because he had an appointment.

21. The heart rate _____ for a number of reasons.

Which word correctly completes the sentence?

A) veries

B) varies

C) varries

D) varys

22. He was hyped for the concert, and planned to show up early so he wouldn't miss any songs.

Which word or phrase from the sentence is slang?

A) hyped

B) show up

C) wouldn't

D) miss

23. The stringent entrance requirements made it difficult for even the best students to be accepted to the school.

Which word best captures the meaning of *stringent* as used in the sentence?

A) demanding

B) confusing

C) despised

D) forgettable

24. Which of the following follows the rules of capitalization?

    A) Mr. Jones, who is a Senator

    B) the representative from maine

    C) President Clinton

    D) Vice-president Biden

25. Which example is a complete sentence?

    A) The girl who always looks out the window during class.

    B) Because he is running late.

    C) Go look for it now.

    D) Under the stars.

26. Which word is an exception to a common spelling rule?

    A) scarves

    B) noticeable

    C) parties

    D) unfortunate

27. I'm not sure how my book ended up at her house but I want it back.

    Which punctuation mark best completes the sentence?

    A) .

    B) ,

    C) ;

    D) :

28. The dress was beautiful, but it was too expensive for her budget.

    The word *expensive* serves as which of the following parts of speech in the sentence above?

    A) adjective

    B) preposition

    C) conjunction

    D) noun

ANSWER KEY

READING

1. C

The first sentence of the passage explains that jazz "reached into many aspects of American culture." The rest of the passage supports this idea by discussing the role of jazz in the growth of urban centers, in the movement for women's rights, and in the Harlem Renaissance.

2. D

This sentence is a supporting idea because it provides another reason why jazz would be considered influential in American culture.

3. B

Expository writing is used to describe, explain, or provide information. It includes a logical sequence of steps or order of events.

4. A

The second paragraph describes how jazz music influenced the struggles of two minority groups—women and African Americans.

5. A

The opening sentence of this passage is the topic sentence and introduces the topic of jazz music.

6. C

The organization of the passage is chronological: it traces the popularity of popcorn from the ancient world through the twentieth century and to the modern day.

7. B

The opening sentence of the passage is the topic sentence and introduces popcorn as the topic of the passage.

8. A

The last sentence of the third paragraph states that "popcorn continued to rule the snack food kingdom until the rise in popularity of home televisions in the 1950s," suggesting that as people watched more television, they went to the movie less, and thus ate less popcorn.

9. D

The sentence is meant to inform the reader when Americans began consuming large amounts of popcorn.

10. C

The passage explains that popcorn is a food that many cultures have eaten and also describes the growth of the popcorn industry over time.

11. B

The popcorn industry will likely continue to thrive because every time it has faced a decline, it has come up with a new way to market its product and make it available to consumers.

12. A

This passage would most likely come from a short-story collection because it tells the story of an individual. It does not focus on information, processes, or historical events.

13. A

The author uses vivid imagery such as "brown orbs seemed lit from within" to entertain the reader with a description of Mason.

14. D

The passage describes how Mason makes friends on a bus and on a team. It also states that "people sought out Mason," meaning that people wanted to be around him.

15. C

The subject line of the memo is "Personal Use of Computers," and this memo is being sent to department leaders.

16. D

The memo states that management will take disciplinary action against employees who use computers for personal matters during work hours. The memo stresses the seriousness of the issue by stating, "These rules must be respected."

17. C

This is an example of persuasive writing because the author is arguing for a particular interpretation of historical events. The statement "but people who try to sell you this narrative are wrong" clearly attempts to sway the reader.

18. A

The author states, "The Civil War was not a battle of cultural identities—it was a battle about slavery" in an attempt to persuade the reader. The rest of the passage supports this idea.

19. B

The author states in the passage that the Civil War was not "a battle of cultural identities [but] … a battle about slavery." *Slavery* and *slave labor* can be considered synonymous terms.

20. B

The passage states that "surgery patients must check in at the main Hospital Admissions Desk" before going to the third floor for surgery.

21. C

The passage states that the nurse at the Surgery Admissions Desk will "ensure that all required paperwork has been completed before the patient is taken to the Surgery Holding Room."

22. A

A primary source is produced by someone with firsthand knowledge of the events being described. Of the choices, only the letter writer was a witness to the Battle of Gettysburg.

23. C

Beech trees are included in the list of species found in temperate deciduous forests.

24. B

The tree species magnolia is included in the list of species that occur in temperate deciduous forests.

25. C

The transition word *overall* is used to indicate a conclusion or summary.

26. D

The entry for short-term memory shows that it begins on page 340.

27. B

The temperature -40°F is equivalent to -34°C.

28. A

If the temperature dropped 10°C, the thermometer would read 30°C, or approximately 82°F.

29. A

The diner has the fewest number of bacon slices (nineteen), and bacon slices occupy the smallest slice of the pie chart.

30. A

Adding 120 buns to the existing eighty buns would provide enough buns for 200 hamburgers.

31. A

There are enough bacon slices to make nineteen burgers, and enough cheese slices to make eighteen burgers ($37 \div 2 = 18.5$). The most hamburgers that Gigi's could make would be eighteen.

32. D

The context clues "wit" and "flair" suggest the president used fun, engaging wordplay, meaning he was well-spoken.

33. D

Topaz Forest is located to the west of Emerald Lake.

34. C

The map's scale shows that ¼ inch = 2 miles. The two camps are approximately 2.5 inches, or 10 miles apart. The other answers do not fit the scale of the map.

35. C

Emerald Lake is located directly south of Tannanite Forest.

36. C

Calculate the cost to buy shoes from each retailer. Use rounding to make the process easier.

Wholesale Footwear: $60 + 11 + 8 =$ **$79**

Bargain Shoes: $66 + 6 + 5 =$ **$77**

Famous Shoes: $80 + 5 = \$85$

Fancy Shoes: $90 + 3 + 9 = \$102$

37. A

Find the cost for shoes from each retailer if Dennis pays shipping and handling but not taxes. Use rounding to make the process easier.

Wholesale Footwear: $60 + 11 =$ **$71**

Bargain Shoes: $66 + 6 = \$72$

Famous Shoes: $80 + 5 = \$85$

Fancy Shoes: $90 + 3 = \$93$

38. B

A glossary is the part of a book that contains brief explanations or definitions of key terms.

39. D

This is the site of a government agency. This site will focus on studies and factual data rather than personal opinions or consumer products.

40. C

All of these titles are subheadings (marked with the letters A or B) that fall under a major heading (marked with a number).

41. B

In this passage, bold print is used to make certain words stand out from the rest of the text.

42. B

Work through each step.

1. $20
2. $20 - 5 = \$15$
3. $15 + 20 = \$35$
4. $35 - 10 = \$25$
5. $25 + 10 = \$35$
6. $35 - 30 =$ **$5**

43. A

Maximum Tees has the lowest price per shirt when a customer orders fifty shirts.

44. D

Find the cost for 100 shirts from each company. Use rounding when necessary.

Maximum Tees: $15.99

Wholesale Tees: $16.50

Total Tees: Half the shirts will cost $19.99, and the other half will cost $14.99. The average cost per shirt will be $(20 + 15) \div 2 = \$17.50$

Classic Tees: Half the shirts will cost $16.50, and the other half will cost $11.50. The average cost per shirt will be $(16.5 + 11.5) \div 2 = $**$14**

45. C

Work through each step.

1. 3 gallons
2. $3 - 0.5 = 2.5$ gallons
3. $2.5 - 1 = 1.5$ gallons
4. $1.5 - 0.5 = $**1 gallon**

46. A

The context clue "poor night's sleep" suggests that Elaine was feeling tired.

47. C

"Recipes for Common Dishes" is the only heading that is not about an art form.

48. B

Work through each step.

1. 0 miles north, 0 miles west
2. 10 miles north, 0 miles west
3. 10 miles north, 5 miles west
4. 8 miles north, 5 miles west
5. 8 miles north, 6 miles west

49. A

"Deep cut" is the only option that would require stitches and not another form of treatment.

50. D

The best heading would be "Road Trips" because it is the only option that suggests another method of travel.

51. B

Work through each step.

1. 1 red, 2 green
2. 0 red, 2 green
3. 0 red, 3 green
4. 1 red, 3 green
5. 1 red, 4 green
6. 0 red, 4 green
7. 0 red, 3 green
8. 3 red, 3 green
9. 3 red, 5 green

52. D

Based on context clues in the paragraph, it appears the couple has no plan or set ideas about their travels. Therefore, the word is used with irony or sarcasm.

53. C

Alphabetically, the word *license* would appear after the word *lexicon* and before the word *lipid*.

MATHEMATICS

1. C

total seats = 4,500 + 2,000

$$\frac{\text{lower seats}}{\text{all seats}} = \frac{4,500}{6,500} = \frac{9}{13}$$

2. D

A rational number is one that can be written in the form of a fraction. Only option D) represents a number which cannot be written in the form of a fraction.

3. D

Write a proportion and then solve for x.

$$\frac{40}{45} = \frac{265}{x}$$

$40x = 11,925$

$x = 298.125 \approx \mathbf{298}$

4. C

Use the formula for percentages.

$percent = \frac{part}{whole}$

$= \frac{42}{48}$

$= 0.875 = \mathbf{87.5\%}$

5. C

The digit in the hundredths place is 3. The digit to the right of the hundredths place is 2; therefore, the 3 remains the same. The number rounds to **1230.93**.

6. C

There are two ways to solve this question. First, you can add all the given numbers and find the exact answer. This method is time-consuming and is less efficient.

The second method to solve this question is by adding only the numbers on the left of the decimal and then comparing your answer with the answer choices that you are given. We add 45, 32, and 31 to get 45 + 32 + 31 = 108. Therefore, the answer must be close to, and greater than, 108. In the answer choices, only option C) fits these criteria. (Note that this method of approximation saves time but it is not very accurate if all the answer choices are very close to each other.)

7. C

Use the area to find the length of a side of the square:

$A = s^2$

$5,625 \text{ ft}^2 = s^2$

$s = \sqrt{5,625 \text{ ft}^2} = 75 \text{ ft}$

Now multiply the side length by 4 to find the perimeter:

$P = 4s$

$P = 4(75 \text{ ft}) = \mathbf{300 \text{ ft}}$

8. C

From the given information in the question, we know that 25% of the actual price of a desk is $45. If we write this in the form of an equation, it becomes:

$\left(\frac{25}{100}\right) \times x = \$45$ (25% of x equals $45)

$x = \frac{45}{0.25} \rightarrow \$180$

Therefore, the actual price of the desk equals **$180**.

9. B

In order to find 5% of 2000, we need to multiply 2000 by $\frac{5}{100}$, i.e., $2000 \times 0.05 = \mathbf{100}$

10. B

Multiply the ratios so that pants cancel out in the numerator and denominator:

$$\frac{4 \text{ shirts}}{1 \text{ pants}} \times \frac{5 \text{ pants}}{2 \text{ pairs shoes}} = \frac{20 \text{ shirts}}{2 \text{ pairs shoes}}$$

Divide by the greatest common factor to reduce the ratio:

$$\frac{20 \text{ shirts}}{2 \text{ pairs shoes}} \div \frac{2}{2} = \frac{\mathbf{10 \text{ shirts}}}{\mathbf{1 \text{ pair shoes}}}$$

11. D

The money Jane earns is equal to $15 times the number of hours she babysits: $15h$

The total money in Jane's bank account is equal to the money she started with plus the money she earns: $275 + 15h$

Set this expression equal to $400:

400 = 275 + 15h

12. C

22 kg − 3.2 kg = 18.8 kg remaining for coffee

18.8 kg = 18,800 g

$18{,}800 \text{ g} \times \frac{1 \text{ bag of coffee}}{800 \text{ g}} = 23.5$ bags of coffee

Round down to 23 bags. Although 23.5 would normally round up to 24, a 24th bag of coffee would cause the suitcase to exceed the weight limit.

13. B

There are twice as many red marbles as blue marbles, so (red) = 2(blue).

The number of blue marbles is 88% the number of green marbles, so (blue) = 0.88g.

Substitute this expression for blue marbles in the one above:

(red) = 2(0.88g)

(red) = 1.76g

The total number of marbles is equal to red plus blue plus green:

(red) + (blue) + g

1.76g + 0.88g + g

3.64g

14. D

Write each value in decimal form and compare.

−0.95 < 0 < 0.4 < 0.35 < 0.75 FALSE

−1 < −0.1 < −0.11 < 0.8$\overline{3}$ < 0.75 FALSE

−0.75 < −0.2 < 0 < 0.$\overline{66}$ < 0.55 FALSE

−1.1 < −0.8 < −0.13 < 0.7 < 0.$\overline{81}$ **TRUE**

15. C

Consider the given inequality:

$\frac{2x+7}{9} < 2$

Multiplying by 9 on both sides, we get:

2x + 7 < 18

Subtracting 7 on both sides, we get:

2x < 18 − 7

2x < 11

Dividing by 2 on both sides, we get:

$x < \frac{11}{2}$

16. B

A simple trick in solving these complex fraction-multiplication questions is to look for the numbers which can cancel each other. For example, in this given question, we see that 3 × 3 = 9 which cancels the 9 of the denominator. Similarly, $\frac{125}{25} = \frac{5}{1} = 5$.

The net result of this multiplication after cancellation of numerators and denominators becomes:

$\frac{2}{6} \times 5 \times \frac{1}{10} = \frac{1}{6}$

17. B

Finding the sum of the expressions in parentheses first, we get:

$\left(\frac{3}{4} + \frac{1}{5}\right) \rightarrow \frac{15+4}{20} = \frac{19}{20}$

$\left(\frac{2}{3} + \frac{3}{2}\right) \rightarrow \frac{4+9}{6} \rightarrow \frac{13}{6}$

$\frac{19}{20} - \frac{13}{6} = \frac{19(6) - 13(20)}{120} \rightarrow \frac{-146}{120} \rightarrow -\frac{73}{60}$

18. C)

3x + 2 > 5

3x > 3

x > 1

19. A

Add the number of cupcakes he will give to his friend and to his coworkers, then subtract that value from 48.

# of cupcakes for his friend:
$\frac{1}{2} \times 48 = 24$

# of cupcakes for his coworkers:
$\frac{1}{3} \times 48 = 16$

48 − (24 + 16) = **8**

20. C

Finding the difference of the fractions given in the parentheses first, we get:

$\frac{5}{6} - \frac{1}{2} = \frac{5-(3)}{6} = \frac{2}{6} = \frac{1}{3}$

$\frac{2}{9} + \frac{1}{3} \rightarrow \frac{2+3}{9} \rightarrow \frac{5}{9}$

21. A

In 2003, the profit was about $4 million. In 2004, the profit jumps to just over $6 million.

6 − 4 = 2, so we know answer choice A) is correct because it is the closest to the estimate.

22. B

The question asks for the difference in profit between 2001 and 2000. In 2001, approximately $2 million was earned and in 2000, approximately $1 million was earned.

$2 - 1 = $ **1 million**

23. A

Use the equation for percentages.

part = *whole* × percentage =

$9 \times 0.25 = $ **2.25**

24. C

The three legs of the trip make a right triangle.

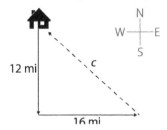

Use the Pythagorean theorem to find the distance she traveled from her final point back to her home:

$a^2 + b^2 = c^2$

$12^2 + 16^2 = c^2$

$144 + 256 = c^2$

$400 = c^2$

$c = 20$

Finally, add the three legs to find the total distance she traveled:

$12 + 16 + 20 = $ **48 miles**

25. C

One way to find the answer is to draw a picture.

Put 24 cans into groups of 4. One out of every 4 cans is diet (light gray) so there is 1 light gray can for every 3 dark gray cans. That leaves 18 dark gray cans (regular soda).

Alternatively, solve the problem using ratios.

$\frac{Regular}{Total} = \frac{3}{4} = \frac{x}{24}$

$4x = 72$

$x = $ **18**

26. D

Find the area of the square as if it did not have the corners cut out.

$12 \text{ mm} \times 12 \text{ mm} = 144 \text{ mm}^2$

Find the area of the four cut out corners.

$2 \text{ mm} \times 2 \text{ mm} = 4 \text{ mm}^2$

$4(4 \text{ mm}^2) = 16 \text{ mm}^2$

Subtract the area of the cut out corners from the large square to find the area of the shape.

$144 \text{ mm}^2 - 16 \text{ mm}^2 = $ **128 mm²**

27. D

$300 \div 12 = 25$

Test each answer choice to see if it equals 25.

A. $2(150 - 6)$

$= 2(144)$

$= 288 \neq 25$

B. $(300 \div 4) \div 6$

$= 75 \div 6$

$= 12.5 \neq 25$

C. $(120 \div 6) + (180 \div 6)$

$= 20 + 30$

$= 50 \neq 25$

D. $(120 \div 12) + (180 \div 12)$

$= (10) + (15)$

$= $ **25**

28. A

Isolate the variable x on one side of the equation.

$5x - 4 = 3(8 + 3x)$

$5x - 4 = 24 + 9x$

$-4 - 24 = 9x - 5x$

$-28 = 4x$

$\frac{-28}{4} = \frac{4x}{4}$

$x = $ **−7**

29. A

$20\% - 18\% = 2\%$

part = *whole* × *percent*

$3{,}000{,}000{,}000 \times 0.02 = $ **60,000,000**

30. C

Use the formula for finding percentages. Express the percentage as a decimal.

part = whole × percentage = **1560 × 0.15**

31. D

Set up a proportion and solve.

$$\frac{8}{650} = \frac{12}{x}$$

$$12(650) = 8x$$

***x* = 975 miles**

32. D

Set up an equation. The original price (*p*) minus 30% of the original price is $385.

$$p - 0.3p = 385$$

$$p = \frac{385}{0.7} = 0.7p = 385 = \mathbf{\$550}$$

33. A

His profit will be his income minus his expenses. He will earn $40 for each lawn, or 40*m*. He pays $35 is expenses each week, or 35*x*.

profit = **40m − 35x**

34. A

If $\frac{2}{5}$ of the houses are painted yellow, then $\frac{3}{5}$ of the houses are NOT painted yellow. Since there are 24 houses that are not yellow, divide 24 by $\frac{3}{5}$ to find the total number of houses. Then subtract to find the number of yellow houses.

$$24 \div \frac{3}{5} = 24 \times \frac{5}{3} = 40$$

$$40 - 24 = \mathbf{16}$$

35. A

The average of 5 numbers is the sum of the numbers divided by 5. Multiply the average by 5 to find the sum; subtract to find the 5th number.

$$\frac{sum}{5} = 16$$

$$sum = 16 \times 5 = 80$$

$$80 - 68 = \mathbf{12}$$

36. C

Two of the walls are 5 feet by 7 feet. The other two walls are 4 feet by 7 feet. Therefore, the total area of the four walls is:

$$2(5)(7) + 2(4)(7) = 70 + 56 = \mathbf{126 \ square \ feet}$$

SCIENCE

1. C

The left ventricle receives oxygenated blood from the left atrium, then pumps the blood to the rest of the body.

2. D

The trachea, or windpipe, is a passageway for air as it moves from the mouth, nose, and throat to the bronchi.

3. A

Digestive juices are produced by the pancreas.

4. C

Erythrocytes are red blood cells that contain hemoglobin, which is responsible for carrying oxygen within the blood cell.

5. A

Capillaries are very small blood vessels found where veins and arteries meet. They are the site of material exchange.

6. A

During exhalation, the diaphragm relaxes causing the tissue to move up into the chest cavity. This movement reduces the space available for the lungs and forces air out of the lungs.

7. B

The two oxygen atoms in a covalent double bond share two pairs of electrons, or four total.

8. C

The tibia, or shin bone, is the larger of the lower leg bones and is located slightly to the front of the smaller fibula.

9. D

The hypothalamus links the nervous and endocrine systems by regulating hormone production of the pituitary gland

10. B

The humerus and ulna connect at the elbow to form a hinge joint.

11. B

The patella is a thick, flat, triangular bone that covers and protects the knee joint.

12. C

The origin is the fixed attachment of muscle to bone that remains in place while the insertion of the muscle moves during contraction.

13. B

Condensation is a phase change that occurs when gas, such as water vapor, is converted to liquid, such as water.

14. A

The quadriceps is a large muscle located at the front of the thigh and is composed of four sections, which all work to extend the knee joint.

15. B

The cerebral cortex is the most developed part of the human brain and is responsible for memory, language processing, and other higher brain functions.

16. C

There are twelve thoracic spinal nerves located in the upper body, centralized in the chest area.

17. A

The special senses are found in organs in the head region; touch is a sense that is found in the body region, making it a somatic sense instead of a specialized sense.

18. A

The jejunum, the middle section of the small intestine, is the site of most of the food absorption in the body after it is broken down in the duodenum.

19. A

Trypsin is a digestive enzyme that breaks down protein into peptides and amino acids.

20. C

The iliac artery receives blood from the aorta to supply blood to the lower body.

21. A

Osteoclasts break down and absorb bone tissue.

22. D

Group 1 elements contain one valence electron. They are more reactive than Group 2 elements because they have a full valence shell when they lose their one valence electron, meaning they lose that electron very easily.

23. C

During phagocytosis a cell actively engulfs other cells or food particles. For example, white blood cells use this process to engulf and kill invading bacteria.

24. A

The release of oxytocin during childbirth is a positive feedback loop because it moves the body further from homeostasis rather than toward it.

25. D

The mitochondria found in cells are what power the cell and provide it with the energy it needs to carry out its life functions. Muscle cells need a lot of ATP in order to provide the energy needed for movement and exercise.

26. D

Water will leave the cell through osmosis when the concentration of solute outside the cell is greater than that inside the cell. Water will leave the cell when it's placed in a 20 percent solute solution, decreasing the mass of the cell.

27. C

The cardiovascular system distributes oxygen to the rest of the body.

28. A

Electronegativity increases from left to right and bottom to top along the periodic table. Chlorine is higher and more to the right on the table than the other answer choices, so it is the most electronegative.

29. A

mRNA is a sequence of nucleotides in which each triplet codes for a particular amino acid. The sequence of triplets in the mRNA would translate into the sequence of amino acids that make up a protein.

30. D

The solubility for Na_2HAsO_4 at 50°C is around 55 grams/100 grams of water. This is the highest for the solutes listed on the graph.

31. B

Scientific models are simplifications or metaphors for observations that allow the observations to be more easily understood.

32. A

The independent variable is deliberately changed in the course of the experiment.

33. B

Sandy water is not a homogeneous mixture. Sand and water can be easily separated, making it a heterogeneous mixture.

34. B

The Punnett square shows that there is a 75 percent chance the child will have the dominant B gene, and thus have brown eyes.

	B	**b**
B	BB	Bb
b	Bb	bb

35. C

Subtracting the atomic number from the mass number gives the number of protons: $A - Z = 88 - 38 = 50$.

36. B

Solid ice is melting into liquid water between points B and C.

37. D

The cell wall is the structure that gives plant cells their rigidity.

38. D

This is a decomposition reaction where one reactant breaks apart into two products.

39. C

Ca+ has nineteen electrons. All the other ions have eighteen electrons.

40. C

Keratin, produced by keratinocytes, makes up the majority of the epidermis structure, hair, and nails.

41. B

The parathyroid controls calcium and phosphate levels, which are maintained by producing and reabsorbing bone tissue.

42. C

Ribosomes are the organelles primarily responsible for translating mRNA into proteins; the primary function of the smooth endoplasmic reticulum is the synthesis of lipids.

43. B

Both urine and semen travel through the penile urethra, the longest portion of the male urethra, to be expelled through the urethral opening.

44. B

The rib cage, which consists of the ribs and the sternum, is part of the axial skeleton.

45. C

Antibodies are proteins produced by plasma cells, a type of lymphocyte, which is a type of white blood cell.

46. A

Salivary amylase in the mouth begins the breakdown of carbohydrates.

47. A

The pituitary gland does not play a role in processing sensory information.

48. B

The gram is the appropriate unit to measure the mass of light objects, such as ants.

49. A

Facilitated diffusion is a form of passive transport across the cell membrane and does not use energy.

50. A

Females have two X chromosomes, so it is possible for the recessive X-linked condition to be masked by the mother's dominant allele. A female would have to have mutations on both X chromosomes in order to be symptomatic.

51. A

The prostate is an exocrine gland that secretes the alkaline fluid found in semen. It does not produce hormones.

52. B

The autonomic nervous system regulates involuntary functions of the heart, digestive tract, and other smooth muscles; it is further subdivided into the sympathetic and parasympathetic nervous systems.

53. C

The growth rate is the variable that is dependent on the changes to water temperature and concentration of salt in the water.

ENGLISH AND LANGUAGE USAGE

1.   B

Tidy is the only answer choice that is a verb and is in the infinitive form (*to tidy*).

2.   D

The female third person pronoun *she* replaces *my sister*.

3.   A

No punctuation is needed to join a dependent clause ("because he had more cavities") to the end of an independent clause.

4.   D

Diner should be spelled *dinner*. A *diner* is a restaurant; *dinner* is the meal eaten in the evening.

5.   D

The singular subject *organization* agrees with the singular verb *has*.

6.   A

A simple sentence has one independent clause and no dependent clauses.

7.   C

But links two ideas that contrast each other: it suggests that one thing has to be done in spite of the other.

8.   C

A customer who is "shouting angrily" is furious.

9.   B

The comma after *party* creates a comma splice, where two independent clauses ("We agreed that Chris would plan our mom's birthday party" and "he had already picked out a restaurant") are joined with a comma but no conjunction.

10.   D

The word *quickly* is an adverb that describes the verb *run*.

11.   C

The paragraph is about a child's wish to be an actor. All the sentences relate to this topic except choice C, which does not mention the child.

12.   B

The complete subject is the simple subject (*fire truck*) and all of its modifiers (*the, shiny, new*).

13.   A

Choice A combines the sentences in a way that accurately describes the logical relationship between events and also uses clear, grammatically correct sentences.

14.   B

A complex sentence has one independent clause ("I forgot my homework") and one dependent clause ("but my teacher said I can turn it in tomorrow").

15.   C

He is a third person pronoun, *you* is a second person pronoun, and *I* is a first person pronoun. In choice B, the subject *you* is implied.

16.   D

The context clue "she wasn't taking their complaints seriously" suggests that the boss was *disinterested*, or not interested in making a real apology to her employees.

17.   A

Choice A includes commas to set apart the items in a list and does not include unnecessary punctuation to introduce the list.

18.   B

This sentence introduces a topic (housing for animals in zoos) that could be explored in a passage. Choices A and C would work best as supporting details. Choice D belongs at the end of a passage because it contains references to previously discussed details.

19. A

Personal means something private; *personnel* are people employed by an organization.

20. A

Adding the phrase *for the bus* creates a simple sentence with only one independent clause and no dependent clauses.

21. B

The correct spelling is *varies* (the singular version of the verb to *vary*).

22. A

Hyped is a slang term that means *excited*.

23. A

If "even the best students" can't gain acceptance to the school, the entrance requirements must be *demanding*, or difficult to achieve.

24. C

President Clinton is the answer choice that is properly capitalized. The name and position are capitalized.

25. C

The sentence "go look for it now" is an independent clause that has a subject (implied *you*) and a verb (*go*). Choice A is a noun phrase, and Choice D is a prepositional phrase. Choice B is a dependent clause.

26. B

The word *noticeable* is an exception to the rule that the final e is dropped before adding a suffix that begins with a vowel (drive + ing = driving; observe + ance = observance).

27. B

A comma is used to separate two independent clauses with a conjugation (*but*).

28. A

The word *expensive* is an adjective that describes *dress*.

Follow the link below to take your second ATI TEAS practice test and to access other online study resources:

www.triviumtestprep.com/ati-teas-online-resources

WANT MORE?

Try our online *ATI Teas 6 Prep Course*

Dear Reader,

Here at Trivium Test Prep, we understand how important scoring well on the ATI TEAS 6 exam is for your future. We believe you can never be "too prepared" for such a life-changing test. We are excited to offer you a comprehensive online course devoted to the ATI TEAS 6! Our *ATI Teas 6 Prep Course* includes:

- a complete review of all content on the ATI TEAS VI exam, with **trackable course progress** so you know exactly what you still need to review;
- subject quizzes at the end of each section, so you can **assess your retention** before moving on to new units;
- two full practice exams with **fully explained answer rationales** and **trackable scoring**, so you can measure your progress and understand what you need to improve on;
- and full accessibility via your computer, tablet, and mobile phone 24/7, enabling you to **learn at home or on-the-go!**

Best of all, our unique material and practice questions are available exclusively through *ATI Teas 6 Prep Course*, ensuring you get double the study time when coupled with this book!

Trivium Test Prep's *ATI Teas 6 Prep Course* is available to current customers like you at the promotional price of only **$39.99!** Many less convenient programs retail for hundreds of dollars online. To enroll today and start learning immediately, please visit:

http://course.triviumtestprep.com/

Thank you for choosing Trivium Test Prep for all your ATI TEAS 6 study needs! Best of luck with your studies,

— *The Trivium Test Prep Team*

Made in the USA
Coppell, TX
04 May 2021

55035364R00129